The Practice of English Language Teaching

Longman Handbooks for Language Teachers
General Editor: Donn Byrne

The Teaching of Pronunciation – Brita Haycraft
The Language Laboratory and Language Learning – Julian Dakin
Writing English Language Tests – J B Heaton
Visual Materials for the Language Teacher – Andrew Wright
Teaching Oral English – Donn Byrne
Selections from 'Modern English Teacher' – edited by Helen Moorwood
Second Selections from 'Modern English Teacher' – edited by Susan Holden
An Introduction to English Language Teaching – John Haycraft
Teaching Writing Skills – Donn Byrne
Drama in Language Teaching – Susan Holden
Communication in the Classroom – edited by Keith Johnson and Keith Morrow
Teaching English through English – Jane Willis
Role Play in Language Learning – Carol Livingstone
The Practice of English Language Teaching – Jeremy Harmer

Longman Handbooks for Language Teachers
General Editor: Donn Byrne

Jeremy Harmer

The Practice of English Language Teaching

Longman

London and New York

Longman Group Limited
Longman House, Burnt Mill, Harlow,
Essex CM20 2JE, England
and Associated Companies throughout the world.

© Longman Group Limited 1983

Published in the United States of America by
Longman Inc., New York

First published 1983
Fifth impression 1986
ISBN 0 582 74612 4

BRITISH LIBRARY CATALOGUING IN PUBLICATION DATA
Harmer, Jeremy
 The practice of English language teaching.
 — (Longman handbooks for language teaching)
 1. English language — Study and teaching
 — Foreign students
 I. Title
 428.2′4′07   PE1128.A2

LIBRARY OF CONGRESS CATALOGING IN PUBLICATION DATA
Harmer, Jeremy.
 The practice of English language teaching.
 (Longman handbooks for language teachers)
 Bibliography: p.
 Includes index.
 1. English language — Study and teaching — Foreign
 speakers. I. Title. II. Series.
 PE1128.A2H34   1983   428′.007   83-1020

Set in 10/12pt Times
Produced by Longman Group (FE) Ltd
Printed in Hong Kong

Contents

Acknowledgements

We are grateful to the following for permission to reproduce copyright material:
Barnaby's Picture Library for page 154 (bottom); Cambridge University Press for
page 119 (bottom), from *Mind Matters* by Maley & Grellet 1981, and for page 120, from *A Case For English, SB* by Hicks *et al* 1979, and for pages 128 & 129, from *A Case For English, TB* by Hicks *et al* 1979; Camera Press Ltd for page 156; Evans Brothers Ltd for page 91, from *Tandem* by Matthews & Read 1981; Heinemann Educational Books for page 73, from *Encounters, SB* by Garton-Sprenger, Jupp, Milne & Prowse 1979, and for page 74, from *Encounters, Complete Edition* by Garton-Sprenger, Jupp, Milne & Prowse 1979, and for pages 103, 148, 159 (bottom), 162 & 163 (top), from *Reasons For Reading* by Davies & Whitney, 1979; Longman Group Ltd for pages 71, 72, 104, 163 (bottom) and 185 (middle), from *Starting Strategies, SB* by Abbs & Freebairn 1978, and for page 76 (top), from *Going Places* by Byrne & Holden 1981, and for page 84, from *Developing Strategies, SB* by Abbs & Freebairn 1982, and for page 122, from *Follow It Through* by Byrne & Holden 1978, and for page 130 (right) and 131 (top), from *Advanced Speaking Skills* by Arnold & Harmer 1978, and for pages 160 & 161, from *Functional Comprehension* by Byrne 1978, and for pages 78 & 79, from *Starting Points* by Scott & Arnold 1978, and for pages 80 & 169, from *Advanced Writing Skills* by Arnold & Harmer 1980, and for page 105, from *Building Strategies, SB* by Abbs & Freebairn 1979, and for page 158, from *Looking For Information* by Jordan 1980, and for page 166, from *In Touch* by Castro & Kimbrough 1979, and for page 186, from *Mainline Beginners A, SB* by Alexander 1978, and for page 191, from *It Happened To Me* by Kingsbury & Scott 1980, and for page 193, from *Listening To Maggie* by Gore 1979; Longman Photographic Unit for pages 130 (left) & 190 (bottom); Macmillan, London & Basingstoke for page 82, from *Contemporary English, PB 1* 1979, and for page 147, from *Active Context English, Book 2* by Brinton *et al* 1971; Mary Glasgow Publications Ltd. for page 165, from *Holiday English, Level 5 Students Workbook* by Mugglestone 1979; Oxford University Press for page 69, from *Streamline English: Connections* by B Hartley & P Viney, © O.U.P. 1979, and for pages 178–179, from *Crosstalk, Book 2* by M M Webster & E W Castañón, © M M Webster & E W Castañón 1980; From Peter Watcyn-Jones: Penguin Functional English *Pairwork, Student A*, p. 27 and *Pairwork, Student B*, p. 27, (Penguin Education 1981), © Peter Watcyn-Jones 1981, reprinted by permission of Penguin Books Ltd for pages 92 & 93, and from Geoffrey Broughton *Success With English: Coursebook 1*, (Penguin Education, revised edition 1977), p. 40, © Geoffrey Broughton 1968, illustrations by Quentin Blake, reprinted by permission of Penguin Books Ltd for page 149.

Associated Book Publishers Ltd for extracts from Jean de Brunhoff's *The Story of Babar* translated by Nellie Rieu and published by Methuen Children's Books; the author, Judith Cook for an extract from 'The Tent People' from *The Guardian* April 25, 1978; W H Freeman & Co for an extract from John Maynard Smith's 'The Evolution of Behaviour' from *Scientific American* September 1978; Heinemann Educational Books for extracts from *Listening Links* by M Geddes and G Sturtridge; Longman Group Ltd for extracts from *Advanced Speaking Skills* by Harmer & Arnold and *Building Strategies, Teachers' Book* by Abbs and Freebairn; Macmillan, London and Basingstoke for extracts from *Contemporary English* Books 1, 2, 6 and Teachers Notes by Rossner *et al*; Oxford University Press for an extract from *Crosstalk, Teachers' Book* by M M Webster and E W Castañón.

Short extracts from the following titles are also included on the pages indicated: page 115 from 'Take your Partners', N Bullard in *Modern English Teacher* 8/3 1981; pages 119 and 120 from *Mind Matters*, A Maley and F Grellet (Cambridge University Press 1981); page 150 from *Mainline Beginners A, Teacher's Book*, L G Alexander (Longman 1978); page 157, 158, 159 and 168 from *Looking for Information*, R R Jordan (Longman 1980); page 167 (bottom) from *Functional Comprehension*, D Byrne (Longman 1977); page 170, recipe from *Mediterranean Food*, E David (Penguin 1965); page 172 from *Read in English*, M Scott (Longman 1981); page 173, *Notes* (Simon and Schuster 1979); page 176 from *It Happened to Me*, R Kingsbury and R Scott (Longman 1980); page 179 from *Crosstalk, Book 2*, M M Webster and E W Castañón (Oxford University Press 1980); pages 182 and 185 from *Building Strategies*, B Abbs and I Freebairn (Longman 1979).

Preface

English language teaching is perhaps healthier now as a profession than it has ever been: certainly it is better informed. There are more good materials than ever before. More articles and books about teaching and those areas of applied linguistics which concern it are published every day. This happy situation, however, may in fact be almost too good for the teacher in training or the teacher recently embarked on a career in English language teaching, for he may find the vast amount of literature overwhelming and somewhat indigestible. (Teacher and student are referred to as 'he' throughout the book, this being the most commonly accepted pronoun.) *The Practice of English Language Teaching* aims to make the teacher's job easier by drawing together many of the theoretical insights of recent years, and putting them at the service of a broad methodological approach (called, in this book, the 'balanced activities approach') to the teaching of English as a foreign or second language.

This book has two major aims. The first is to provide a theoretical background to a methodology for English teaching and the second is to detail techniques that are helpful in the realisation of that methodology. The book is divided into three parts. In Part A: Theory, the concerns of applied linguistics that have influenced English teaching are explained in a way that is, I hope, accessible to those people who have not had the opportunity to study that discipline. Part B: Practice, is concerned with the specific techniques and materials within the general methodological approach outlined in Part A. Part C: Management and planning, looks at teaching in terms of the teacher's attitude to students and to teaching in general and attempts to put forward an approach to classroom procedure that brings together the concerns of the first two parts. The Appendix: Evaluating materials, should be useful if teachers have to choose textbooks; the bases for deciding that materials are appropriate are those qualities that are advocated as being beneficial throughout the book.

At various points in each chapter the reader will find numbers that are picked up at the end of that chapter, forming a list of references for those people who wish to continue reading on the subject matter of the chapter. With these references the reader can turn to the Bibliography at the end the book.

The Practice of English Language Teaching is concerned with Teaching English as a Foreign Language (often referred to as TEFL). It is not necessarily concerned with second language learning, although much of the contents of this book can be applied to that slightly different teaching situation. The book is directed towards the teaching of 'general' classes, that is a group of students whose interests are not necessarily the same. Teaching English for Specific Purposes (ESP) is of course mentioned, but does not form a major part of the book.

It is suggested that *The Practice of English Language Teaching* should be read in sequence. Part A describing the background should be read before Part B which looks at specific techniques. Part C then draws theoretical and practical together. The reader can thus perceive a gradually evolving overall plan to *The Practice of English Language Teaching*. This does not prevent anyone, of course, dipping into particular parts of the book at their own whim or convenience!

Author's acknowledgements

The Practice of English Language Teaching is to a large extent, the result of working as a teacher trainer for the Instituto Anglo-Mexicano de Cultura both in Mexico City and in Guadalajara, but a book of this nature is necessarily the result of a great number of diverse influences. Where possible (and where I have known what these influences are!) credit has been given in the references at the end of each chapter; if I have failed to acknowledge the source of an idea or a technique it is because the source is for some reason unknown to me. In the rapidly expanding world of TEFL it is often impossible to know where an idea really originated.

There are, however, a number of people who have had a very direct influence on the writing of this book. First among these is Richard Rossner who originally involved me in teacher training, and whose example and guidelines for this most important of tasks have remained constantly inspiring. The early material on which this book is based was written in close collaboration with Walter Plumb whose clear thinking and comments on the material as it has evolved have been completely indispensable. I have also had the opportunity of working in teacher training with Jean Pender who has had an undoubted influence on much of the content of *The Practice of English Language Teaching*. Especially important in the writing of this book have been the excellent and stimulating comments of Jane Willis and of Donn Byrne, the general editor of the Longman *Handbooks for Language Teachers* series. At Longman Tim Hunt's patience and continual encouragement have been of great importance to me, and the excellent and cheerful work of Graciela Padilla, who has typed and put together different versions of an invariably chaotic manuscript, has made the book possible. Lastly I should pay tribute to the help, support, forbearance and professional advice of my wife Anita. Without these people the book could not have been written. I can only hope that they will all look upon the results of their influence and endeavours with pleasure.

J.P.H.H.

1

Why do people learn languages?

In this chapter we are going to look at the reasons people have for learning languages (particularly English) and the reasons for their success as language learners.

1.1 Reasons for learning languages

People who wish to learn a foreign language may have any one of a great number of reasons for doing so. If we take English as an example we can make a tentative list of these reasons. It will not of course be complete, but will at least show the great variety of both the needs and desires of students of English.

(a) Target language community
Students may find themselves living either temporarily or permanently in the target language community. (Target language means the language the students are trying to learn: a target language community for students of English would be an English-speaking country, e.g. England, North America, Canada, Jamaica, etc.) These students will have to speak the target language to survive in that community.

(b) ESP[1]
The term *English for Special* or *Specific Purposes* has been applied to situations where a student has some specific reason for wanting to learn the language. For example, an air traffic controller needs English to guide aircraft through the skies. This may be the only time in his or her life when English is used. The businessman may need English for international trade. The waiter may need English to serve his customers. These needs are often referred to as EOP (*English for Occupational Purposes*). The student who is going to study at an English university may need English so that he can write reports or essays and function in a seminar situation. This is often called EAP (*English for Academic Purposes*). The student of medicine or nuclear physics (studying in his own country) may need to be able to read articles and textbooks about

1

that subject in English. This is often referred to as EST (or *English for Science and Technology*). What is interesting about all these examples is that the English the students may want to learn is different. Whereas the waiter might want to speak, the medical student might want only to read in English.

(c) School curriculum

Many students study English only because they have to! English is part of the school curriculum because a decision has been taken by someone in authority that it should be so.

(d) Culture

Some students study a foreign language because they are attracted by the culture of one of the target language communities (see above). They learn the language because they want to know more about the people who speak it and the place(s) in which it is spoken.

(e) Advancement

Some people want to study English (or another foreign language) because they think it offers, in some general way, a chance for advancement in their daily lives. It is possible that a good knowledge of a foreign language will help you to get a better job than if you only know your native language. This is particularly so of English, which is rapidly becoming the language of international communication.

Businessmen (see above) need English and a young person wanting to go into business might well get a better starting position simply because he or she has a sound working knowledge of the language.

(f) Miscellaneous

There are a number of other reasons for learning languages which are possibly less important than those above. We could mention the student who goes to English (or French or German) classes just 'for fun', for something to do. A student might well go to a class because he likes a particular person in the class, or in general likes the atmosphere of the class: perhaps the student has simply heard that English classes at a certain school are enjoyable or prestigious, etc.

It will be clear from the list above that there are many possible reasons for studying a language. What will also be clear is that not all the students mentioned above can necessarily be treated in the same way. The students whose interest is only in some form of ESP may be taught in a very different way from the student who is learning English 'for fun'. The student who studies English because it is in the curriculum should be treated in a very different light from the student who voluntarily goes to a language teaching institute.

Most students who decide to go to a language school do so for a mixture of the reasons mentioned above. In this book we will be considering these students especially. We will also be considering the students for whom English is a part of the curriculum. The student of specialist English will not be specifically concentrated on, although we will be mentioning him throughout the book.

1.2
Success in
language learning

We will now consider why it is that students achieve success in language learning. It should be said immediately that if we knew the answer to this question the job of teaching a language (and learning it) would be extremely easy! There are a number of factors, though, that we can mention and that seem to have a strong effect on success or failure in language learning.

1.2.1
Motivation

It has often been said by people involved in language teaching that a student who really wants to learn will succeed whatever the circumstances are under which he studies. It is certainly true that students do learn in unfavourable conditions, and it is also true that students often succeed using methods that experts have considered unsatisfactory. All teachers can think of situations in which certain 'motivated' students do significantly better than their peers, and it seems reasonable to suggest that the motivation of the student is perhaps the single most important thing that he brings to the classroom.

Motivation is some kind of *internal drive* that encourages somebody to pursue a course of action. It seems to be the case that if we perceive a *goal* (that is something we wish to achieve) and if that goal is sufficiently attractive, we will be strongly motivated to do whatever is necessary to reach that goal. Goals may be of many different types; for example we may work overtime in order to earn more money and reach the goal of owning a new car or stereo set. The tennis player who wishes to win an important competition (the goal) may be motivated to put in incredibly long hours of practice.

Clearly language learners who are motivated also perceive goals of various types, and here we might immediately make a distinction between *short-term goals* and *long-term goals*. Long-term goals might have something to do with a student's wish to get a better job or become a member of the target language community (see 1.1(a) above). Short-term goals might include such things as the urge to pass an end-of-term or end-of-semester exam or complete a unit successfully. It seems possible to suggest that a teacher will find a strongly motivated student with a long-term goal easier to teach than a student who has to study the language because it is on the curriculum and who does not have such a goal. For the latter type of student short-term goals will often be the source of any motivation he has.

At this point we will separate motivation into two main types: *extrinsic motivation*, which is concerned with factors outside the classroom, and *intrinsic motivation* which is concerned with what takes place in the classroom.

1.2.2
Extrinsic
motivation

Students who decide to go and study a language usually do so because they have some goal which they wish to reach. It has been suggested that there are two main types of goal.

(a) Integrative motivation
Here the student is attracted by the culture of the target language community, and in the strong form of integrative motivation wishes to integrate himself into that culture. A weaker form of such motivation would be the student's desire to know as much as possible about the culture of the target language community.

3

(b) Instrumental motivation

Here the student believes that mastery of the target language will be instrumental in getting him a better job or position. The language is an instrument to be used by such a student.

Two researchers, Gardner and Lambert,[2] suggested that the most successful students were integratively motivated, but this conclusion has not really been adequately substantiated. Indeed it seems that it is not so much the type of motivation that counts as its strength. Certainly a student who has strong integrative motivation will be likely to succeed, but the same is also true of the student who has strong instrumental motivation!

There are a number of other factors, however, that have an effect on extrinsic motivation, and most of these have to do with a student's attitude to the language. A student's attitude will be strongly influenced by those around him. If, for example, a young student's parents are very much against the culture of the target language community it is possible that this will negatively affect the student's attitude. Conversely a positive attitude on the part of the parents might have a very positive effect. The attitude of the student's *peers* (his equals) will also be very important in the same way. Indeed any members of the community in which the student lives may affect his attitude to the target language. Thus, for example, if the student's friends are all studying the language, and if this seems a prestigious thing to do, the student may be favourably disposed towards that language.

Another major factor that will influence the student's attitude will be (in the case of more adult learners especially) his previous experiences as a student. If the student remembers being humiliated by a lack of success as a learner he will find his extrinsic motivation negatively affected. Previous success, of course, will have the opposite effect.

What can the teacher do about extrinsic motivation and student attitude? It is probably true that he cannot create it, since we have suggested that extrinsic motivation is the result of factors outside the classroom. But the teacher can clearly have an effect on that motivation. If the teacher is negative about the culture of the target language this will be disadvantageous, and it is equally true that a positive attitude towards the culture (by which we do not mean uncritical) will help. The teacher's treatment of the student will also affect the student's motivation and attitude where it either reinforces or undermines previous learning experience. The teacher who (albeit unwittingly) humiliates a student whose previous learning experience was unhappy will be doing a grave disservice to that student, but a teacher who is able to encourage a previously unsuccessful student will be helping that student's motivation and attitude.

1.2.3 Intrinsic motivation

While it is reasonable to suppose that many adult learners have some degree of extrinsic motivation, and while it is also true that a student's attitude may be affected by members of his community, it would seem to be the case that intrinsic motivation plays by far the larger part in most students' success or failure as language learners. Many students bring no extrinsic motivation at all to the classroom (see 1.2.1) and may well, in the case of schoolchildren, have neutral, or even negative feelings about language learning. For them what happens in the classroom will be of vital importance in determining their attitude to the language, and in supplying motivation, which we have suggested is a vital component in successful language learning. As we have also suggested above, what happens in the classroom will have an important effect on students who are already in some way extrinsically motivated. We can consider factors affecting intrinsic motivation under the headings of *physical conditions, method, the teacher* and *success*.

(a) Physical conditions

It is clearly the case that physical conditions have a great effect on learning and can alter a student's motivation either positively or negatively. Classrooms that are badly lit and overcrowded can be excessively de-motivating, but unfortunately many of them exist in schools. Vitally important will be the blackboard: is it easily visible? Is the surface in good condition?, etc. In general, teachers should presumably try to make their classrooms as pleasant as possible. Even where conditions are bad it may be possible to improve the atmosphere with posters, students' work, etc. on the walls.

We can say, then, that the atmosphere in which a language is learnt is vitally important: the cold greyness of much institutionalised education must be compensated for in some way if it is not to have a negative effect on motivation.

(b) Method

The method by which students are taught must have some effect on their motivation. If they find it deadly boring they will probably become de-motivated, whereas if they have confidence in the method they will find it motivating. But perhaps this is the most difficult area of all to be certain of. We said earlier that a really motivated student will probably succeed whatever method (within reason) is used. It is also true that different students are more or less sympathetic to any particular method depending upon their expectations. Teachers can easily recall students who felt that there was not enough grammar or enough conversation! Despite various attempts there is unfortunately no research which clearly shows the success of one method over another. What, though, is clear is that if the student loses confidence in the method he or she will become de-motivated. And the student's confidence in the method is largely in the hands of the most important factor affecting intrinsic motivation, *the teacher*.

(c) The teacher

Whether the student likes the teacher or not may not be very significant. What can be said, though, is that two teachers using the same method can have vastly different results. How then can we assess the qualities a teacher needs to help in providing intrinsic motivation?

In 1970 a study done by Denis Girard attempted to answer this question.[3] A thousand children between the ages of twelve and seventeen were asked to put a list of teacher 'qualities' in order of preference. The children showed what their learning priorities were by putting these qualities in the following order (1 = most important, 10 = least important):

1 He makes his course interesting.
2 He teaches good pronunciation.
3 He explains clearly.
4 He speaks good English.
5 He shows the same interest in all his students.
6 He makes all the students participate.
7 He shows great patience.
8 He insists on the spoken language.
9 He makes his pupils work.
10 He uses an audio-lingual method.

Interestingly, the main point of the study – to see if the audio-lingual method was popular – only comes tenth. Students were concerned that classes should be interesting, and three of the top ten qualities (5, 6 and 7) are concerned with the relationship between teacher and student. We can speculate that these qualities would emerge whatever subject were being taught.

The students were also asked to list any additional qualities they thought were important. The most popular were:

– He shows sympathy for his pupils.
– He is fair to all his students (whether good or bad at English).
– He inspires confidence.

Clearly this study on its own is in no way conclusive, but it does suggest certain conclusions:

1 The teacher has to make his classes interesting.
2 The teacher must be fair, treat his students equally and as far as possible understand and act on the worries and aspirations of his pupils.
3 The teacher must offer a good model as the target language user.
4 The teacher must be a good technician: his students should understand what is wanted of them, be able to pronounce correctly, and be stimulated into activity in the target language.

(d) Success

Success or lack of it plays a vital part in the motivational drive of a student. Both complete failure and complete success may be de-motivating. It will be the teacher's job to set goals and tasks at which most of his or her students can be successful – or rather tasks which he or she could realistically expect the students to be able to achieve. To give students very *high challenge* activities (high, because the level of difficulty for the students is extreme) where this is not appropriate may have a negative effect on motivation. It will also be the case that *low challenge* activities are equally de-motivating. If the students can achieve all the tasks with no difficulty at all they may lose the motivation that they have when faced with the right level of challenge.

Much of the teacher's work in the classroom concerns getting the level of challenge right: this involves the type of tasks set, the speed expected from the student, etc.

Of course ultimately a student's success or failure is in his own hands, but the teacher can influence the course of events in the student's favour.

**1.3
Motivational
differences**

We have been talking about how students in general are motivated, and we have suggested different types of motivation (see 1.2.2 and 1.2.3). To know exactly how or why your students are motivated will mean finding out at the beginning of a course how they feel about learning English. It is unlikely that everyone in the class will have the same motivation, and a student's motivation may be a mixture of the factors we have been discussing. However, it is possible to make some general statements about motivational factors for different ages and levels of learners of English as a foreign language.[4] We will look at *children, adolescents, adult beginners, adult intermediate students and adult advanced students.*

**1.3.1
Children**

More than anything else, children are curious, and this in itself is motivating. At the same time it is probably true to say that their span of attention or concentration is considerably less than that of an adult. Children will often seek teacher approval: the fact that the teacher notices them and shows appreciation for what they are doing is of vital importance.

It is suggested that children need constant changes of activity: they need activities which are exciting and stimulate their curiosity: they need to be involved in something active (they will usually not sit and listen!), and they need to be appreciated by the teacher, an important figure for them. It is extremely unlikely that they will have any motivation outside these considerations, and so almost everything for them will depend on the attitude and behaviour of the teacher.

**1.3.2
Adolescents**

Adolescents are perhaps the most exciting students to teach, but they can also present the teacher with more problems than any other age group.

We can certainly not expect any extrinsic motivation from the majority of our students – particularly the younger ones. We may hope, however, that the student's attitude has been positively influenced by those around him. We have to remember that adolescents are often brittle! They will probably no longer be inspired by mere curiosity, and teacher approval is no longer of vital importance. Indeed, the teacher may no longer be the leader, but rather the potential enemy. *Peer approval* will, however, be important.

The teacher should never, then, forget that the adolescent needs to be seen in a good light by his peers, and that with the changes taking place at that age he is easily prone to humiliation if the teacher is careless with his criticism. But the adolescent is also highly intelligent if stimulated, and dedicated if involved. At this age, getting the level of challenge right (see 1.2.3(d) is absolutely vital. Where this level is too low the student may simply 'switch off': where it is too high he may become discouraged and de-motivated. It is the teacher's task, too, to put language teaching into an involving context for his pupils. More than anything else they have to be involved in the task and eager to accomplish it.

**1.3.3
Adult beginners**

Adult beginners are in some ways the easiest people to teach! Firstly they may well come to the classroom with a high degree of extrinsic motivation. Secondly they will usually succeed very quickly. Goals within the class (learning a certain piece of language or finishing a unit) even though less than satisfactory are easy to perceive and relatively easy to achieve.

But it is still difficult to start learning a foreign language, and unrealistic challenge coupled with a negative teacher attitude can have disastrous effects on students' motivation.

1.3.4 Adult intermediate students

The adult intermediate student may well be motivated extrinsically. He may have very positive feelings about the way he is treated in the classroom where he is studying. Success may also be motivating, and the perception of having 'more advanced English' may be a primary goal. It is for this latter reason that problems sometimes arise. The beginner, as we have said, easily perceives success; since everything is new, anything learnt is a success. But the intermediate student already 'knows' a lot and may not perceive any progress. Conversely he may find the complexity of the language too much.

The teacher's job would seem to be that of showing the student that there is a lot to learn (without making this totally demoralising!) and then setting realistic goals for the student to achieve. Once again, a major factor will be getting the level of challenge right.

1.3.5 Adult advanced students

These students are often highly motivated. If they were not they would not see the need to continue with language study when they have already achieved so much. Like some intermediate students (but even more so) they will find progress more difficult to perceive. Much of the time they may not be learning anything 'new' but learning better how to use what they already know.

The teacher has a responsibility to point this fact out and to show the students what it is they will achieve at this level: it is a different kind of achievement. Many advanced teachers expect too much from their students, feeling that the setting of tasks and goals is in some way demeaning. But just because advanced students have difficulty in perceiving progress and success they may well need the clarity that the setting of short-term goals, tasks, etc. can give them.

1.4 Conclusions

We have seen, then, that there are many different reasons for learning a language, and we have said that we are mainly concerned with a classroom situation in which 'general' English is being studied. We have included both those students who have themselves made the decision and also those for whom the study of a language is a compulsory part of their education.

We have suggested many different factors that may affect a student's motivation stressing that a strongly motivated student is in a far better position as a learner than a student who is not motivated.

Most importantly we have said that both positively motivated students and those who do not have this motivation can be strongly affected by what happens in the classroom. Thus, for example, the student with no long-term goals (such as a strong instrumental motivation) may nevertheless be highly motivated by realistic short-term goals within the learning process.

We have seen that the teacher must strive to make his classes interesting and treat the students fairly, that he must be a good model as a speaker of the target language, and that he must be technically adept at ways of getting the students to learn and practise. Much of the second part of this book will concentrate on just that technical ability.

Teachers, too, must realise the important effect success has on motivation. They must be able to assess the students' ability so that the latter are faced with the right degree of challenge: success, in other words, should not be too easy or too difficult.

Discussion

1 Can you think of any other reasons why people learn languages apart from those given in 1.1?
2 Why are your students learning English?
3 Can you come to any conclusions about what a good method is? (See 1.2.3(b).)
4 Which of the different types of student in 1.3 would you like to teach? Why?

Exercises

1 Write a questionnaire which would tell you:
(a) Why your students are learning English.
(b) If they are extrinsically motivated.
2 In consultation with a colleague decide on three more qualities a teacher needs apart from those mentioned in 1.2.3(c).
3 With a colleague choose one of the different ages/levels of students from 1.3 and make a list of things you could do with them that would not be suitable for the other ages/levels mentioned.

References

1 For more information on ESP see P Strevens (1977) Chapter 8 and R Mackay and A Mountford (1978) and C J Brumfit (1980) pages 106–110.
2 The results of Gardner and Lambert's research into integrative and instrumental motivation can be found in R Gardner and W Lambert (1972). See also E Hoadley-Maidment (1977). A more general approach to the subject can be found in P Mugglestone (1977).
3 This study is described in D Girard (1977). See also R Allwright (1977a) on the relationship between the teacher and motivation.
4 For more on differences between children, adolescents and adults see P Strevens (1977) pages 17–18.

2

What a native speaker knows

In this chapter we will analyse what it is that a native speaker knows which enables him to use his language effectively. Our model of the native speaker is somewhat idealised, but most speakers of their native languages share most of the characteristics we will be concerned with. The native speaker's knowledge is usually subconscious – or at least is not something that he consciously 'thinks about' – and has to do not only with his actual language (e.g. grammar, etc.) but also with what he knows about the world and the society he lives in. We will look at the following areas of native speaker knowledge: *sounds, grammar, appropriateness, interaction with context* and *language skills.*

2.1 Sounds[1]

If we consider the spoken language, it will be obvious that it is made up of sounds. The baby crying is making a sound just as the politician making a speech is, although it is to be hoped that the latter's sounds will be somewhat more sophisticated! But how do the sounds work?

On their own, sounds may well be meaningless. If you say /t/ (the lines show that this is phonetic script) a few times, e.g. '*tu, tu, tu*' it will not mean very much in English. The same will be true of the sound /k/ or the sound /a/ or /s/. On their own they are meaningless, but rearrange those sounds in a different order and you will come up with the word 'cats', instantly recognisable to any speaker of English.

All words are made up of sounds like this, and a speaker of a language needs to know the sounds of that language. Indeed many problems are caused when people speak foreign languages because they can not reproduce the correct sounds. The native speaker of Spanish, for example, often has difficulty with the /v/ in English, and may say 'bery' instead of 'very'. The native speaker of Japanese has problems when speaking English with the sounds /l/ and /r/ and may say 'light' when meaning to say 'right'. The native speaker of English, however, will not make these mistakes for he knows what the sounds of English are and he knows how they are put together. He will have considerable difficulty, though, with Spanish or Japanese sounds!

There are two other types of sound that the native speaker knows about: they are *stress* and *intonation.*

2.1.1
Stress

A native speaker knows which part of a word is the most important. For example, in the word 'photograph' not all the parts are of equal importance. We can divide the word into three parts: '*pho*', '*to*', and '*graph*'. The native speaker of English will say the word in the following way, '*PHOtograph*', making the first part, or syllable, more important and stronger than the other two parts. The situation changes with the word 'photographer', however, and we get '*phoTOgrapher*' with the stress falling on the second syllable. More examples will show the importance of word stress: the word '*perMIT*' is a verb, but the word '*PERmit*' is a noun! The same is true of the words, '*imPORT*' and '*IMport*'.

Stress is also very important in sentences. For example if I say '*I can RUN*' I am probably only telling you about my ability to run. But if I say '*I CAN run*' I am probably stressing the word *can* because someone has suggested that I am not able to run and I am vehemently denying it. If somebody said to you '*Is this your PENcil?*' it would probably be a simple question with no deep meaning, but if the same person said '*Is this YOUR pencil?*' he might be showing, by stressing the word '*your*' that there was something very surprising about your possession of the pencil.

The native speaker unconsciously knows about stress and how it works. He knows which parts of individual words should be stressed and he knows how to put special meaning into sentences by making different words more or less important.

2.1.2
Intonation[2]

Closely connected with stress is intonation, which means the tune you use when you are speaking, the music of speech.

One of the famous plays of the writer Oscar Wilde is *The Importance of Being Earnest* in which, during a particular scene, a young man is explaining to a rather aristocratic lady that he was abandoned, as a baby, at Victoria Station. In fact it turns out that he was left at the station in a handbag. The aristocratic lady's reaction to this piece of information is, for various reasons, one of outraged surprise, and she shows this by saying 'A handbag?'. Well, written like that, there is no sense of outrage or surprise. But if the two words are spoken this feeling can be clearly shown: the lady's voice starts by being high pitched, then swoops down and finally rises again. It is one of the most famous moments in English theatre, and the effect is achieved purely through intonation, the rising and falling of the voice.

More commonplace examples will make the idea even clearer. If I say '*You're from Australia, aren't you?*' and my voice drops down on the words '*aren't you?*', this will indicate to the native speaker that I am simply stating a fact about which I have no doubt. If I say the same sentence but make my voice rise on the last two words the native speaker will understand that something has made me doubt the listener's nationality and I am asking the question to try and confirm what I originally thought. If someone tells me a story and I say '*How interesting*' I can show by my intonation whether I really thought the story was interesting, whether I was indifferent to it, or whether it bored me completely. For example, if the pitch of my voice is high on the word '*how*' and either rises or falls only very slightly on the 'int' of '*interesting*' then it suggests that I really am interested. If the pitch of the word '*how*' is fairly low and my voice drops considerably on the 'int' of '*interesting*' then I am indicating that the story was not interesting for me. The greater the difference between the high pitch of '*how*' and the low falling tone of 'int' is, the more obvious my lack of interest becomes.

Clearly, then, intonation is vitally important in spoken language, and the native speaker knows how the intonation in his own language works and therefore knows how to use it to create the desired effect.

2.2
Grammar

If you ask the average Englishman about his knowledge of grammar he will say he doesn't know any. What is meant by this, of course, is that he cannot tell you what the rules of grammar are, or rather, how English works grammatically. The same man, however, can say a sentence like '*If I had known I'd have come earlier*'. How is this possible?

Linguists have been investigating a native speaker's knowledge for many years, and perhaps the most famous work in this respect is that of Noam Chomsky.[3] His suggestion is that a native speaker has, somewhere in his brain, a set of grammar rules which he can use to make sentences with. We will look at his representation of the rule governing a simple English sentence. '*The boy kicked the dog*'. Chomsky might represent that sentence in the following way:

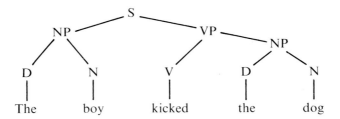

The rule says that the sentence (S) contains a noun phrase (NP) and a verb phrase (VP). The noun phrase contains a determiner (D) and a noun (N) and the verb phrase contains a verb (V) and another noun phrase which we already know contains a determiner and a noun.

The realisation of this rule is not important for our purposes, but what is interesting is that if we slot bits of vocabulary into this tree, or frame, we get a sentence. By changing the bits of vocabulary we get completely different sentences, for example, '*The girl loved the man*', '*The American ate the hamburger*', '*The artist painted the nude*', etc. In other words the rule has not changed, but the sentence has. By using the rule as a base we can select the vocabulary to mean the things we want.

Chomsky's contention is that there are a *finite* number of such rules that all native speakers know: the native speaker knows all the rules. With these rules it is possible to create an *infinite* number of sentences. Our example above showed that with one rule we could make many thousands of sentences and if we use all the rules at our disposal the possibilities are literally endless.

A moment's thought will convince anyone of this: in our lifetime we will never say all the possible sentences in our language, neither will we and twenty of our friends. It is just not possible. And yet we all subconsciously know the rules of our language otherwise we would hardly be able to say anything at all.

Chomsky made a difference between this knowledge and the sentences it produced. He calls the grammatical knowledge *competence* and the realisation of these rules as sentences such as 'The boy kicked the dog' *performance*.

The man, then, who says he doesn't know any grammar is both right and wrong. He could not formulate a grammar rule in the way we have seen above – or perhaps in any other way. But he has language competence, or in other words a subconscious knowledge of the grammar rules of his language, which allows him to make sentences in that language.

2.3 Appropriateness

Although the type of rules explained by Chomsky may account for a native speaker's knowledge of grammar, it may not be sufficient to explain everything a native speaker knows about his own language. One researcher in particular thought that Chomsky had missed out some very important information. Dell Hymes[4] wrote, 'There are rules of use without which the rules of syntax are meaningless'. In other words, the competence that Chomsky talked about (a knowledge of grammar rules) was no good to a native speaker if he did not know how to use the language those rules produced. It is not much help to know that '*Would you like to*' takes the infinitive unless you know that 'Would you like to come to the cinema?' is performing an inviting function.

Hymes, then, said that competence by itself was not enough to explain a native speaker's knowledge, and he replaced it with his own concept of *communicative competence.*

2.3.1 Communicative competence

Hymes separated the native speaker's knowledge about language into four categories.

(a) Systematic potential

The native speaker possesses a system that has potential for creating a lot of language. This is much like Chomsky's original competence.

(b) Appropriacy

The native speaker knows what language is appropriate in a given situation. In broadly social terms the idea could be explained with the old example of the British railway carriage. If you get onto a commuter train to London one morning which is full of businessmen going to work it is most inappropriate to be very cheerful and try and get a carriage full of these men to have a stimulating conversation. It offends against the social customs of that part of English society. Likewise it is possible to suggest that if you wish to invite the managing director of your company to dinner, and you are considerably junior to him, it may not be a good idea to say, '*Hey, d'you fancy a bite to eat this evening?*' since this might be inappropriate when talking to a superior whereas the question '*I was wondering if you'd like to come to dinner this evening*' might not.

Appropriacy, then, accounts for many of the rules of use mentioned in 2.3 and we will look at the concept in greater detail below (see 2.3.2).

(c) Occurrence
A native speaker knows how often something is said in the language. In other words he knows how common a piece of language is. The more common a piece of language is, the more likely it is that it will be clearly understood.

(d) Feasibility
A native speaker knows whether something is possible in the language or not. Systematic potential (see (a) above) might possibly allow for a construction like '*He has been being beaten*', but a native speaker knows that this is not feasible or possible in real life. Again, there are no rules to say how many adjectives you may have before a noun, but at some point the native speaker will say that there are too many to make sense. It is no longer feasible.

Obviously Hymes has included categories that are very different from Chomsky's original idea of competence, and his ideas are considerably more complex in their original form than we have represented here. But it seems clear that the native speaker does in some way 'know' the rules of use Hymes talks about and that these make it possible not only for him to 'get the grammar right' but also to say 'the right thing'. We will now examine that idea in more detail with particular reference to the idea of *appropriacy*.

2.3.2
Appropriacy

We have said that the idea of appropriacy is that a native speaker knows how to choose the suitable thing to say in a given situation. How is that choice made? Hymes says that when we speak we base our choice on the following variables (among others).

(a) Setting
Where are we when we speak; in what situation are we?

(b) Participants
Who is taking part in the conversation?

(c) Purpose
What is the purpose of the speaker? What is he trying to say with the words he is using? Is he trying to complain or apologise? Explain or demand?

(d) Channel
Are the words said face to face or over the telephone? In a telegram or in a letter?

(e) Topic
What are the words about? A wedding or nuclear physics? Cigarettes or films?

All these factors (Hymes also mentions some others) influence a native speaker in his choice of words. For example, if the setting is a church and you are trying to talk to someone three seats away without attracting too much attention you may use as few words as possible but which are nevertheless completely clear, for example, 'Your father?' (said in a whisper) instead of 'How's your father these days?' which you might say if you met the same person in the street. We have already said that you will choose what you say on the basis of who you are talking to. You might say to a friend 'I think you're talking a lot of old rubbish', but you would probably not say the same thing to someone you have invited to your house for the first time! When you say something you have decided what you want to *do*: in other words the Englishman who says 'I'm terribly sorry for being late' says this because he has decided to apologise. If he says 'Yesterday I went to the cinema' he has decided to tell you about a past experience. Most people say things, then, because they have a purpose such as *apologising, greeting, talking about the past, denying, making statements of probability*, etc. Yet another deciding factor will be what you are talking about, and this is obvious since if you are talking about guitar playing the vocabulary you use (apart from anything else) will be different from that of a conversation about newborn babies.

These variables, and the way they affect the native speaker's choice, are what Hymes means when he talks about the rules of use (see 2.3). The problem remains, though, that no-one has satisfactorily arrived at a way of stating such rules!

2.3.3 Situation and context

The fact that rules of use have never been clearly stated need not, however, cause too much alarm. In a general way the discussion of appropriacy is suggesting that language is not an abstract system. In other words people use language in context, in a real-life situation, and it is one of the jobs of the linguist to identify these contexts.

2.4 Interaction with context[5]

Any use of language, of course, is not static. You do not decide on an appropriate piece of language, say it, and then walk away (except in especially dramatic situations). In conversation with another person you constantly have to interpret what is being said as the conversation continues. The listener in a conversation uses what has already been said to help him understand the message that is being conveyed. Based on what has gone before in the conversation he will also predict what is coming next, thus preparing himself to understand it (although of course his prediction may be wrong).

What a good listener is able to do, then, is to process what he hears on the basis of the context it occurs in. And this does not just mean the context variables that govern appropriacy (see 2.3.2): it also involves the verbal and informational context that is created by the sentences before and after the language the listener is processing. In other words you will probably not understand an isolated sentence from a lecture unless you can relate it to what the speaker has already said.

The listener in a conversation is in a similar position to a reader of written text, for the latter too processes what he reads on the basis of what comes before and after it. Both the reader and listener, then, are constantly interacting with the language they see or hear, analysing the context in which it occurs.

**2.5
Language skills**

In 2.3.2(d) we mentioned the concept of channel as being important in determining a native speaker's choice of language. If we examine this concept more closely we can identify certain *language skills* that native speakers possess.

Anyone who uses language well has a number of different abilities. He may read books, write letters, speak on the telephone, listen to the radio, etc. In the most general way we can identify four major skills: *listening and understanding, speaking, reading and understanding* and *writing*. Speaking and writing are obviously skills and involve some kind of production on the part of the language user. Listening and reading are receptive skills in that the language user is receiving written or spoken language. But they are, of course, skills which involve language use because of the interaction with the context that we have just considered in 2.4.[6] Very often the language user is involved in using a combination of skills (see 5.5) so that a participant in a conversation, for example, is involved with both the speaking and the listening skill.

We can summarise the four major language skills in the following way:

MEDIUM / SKILL	SPEECH	WRITTEN WORD
RECEPTIVE	Listening and understanding	Reading and understanding
PRODUCTIVE	Speaking	Writing

This summary is, however, general, and we might well isolate a number of more detailed *sub-skills*. If we consider the skill of writing we can identify a great number of such skills. The writing of an academic paper is very different from the writing of an informal letter. These will be different from the writing of a travel brochure or the taking of notes. We could summarise this in the following way:

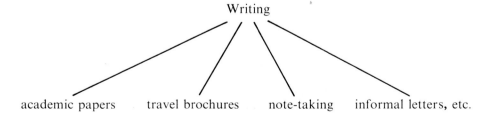

Writing — academic papers, travel brochures, note-taking, informal letters, etc.

Different native speakers will have different sub-skills. Not all Englishmen are good at writing academic papers! It is also true that not all native speakers are competent in the use of the four major skills. There are a great number of illiterate people in the world, so called because they can neither read nor write.

2.6 Conclusions

We have seen that what the native speaker knows is extremely complex. In formal terms he knows the sounds of the language and how to join them together to make recognisable words in that language. The same person knows how to use stress and intonation to make his meaning clear.

The native speaker possesses the grammar rules of the language. He will probably be unable to say what these rules are, but they must exist somewhere in his brain otherwise he would not be able to put together grammatically correct sentences in his language.

The native speaker also knows how to use language: he knows, in other words, what language is suitable in a given situation. Language is always used in a context or situation, and it is the native speaker's knowledge of these contexts and how to behave in them that, to a large extent, determines his selection of words. The native speaker also interacts with the language he receives in order to understand messages on the basis of what goes before and after what he is reading or listening to.

The native speaker, too, is a more or less competent user of a number of skills. Almost all native speakers (except the deaf and the dumb) practise the listening and speaking skills, and a great number are users not only of the other two major skills, but also a selection of sub-skills, depending on their training and occupation.

What the native speaker knows, then, is how his language works and how to use it, and we can call this knowledge the ability to communicate. Language is not something to learn out of academic interest (although some people do study 'dead' languages such as Latin or classical Greek) but something to learn in order to be able to use. Language is the tool by which human beings communicate with each other, and it is this ability to communicate that we have been analysing in this section.

Discussion

1 Do you know any grammar rules, either in your own language or in English (if it is not your language)?
2 Can you think of situations in your own language where it would be inappropriate to say certain things? Do you address people in different ways in your own language? Why?
3 How important is it to be able to write well? What sub-skills do you think are essential?

Exercises

1 Take any word in English and say how many sounds it has.
2 Take any sentence in English and see if you can change its meaning by changing stress and intonation.
3 Take a simple English sentence and see how many more sentences you can make which have a different meaning but the same grammatical form.
4 Write down as many ways of disagreeing as you know in English and then say in what situation you would use the different sentences or phrases.
5 Select one of the four skills and see how many sub-skills you can think of.

References

1 Two excellent books on English sounds, intonation and stress are J O'Connor (1967) and P Tench (1981). For a general introduction see D A Wilkins (1972) Chapter 2 and E Stevick (1982) Chapters 17–19.

2 For a detailed study on intonation see M Coulthard (1977) Chapter 6 and D Brazil et al. (1980).

3 Reading Chomsky can be difficult! The best introduction to his work is J Lyons (1970).

4 Hymes' work on appropriacy is clearly summarised in M Coulthard (1977) Chapter 3. On communicative competence and appropriacy in general see E Williams (1979), P Trudgill (1974) Chapter 5, S P Corder (1973) pages 92–93 and D A Wilkins (1972) Chapter 5.

5 See H Widdowson (1979).

6 For a discussion of how native speakers use language skills see H Widdowson (1978) Chapter 3.

3

What a language student should learn

Having talked about the native speaker we will now turn our attention to the student of English as a foreign language. Should he know the same as a native speaker, and if so should he sound like a native speaker? What kind of language should the student know? Should he be good at the four major skills, and do we expect him to possess any sub-skills, etc.? We will start by looking at the *type of syllabus* students should study.

3.1 Type of syllabus[1]

We have said (see 1.1) that students learn English for different reasons and in different circumstances, and we suggested that people might be taught differently depending on such reasons. It is this latter idea that we will consider here.

Before any teaching is done in a classroom, and hopefully before any materials are written, a decision has to be taken about what the students are going to learn. Often decisions about this will appear in list form. The list may contain grammatical terms (e.g. *the present continuous, the past simple*, etc.), items of language (e.g. *'there is/there are', 'how much/how many'*, etc.), different situations (*At the railway station, At the bank*, etc.) or language functions (e.g. *apologising, agreeing*, etc. (see 3.2)). The syllabus, in other words, is the framework for a course of study listing the contents of that course. Once a syllabus exists materials can be written and teachers can decide how long they need to spend on various parts of the syllabus and how long they will need in class to complete it.

The syllabus is clearly important since it says what will be taught! It is clearly not the case, though, that all students will benefit from the same syllabus. What factors, then, should influence the content of a syllabus? We will look at three main areas: *needs, situation* and *students*.

3.1.1
Needs

One of the things a syllabus designer should consider is what the students need. The air traffic controller probably needs a special kind of spoken English so that he can perform in the skills of speaking and listening. The medical student on the other hand probably needs an ability to read scientific English (the reading skill). In both cases we are saying that the student does not necessarily need to cover the four major skills that we talked about in 2.5. When syllabuses are designed, then, it may be decided to restrict the skills depending upon the needs of the students.

If we know that our students are all air traffic controllers (or will soon become air traffic controllers) it is comparatively easy to take syllabus decisions since the needs of the students are clear: this will generally be the case with such homogeneous groups. We will also be able to decide on the *themes and topics* of the teaching material, and the things we ask the students to do in class. In other words we will probably do a lot of reading in class if our students are studying medicine (see 11.3.3(c)). It is this kind of syllabus, where we may only teach one of the four skills, or at least not all of them, that is often referred to as ESP (see 1.1(b)).

Of course we may not only restrict the skills that we teach, we may also restrict the language to be taught. Some experts have argued that we can decide what skills to teach for specific needs, what topics (or subjects) to deal with on the course (e.g. medicine, agriculture, etc.), and what activities to ask the students to perform (e.g. reading, role playing as waiters, etc.). We will also decide what language we should put in the syllabus and what we can leave out.

The problems arise, though, where groups of students are not homogeneous (i.e. do not have the same needs and level). The language classes in schools and institutes that teach general English contain students with different occupations and interests; in other words, different needs. In the case of schoolchildren, particularly, it is difficult to say with any certainty what their needs will be since we do not know what occupations they may have in later life. This situation is in many ways unsatisfactory for the syllabus designer, but it exists all over the world, and it is possible to speculate that by far the greatest number of students fall into this category. This is so since as we have noted in 1.1 students often take language classes for a great variety of reasons. What can be done in this situation?

Since we do not know exactly what the students may need English for it would seem unwise to restrict the skills that we teach them. The first decision, then, will be to teach, in some measure, the four major skills we have detailed. Our choice of themes and topics, likewise, will not be determined by our students' needs in the same way. Here we will try and produce material that satisfies the greatest majority of our students, at the same time making provision for minority interests within the group.

In this context, however, it will still be necessary to try and ascertain what kind of group we have. If the students are largely adult, with professional lives, our emphasis may be different from that in a class of adolescents. The latter will probably be stimulated and interested by different things from a group of children.

In other words, within the framework of a general syllabus teaching the four skills it will still be possible sometimes to place greater emphasis on certain skills and interests if this seems appropriate after getting information about the members of the group. (See Figure 10 'Profile of student needs' in the Appendix).

3.1.2 Situation

In planning our syllabus we will look very carefully at the situation in which the teaching takes place. Clearly a class of twelve in a well-lit, comfortable and quiet classroom may be treated differently from students in over-large classes where continual noise makes learning difficult. The former may, in other words, be expected to achieve better and faster than the latter. Conditions, then, include such factors as the number of students in a class, the type of classroom, and the aids and materials available. The European classroom equipped with the modern technology of video, overhead projector, tape recorders, etc. will get different treatment from the less privileged classes that survive with a textbook alone. Both the syllabus and teaching content will be different in both cases.

Another factor here will be the aims of the institution where the learning takes place and its attitude towards the learning of English. Indeed these factors may affect such things as skill restriction that we have mentioned above: if the English is a backup for another course of study it will be differently approached from the situation in the language institute, where all students have come only to learn English. The attitude of the school may determine the emphasis placed, for example, on writing.

We will also look at the time allotted to the language class. Obviously students can be expected to achieve more if they have a greater number of hours to learn in. A lot will depend, too, on how the classes are sequenced. Does the class meet once a day or twice a week? In the former case it will be easier to assume that the students remember what went on in the class before. At the same time, though, they do not have an equal amount of time to digest what they have learnt as do those studying with less frequency.

The learning-teaching situation, then, will be very important when planning a syllabus, and what is good for the prosperous language institute may not be ideal for the disadvantaged secondary school.

3.1.3 Students

In 1.3 we looked at the motivational differences of students of different ages and levels since it was felt that we might treat students very differently depending on these factors. Clearly the syllabus designer is also very conscious of the type of student the syllabus is designed for. It is unreasonable to expect that a young child in a classroom situation can achieve the same amount of formal grammar as the young adult, nor is he probably able to deal with the same wide range of themes and topics. In the same way we can suggest that a syllabus for adults can be based on the expectation that they know a lot more conceptually than the schoolchild and have a greater knowledge of social interaction – the way people behave when together.

When we talked about motivation we referred to the student's previous learning experience as being a significant factor. The syllabus designer will want to consider, too, the educational background of his students. We may treat students who are postgraduates differently from those who have only just completed secondary education. Students who come from socially underprivileged situations and whose literacy is called into question will clearly need special treatment.

The syllabus designer, then, takes into account what type of students will use the syllabus, concentrating especially on the students' age and their educational background. (See also 11.3.3 and the 'Description of student needs' in the Appendix).

3.1.4
Syllabus:
conclusions

When we consider what the student of a language should know we have to refer to factors that directly affect the design of a syllabus – the blueprint for language study over a given period. We should not forget that the syllabus is only the first stage in planning a language course, but since it provides the framework for that course it is vitally important to consider factors that make groups of students different.

3.2
Type of language

We mentioned briefly in 3.1.1 the possibility of language restriction, and we will now look at what this involves.

The air traffic controller has a special language which comprises vocabulary and language that many of us do not use in everyday life: the same is true of the waiter. This special language is related to what these people have to *do* in their jobs. They will presumably use the language that does what they want to do. This language of 'doing' has been seen as different from the structures that make up the grammar of the language. Whereas the latter are such things as the present simple (e.g. 'He swims') or the past continuous (e.g. 'He was swimming') the former comprises such things as inviting, apologising, disagreeing, etc. The items of language of 'doing' have been called *functions*.

3.2.1
Functions

The idea of a language function is that it describes what is done with the language. If we wish to invite someone we use the language of inviting. We might say, 'Would you like to come to the cinema?' or 'How about coming to the cinema?', and there are a great many other ways of doing the same thing. *Inviting* is a language function. For every function there are a number of different ways in which the function can be expressed as we have seen with *inviting*. If we look at the function of disagreeing we can do it by saying a number of different things (e.g. 'I totally disagree', 'I wouldn't go along with you there', 'I can't agree with you', 'I'm not really sure if I'd agree with you', 'Rubbish!', etc.). There are a great many language functions such as *greeting, inviting, complaining, apologising, offering, requesting, giving advice, agreeing and disagreeing, suggesting, expressing pleasure and displeasure*, etc.

3.2.2
Functions and
structures[2]

Recently a lot of emphasis has been placed on the functions of language and many writers and materials producers have suggested that they should form the basis for a language learning syllabus rather than the traditional grammatical item such as the present simple, present continuous and past simple, for example. It has been suggested that traditional syllabuses and materials failed to teach the use of language: what they seemed to be doing was teaching the grammar of the language without giving the students knowledge of – or practice in – how it used. Functions, on the other hand, are areas of language where the language is actually used to do things (see 3.2.1). A number of textbooks have been produced that have purely functional syllabuses such as we described in 3.1.

It would seem fair to suggest that learners should be taught to understand functional language; they should, in other words, be able to perform functions such as apologising, inviting, asking for directions, etc. Certainly many students will need to be able to use language for these purposes, and it is true to say that some earlier materials writers neglected to include functional items in their textbooks. But the organising of syllabuses along functional lines brings with it a number of problems. Firstly it is very difficult to order them according to any standard of difficulty. This is so because the grammar used to perform them is extremely varied. We could easily show this by listing the many ways in which it is possible to invite someone, for example. A syllabus designer has to take rather haphazard judgments about which way of inviting he should teach his students to use first. Secondly, a lot of functional language in some textbooks tends to be phrase- rather than sentence-like (e.g. 'You must be joking!' for disagreement or 'That's certainly a possibility' for accepting advice). Although teaching phrases may have some value, students will not be given an ability to create new language as they are with grammatical items (see 2.2). Most importantly, though, functions are expressed through the use of grammatically based language: without some understanding of grammar students would not be able to do anything more than utter separate items of language for separate functions. The expression of functional language is only possible through the use of the grammar of the language. (A more contentious argument is that by teaching students how English people, for example, apologise, you are in fact imposing a cultural stereotype on them.)[3]

The suggestion being made, then, is that students must somehow learn the grammar of the language, for this is central to language use. As the grammar is learnt so the students will also be shown how to use it to perform functions that are relevant to their needs. Both grammatical items and functional realisations will be taught side by side.[4]

Particularly in the area of receptive skills an understanding of functional meaning and use will be important. Students will be trained in the ability to recognise what functions are being performed when they read or listen to something and they can be shown how a conversation in which someone invites a friend to the cinema or asks someone for directions may often follow fairly predictable patterns. (For an example of this see 6.5.3(e).)

**3.3
Communicative
efficiency**

When we discussed what a native speaker knew we considered the concept of communicative competence as put forward by Hymes. We said that a native speaker knows about the grammar of the language, and knows especially what is appropriate in certain situations. It was this knowledge that enabled him to select the language he wished to use.

Do we expect our students to have the same kind of competence? Can they really know what is appropriate without actually living for some time in the target language community?

Communicative competence is often talked about but seldom defined in terms of level. For example, are all native speakers communicatively competent? The answer would surely be no if we consider that part of this competence is knowing what is appropriate in certain situations. And it is doubtful whether we can expect, in a classroom, to teach our students communicative competence. Firstly the classroom may be far from the target language community, and it is doubtful whether we can give this knowledge. We should also ask ourselves whether we necessarily want to train students for the type of competence that is closely allied to one particular society (see reference 3 on page 23). Communicative competence, then, may be not only an impossible goal, but also an unnecessary one in the classroom.

What we can aim for, though, is *communicative efficiency*. Here we will expect our students to be able to express what it is they wish to say. In other words, if they wish to express disagreement we can ensure that they are able to do so and that their meaning is understood. We can take an English standard (see 3.4) and teach students how to convey their thoughts and purposes efficiently. We are not teaching our students to be model Englishmen or Americans, etc., but to use the tool of the English language to communicate.

We will now look at how the concept of communicative efficiency applies to *students at different levels, grammar, situation and context, pronunciation and accent* and *skills*.

3.3.1
Students at different levels

Clearly we cannot expect a student to be communicatively efficient after ten hours of class! At that level he will know only a very small part of the language. Our long-term goal as teachers has to be seen in terms of students who have attained a high standard of language. What, then, can we do about students whose knowledge of English is still at an elementary or intermediate level?

At an early stage of the learning process students will have only a limited amount of English at their command. It will be the job of the teacher to make sure that students can communicate with this limited amount of English. If we are talking about language functions, for example, we can say that asking for information is one of the more vital ones. We *could* ask for information by saying 'Excuse me; I wonder if you could tell me where the station is?'. This is, however, rather complicated for the student at the beginner level, and so we might substitute, 'Excuse me; where's the station?'. The latter question performs the same function efficiently, and we can expect a beginner to be able to say it. It terms of the grammatical language the students study it will be necessary to make sure they know how to use the language they've learnt. In other words, if they have learnt to say sentences such as 'He leaves the office at 6 o'clock', etc., we can make sure that the student can use this construction to, for example, ask questions such as 'When does the bus for Coventry leave?'.

What we are saying is that just because a student's knowledge of English is limited, this does not mean he cannot communicate fairly efficiently with the language he has got. Clearly the lower his level is, the less he will be a sophisticated language user. But he can nevertheless be expected to use the language he knows for the purposes of communication. We said that language was not just an abstract system: it is the job of the teacher to make this true for the student at all levels.

3.3.2
Grammar

The following two (unconnected) sentences can illustrate the treatment of grammar in terms of a student's need for communicative efficiency. The sentences are:

1 He arrived yesterday.
2 Not for many years have I felt so exhilarated.

The first sentence is clearly vital to anyone who wishes to speak the language, whereas the second one is a matter of sophisticated style. It is clear that for a student to be communicatively efficient he needs to know the former, needs to know how to talk about what happened in the past using the past simple tense. But it is not necessarily the case that he also needs to know that a phrase such as 'Not for many years' causes the order of the personal pronoun and the auxiliary to be reversed.

In order for students to have communicative efficiency, then, they should have a grasp of the major grammatical concepts that are essential for any language user. Features of sophisticated style such as the example above are not essential. Of course to have an absolute command of the language these features are desirable, but it is not necessarily the case that all students need or even want to cope with literary style.

3.3.3
Situation and context

We said in 3.3.1 that it was the teacher's job to train students in the use of language and that this meant more than just teaching an abstract system. How can we go about this?

Language happens in situations (see 2.3.3) and in order for students to be able to use it they should realise in what situations certain pieces of language are used. Our teaching for communicative efficiency, then, should take place in such a way that students learn the language and the situations it occurs in at the same time. It is easy to teach a student to say 'John is running' but unless we also teach him how, and in what situations and contexts, such language is used we will not be helping him towards communicative efficiency. (See 4.2.4 on this point and 6.1.1 and 6.1.2 for a discussion of context in language presentation.)

3.3.4
Pronunciation and accent

Many teachers and students feel that the only realistic long-term goal of language learning is for the student to sound exactly like an American or an Englishman. A moment's reflection, though, will show that this idea is rather worrying. In the first place there are very few people who do not live in the target language community who will ever achieve this goal! In the second place it is by no means certain that it is desirable to speak 'like a native speaker'. The fact is that a student learning English in classes outside, for example, England will rarely have sufficiently good models of the language throughout his learning life for such proficiency to be achieved. The older the student is, the more difficult it will be for him to break down pronunciation habits of his own native language. If we turn again to our ideal of communicative efficiency we will soon see that such native-speaker accents are unnecessary. Communicative efficiency supposes that a student can say (and be understood to say) what it is he wishes to communicate. The possession of a foreign accent does not necessarily get in the way of such efficiency. It is the teacher's job, presumably, to ensure that a student should be understood, but this is not at all the same thing as ensuring that he will be taken for an Englishman! Much time has been wasted, in the past, in trying to exact impossible standards of pronunciation from students who quite simply do not need it to be so impeccable.

Teachers and students, then, should insist on a level of pronunciation that ensures communicative efficiency.

3.3.5
Skills

We have already said in 3.1.1 that in a 'general' English course we will attempt to give students a grounding in the four skills. Once again it is worth pointing out that we are not expecting an ability to manipulate literary style or write academic papers in the general English class (although there are some students of language for whom these sub-skills may be very important).

We will, however, be asking for an ability to perform in the four skills within the student's language capability. A writing task for a beginner might involve the filling in of a form applying for a job: not a complicated writing or reading task, but necessary. Most importantly the student is using the fairly modest language ability he has to be communicatively efficient in one task.

It is now generally accepted that students can take a higher level of English in the receptive skills than in the productive skills: provided that students are helped to tackle listening and reading material they can probably handle texts which are considerably more complex than the sort of language they themselves are able to produce either in speech or in writing. (See the concept of roughly-tuned input in 4.2.2 and Chapter 9 on receptive skills.)

Communicative efficiency, then, in terms of the four skills means that we will expect our students to be able to perform at their given level of English and be efficient in this performance. In 3.3.1 we talked about using language for the purpose of communication: it is precisely this purpose that the teacher will encourage in his treatment of the language skills for his students.

**3.4
Language
varieties[5]**

A word must be said about the variety of a language that is taught. A moment's reflection will show that English, for example, has many varieties. British English is often very different from the language spoken in the United States. Jamaican English is again different from both these. There are some people that maintain that one of these varieties is in some way superior to the others, but this is clearly ridiculous! They are all varieties that are spoken by large language communities: they are therefore simply different, and we could list many other varieties from different countries which are spoken by the communities in those countries and which are different from English spoken elsewhere in the world.

The situation becomes even more complex, of course, when we consider a country. There is a considerable difference between northern and southern English, and between Scottish and Irish English.

Which variety, then, are we to teach? In general in British-based English language teaching we teach what is called the Southern English Standard, in other words the English spoken by the middle classes from the south of England. One of the great absurdities of English life is that this variety of English is considered superior to all others (except perhaps the exaggerated emphasis of aristocratic English) despite the fact that it is spoken by a minority of the population. Nevertheless it is the language of 'culture', of

British broadcasting, and in general of the arts.

Students are far less preoccupied (at intermediate and advanced levels) by differences of variety than is generally supposed. At the beginner level, however, it is probably wise to stick to a particular variety of English (within certain limits). We cannot expect every teacher to speak the same way, neither should we. But in terms of the basics of the grammatical system (for there are differences between different varieties) it seems wiser to be as unconfusing as possible, so that whether you are teaching American English, British Southern English Standard or British Northern English Standard it is probably wise to stay with it and not overlap with the other varieties.

3.5 Conclusions

We have said that what the student should learn depends to a large extent upon his needs. Where these are clearly defined, such as in the case of a student studying medicine who needs to read textbooks in English, we may design a special syllabus which restricts the amount of language and the language skills being taught. A great number of students, however, do not have such clearly defined needs, and so we will attempt to teach them a 'general' English.

Our syllabus will change depending on certain other factors such as the type of students we are teaching and the situation they are learning in.

We have discussed briefly the idea of language functions, and we have decided that while they are important, they cannot take the place of the grammar of the language. Students obviously need to know the latter, and should know how to perform certain language functions as well.

We have said that the idea of communicative competence discussed in Chapter 2 cannot be immediately applied to the student of a foreign language since it is based on too many cultural assumptions. A more realistic goal will be communicative efficiency. This means that we are not expecting perfection from our students (or even, necessarily very sophisticated style). Our main concern is that they should be able to communicate efficiently with what they have got, even if the level of this language is fairly low. In particular we criticised the idea that students should speak like southern Englishmen (for example) without a trace of a foreign accent. We said that, on the contrary, it might not be desirable for them to speak like Englishmen and it certainly isn't necessary. The greatest demand a student and a teacher need make upon his pronunciation is that it should not impede communication.

In terms of the language skills communicative efficiency means that students should (in a 'general' class) be able to perform efficiently in all of the four skills, and the sub-skills will be determined by level.

Students should be taught within the framework of a definite language variety at the beginner level: once we have decided which one to adopt we should stick to it in the early stages.

Discussion

1 Do you think we should teach all four skills equally in a 'general' course?
2 How important is good English pronunciation to you and to your students?

3 What is the best way, in your opinion, of finding out what your students' needs are?

4 How important is it to teach grammar? What is the best way to do it?

Exercises

1 Write down what you think are the needs of your students. Describe the situation they are in and say what kind of students they are. What does this tell you about the syllabus you would give them?

2 List as many functions as you can. Then select one and see how many ways there are of performing it.

3 Make a list of the varieties of language spoken in your country. If someone was learning your language which of these varieties would you teach them?

4 In what ways would you restrict (if at all) the language to be taught if your students were:
(a) travel agents?
(b) taxi drivers?

References

1 See D A Wilkins (1976) and especially K Johnson (1982) on different types of syllabus.

2 For more on the relative merits of functional and grammatical syllabuses. (and what these differences are and entail) see K Morrow (1977), K Johnson and K Morrow (eds.) (1978) and K Johnson (1981). Much of their work is a result of (or a reaction to) the work of D A Wilkins mentioned in the first reference above. An example of a syllabus that attempted to answer both functional and grammatical criteria is J Van Ek (1978).

3 This argument is put forward by C J Brumfit in the articles 'Notional syllabuses revisited' and 'The English language, ideology and international communication' in Brumfit (1980).

4 C J Brumfit (1981) page 50 explains this idea very clearly. It should be said, however, that there is a stronger case for a purely functional syllabus at advanced levels since the students can already be presumed to have a reasonable knowledge of the grammar.

5 For a general picture of the different varieties of English see P Strevens (1977) Chapter 11.

4

Language learning and language teaching

In this chapter we will lay down the basis for a language learning and teaching methodology which we will show in detail in Part B of this book. The methodology will be based on much that we have already discussed in the first three chapters as well as on significant theories of language learning.

4.1 Language learning

No-one knows exactly how people learn language although a great deal of research has been done into the subject. Certain theories have, however, had a profound effect upon the practice of language teaching (and continue to do so) and it seems sensible, therefore, to consider them.

4.1.1 Behaviourism[1]

In an article published in 1920[2], two psychologists, Watson and Raynor, reported the results of experiments they had carried out with a young baby called Albert. When Albert was nine months old they discovered that the easiest way to frighten him was to make a loud noise (by striking a steel bar with a hammer). At various intervals over the next three months they frightened Albert in this way while he was in the presence of various animals (a rat, a rabbit and a dog). The result of these experiments was that after three months Albert showed fear when confronted with these animals even when the noise was not made, and even showed unease when a fur coat was put in front of him. The psychologists suggested that they would be able to cure Albert's fear but were unable to do so because he was no longer available for experimentation, and they even discussed the possibility of Albert's fear of fur coats when he reached the age of twenty!

The ethics of this experiment are highly questionable, but Albert's experiences are an early example of the idea of *conditioning*. Watson and Raynor had managed to condition Albert to be afraid of the rat, rabbit, dog and fur coat where before he had a neutral emotional reaction to them.

The idea of conditioning is based on the theory that you can train an animal to do anything (within reason) if you follow a certain procedure which has three major stages, *stimulus, response*, and *reinforcement*. In the classic form of the theory a rat is placed in a box. A signal light is operated (*the stimulus*), the rat goes up to a bar in the cage and presses it (*the response*) and a tasty food pellet drops at its feet (*the reinforcement*). If the rat's behaviour is reinforced a sufficient number of times it will always press the bar when the light comes on.

Reinforcement in that example took the form of a reward and was therefore positive. But you could also train the same rat not to do something by giving him negative reinforcement, maybe in the form of a small electric shock.

In a book called *Verbal Behaviour*,[3] the behavioural psychologist Skinner applied this theory of conditioning to the way humans acquire language. Language, he suggested, is a form of behaviour in much the same way as the rat pressing the bar exhibits a form of behaviour. (It is because we are concerned with behaviour that this theory of learning is referred to as *behaviourism*.) The same model of stimulus-response-reinforcement accounts for how a human baby learns a language. An internal stimulus such as hunger prompts crying as a response, and this crying is reinforced by the milk that is subsequently made available to the baby. Our performance as language users is largely the result of such positive (or negative) reinforcement.

Behaviourism, which was after all a psychological theory, was adapted for some time by the language teaching profession, particularly in America, and the result was the *audio-lingual method* still used in many parts of the world. This method used consistent and unending drilling of the students followed by positive or negative reinforcement. Of course the approach wasn't quite as crude as that, but the stimulus-response-reinforcement model formed the basis of the methodology. The language 'habit' was formed by this constant repetition and the reinforcement of the teacher. Mistakes were immediately criticised, and correct utterances were immediately praised.

4.1.2
Cognitivism

The term *cognitivism* is often used loosely to describe methods in which students are asked to think rather than simply repeat. It stems to a large extent from Noam Chomsky's reaction to Skinner's book and is based on his theory of competence and performance that we have already discussed (in 2.2).

In 1959 Chomsky published a strong attack upon Skinner's *Verbal Behaviour* which has become rightly famous.[4] In his review of the book he explained his rejection of the behaviourist model of language acquisition (how a baby learns a language) on the basis of his model of competence and performance.

The strength of the attack can largely be produced by the asking of questions: if all language is learnt behaviour, how is it that young children can say things they have never said before? How is it possible that adults all through their lives say things they have never said before? How is it possible that a new sentence in the mouth of a four-year-old is the result of conditioning?

Language is not a form of behaviour, Chomsky maintained. On the contrary, it is an intricate rule-based system and a large part of language acquisition is the learning of this system. There are (see 2.2) a finite number of grammatical rules in the system and with a knowledge of these an infinite number of sentences can be performed in the language. It is competence that a child gradually acquires, and it is this language competence (or knowledge of the grammar rules) that allows the child to be creative as a language user (e.g. experimenting and saying things that he has not said before). We looked at a simple example of what the concept of competence and performance involved in 2.2.

Language teaching has never adopted a methodology based on Chomsky's work: after all Chomsky never intended that his theory should have anything to do with adult language learning and has repeatedly made this clear. Nevertheless the idea that students should be allowed to create their own sentences based on an understanding of a rule is widely accepted in many classrooms. This idea is clearly in opposition to the audio-lingual method since we are talking about letting the students, on their own, 'have a go' at the language.

4.1.3 Acquisition and learning	Recently a distinction has been drawn between *acquiring* a language and *learning* a language, most notably by the American writer Krashen.[5] He characterises the former as a subconscious process which results in the knowledge of a language whereas the latter, learning, is a conscious process which results only in 'knowing about' the language. Acquiring a language is more successful and longer lasting than learning.

What is being suggested is that second (or foreign) language learning needs to be more like the child's acquisition of his native language. Although there may be some limits on the language a child hears (see below), he is never consciously 'taught' it, nor does he consciously set out to learn it. Instead he hears and experiences a considerable amount of the language in situations where he is involved in communicating with an adult – usually a parent. His gradual ability to use the language is the result of many subconscious processes, based on the experiences in which he began to acquire – without consciously setting out to do so – the ability to enter linguistically into the communication. Traditional foreign language teaching, on the other hand, concentrated on getting the adult student consciously to learn items of language in isolation, often unconnected with any real communication situation. The focus was not on communicating, but on a piece of language which might later be used to communicate.

Many writers see this traditional approach to language learning as being mistaken since there is no guarantee that an item so learnt will be successfully used in communication or remembered for any length of time. Language has to be acquired as the result of some deeper experience[6] than the concentration on a grammar point, just as it is when children learn their first language.

An experiment by the British applied linguist Allwright[7] seems to bear these conclusions out to some extent. He theorised that:

> . . . if the 'language teacher's' management activities are directed exclusively at involving the learners in solving communication problems in the target language, then language learning will take care of itself . . . (1977b: 5)

In other words there is no need for formal instruction (e.g. the teaching of a grammatical point). Instead students are simply asked to perform communicative activities in which they have to use the foreign language. The more they do this the better they become at using the language.

Allwright's experiment took place at the University of Essex where a number of foreign students were about to take postgraduate courses. They were given a number of activities which forced them to use English, but at no time did their teachers help them with the English or tell them anything about English grammar, etc. The students were all at a roughly intermediate level before they arrived at the University of Essex, and the results were, apparently, extremely satisfactory.

Krashen, however, sees successful acquisition as being very bound up with the nature of the language *input* the students receive.[8] Input is a term used to mean the language that the students hear or read. (See receptive skills in 2.5). This input should contain language that the students already 'know' as well as language that they have not yet seen: the input should be, in other words, at a slightly higher level than the student is capable of using, but at a level that he is capable of understanding. Krashen calls this 'rough-tuning' and compares it to the way adults talk to children. Mothers tend to simplify the language they use to children so that the children can more or less understand it. They do not only use certain structures, however. Rather they get the level of their language more or less right for the child's level of understanding. If foreign language students constantly receive input that is roughly-tuned – that is, slightly above their level – they will acquire those items of language that they did not previously know without making a conscious effort to do so.

The suggestion being made by Krashen, then, is that students can acquire language on their own provided that they get a great deal of comprehensible input (e.g. that is roughly-tuned in the way we have described). Allwright, on the other hand, sees language learning taking place most successfully when students are put in communicative situations in the target language. Both writers are claiming that these approaches to acquisition and learning will be more effective than the conscious learning of grammar and teaching of language that characterises much traditional methodology.

4.1.4
Foreign language
learning

What conclusions can we draw from this discussion of various theories of foreign language learning? Is the idea of conscious learning and teaching absurd, and if there is some merit in it, should it be based solely on the students' cognitive abilities and exclude all conditioning? Is a programme based exclusively on acquisition theory necessarily the most effective way of teaching?

There seems to be little doubt that comprehensible input does help the acquisition process. This type of input shows students how language is used and gives them examples of 'new' language that they will later want to have available in communication. It also seems true that the more a language learner uses language to communicate, the better he becomes at communicating, as Allwright suggests. But there do seem to be worries about an approach based either exclusively on comprehensible input or on communicative activities.

In the first place it is difficult to predict exactly when a language will be acquired subconsciously and when it will be consciously learnt, for that depends on the individual learner. A student who receives roughly-tuned input may make a conscious attempt to learn the new language; another may not do so. It would be difficult to say that either student were using a superior learning strategy! More importantly, though, adults learning a foreign language are not children learning their native language. The latter have a tremendous amount of time to acquire their language, and it is a slow process. The former, however, may be very limited in the amount of time they have to learn, and they may want or need to see results quickly. One way of assuring such results is to help students to learn consciously items of the grammar of the language that they can study (side by side, of course, with a great deal of input and language use in communicative situations). A major reason for such formal instruction is that adult students generally expect it and want it, and it does seem to be true that language that is 'learnt' in this way, and then practised, can become part of the acquired store. Indeed one writer[9] suggests that communicative activities may act as a *switch* that allows 'learnt' language to pass to this acquired store. And whereas younger learners of English may not benefit greatly from an emphasis on conscious learning, adults have a wide variety of learning strategies that they can draw upon, and it is being suggested that conscious learning is one way of helping them to internalise rules for later 'acquired' knowledge.

An approach based entirely on the methods Allwright describes must also cause some concern. His students, after all, already had a reasonable basic knowledge of English. At the same time we would expect them to be above average intelligence and to have a powerful extrinsic motivation (they would all need good English to complete their postgraduate courses successfully). They were studying the target language (English) in a target language community (England) which the great majority of English learners throughout the world are not.

If we accept, then, that conscious learning has a place in the language classroom, how are we to balance the claims of behaviourism and cognitivism? Human beings are thinking people who, hopefully, can rationalise, and it seems sensible to give them an opportunity to use their reasoning powers when learning new language in the unnatural situation of the classroom. We should, in other words, allow them to 'create' language on the basis of rules we introduce them to, as we suggested in 4.1.2. Students will be encouraged to use their new knowledge of grammar rules to make, at an early stage, their own sentences and language. The use of this knowledge will be encouraged, too, at stages of practice where students are prompted to use the new language in different contexts and in combination with other items. At the same time, though, it is clearly the case that students derive great comfort and benefit from some of the repetition techniques that audio-lingual methodology used. Particularly where students are learning new grammar with difficult pronunciation, the use of clear teacher models followed by repetition may help them to overcome these problems.

What is being suggested, then, is that roughly-tuned input and the use of the foreign language in communicative situations can satisfactorily exist side by side with work which concentrates on conscious learning where new language is introduced and practised. The major difference between the methodology being advocated here and more traditional teaching is that we will place increasingly greater importance on roughly-tuned input and communicative activities than earlier methodologies tended to do. Conscious learning is thus seen only as one part of the methodological approach, which encourages language acquisition through a large amount of input and a significant emphasis on the use of language in communicative activities.

4.2
A language learning and teaching model

We are now in a position to lay down guidelines for a methodological approach to the teaching of foreign languages based on the previous discussion. We will look at *input and output, roughly-tuned input, finely-tuned input, signification and value, practice output* and *communication output.*

4.2.1
Input and output

We can divide classroom activities into two main categories: those that give the students language input, and those which encourage them to produce output. Whether acquisition or conscious learning take place, there will be stages at which language is somehow being 'put into' the student's brain. If students only get this language input, however, they may end up with a lot of language items separately stored away, but with no ability to retrieve these items when they need them. It is only when the students are asked to produce and use language that they are forced to assess the language they have stored in their brains. The ability to retrieve this stored language is clearly vital to any language user: he will have to select items of language appropriate to the purpose he has for talking (see 2.3.2(c)), and he will have to combine these items in various ways in order to communicate effectively.

Language output can be divided into two distinct sub-categories. In the first, *practice*, students are asked to use new language in different contexts. Activities are organised which specifically promote the use of the new language, often in combination with English the students already know. The aim is to encourage communication while ensuring that specific language items are used. *Communication output*, on the other hand, is more fundamental in that we put students in situations in which they have to select appropriate language from the total language store. Their job is to retrieve any and/or all the language they know in order to complete the communication task. This type of output is absolutely vital in the encouragement of communicative efficiency. If there is no output work of this or the practice type (but especially communication output) students may learn the language but not be able to use it. We will examine the characteristics of practice and communicative activities in greater detail in Chapter 5.

In very general terms, then, classroom activity can be divided into two large areas: those that are concerned with language input (where students receive new language that is stored in the brain) and those that foster language output (where students are forced to use any of the language they have learnt which is necessary).

A further distinction needs to be made, however, between two different types of input: *roughly-tuned* input and *finely-tuned* input.[10] The former (as we have already said) is language at a level slightly above the students' abilities. The latter is language selected very precisely to be at exactly the students' level. For our purposes finely-tuned input can be taken to mean that language which we select for conscious learning and teaching (see 4.2.3 and Chapter 6).

4.2.2
Roughly-tuned input

The need for roughly-tuned input (where students have to deal with language that is at a higher level than they are capable of producing) has already been extensively argued. We have said that it is this kind of input that helps students to acquire new language. In our methodological approach, then, we will make sure that we include a considerable amount of such input.

Input of this type can come from a number of sources. The teacher talking to the class is giving them input; any reading passage has the same function (among others) as does a listening exercise on tape.

It is clearly necessary to give students a lot of reading and listening material. This is so because one of our major aims will be to teach students how to read and listen to English. As we shall see in Chapter 9 much of this teaching will involve students in reading (or listening) to achieve some kind of purpose. In other words, we will ask our students to read a text in order to be able to extract two or three pieces of specific information, for example. The more they do this, we suppose, the better they become at reading for that purpose. The same is true of listening activities.

But reading and listening texts that are roughly-tuned do not only train the students to read and listen. They also provide exactly the kind of input that we have suggested is necessary. While students are involved in reading and listening training, in other words, they will be subconsciously acquiring 'new' language that appears in the text.

The training of students in receptive skills (which we will consider in detail in Chapter 9) is thus a major part of the methodological approach since it serves both the training function, and at the same time promotes language acquisition.

4.2.3
Finely-tuned input

Finely-tuned input is language which has been selected for conscious learning, such as the present simple, the past continuous, the language of invitation, etc. Such language is introduced to the students at a stage (often called *presentation*) where repetition practice is used and where students are encouraged to employ the cognitive strategies we mentioned in 4.1.2.

During a presentation stage the teacher acts as a controller, selecting the language the students are to repeat and insisting on accurate reproduction of the new item. This means that students' errors and mistakes will be dealt with when they occur. An *error* is the result of incorrect rule learning; language has been stored in the brain incorrectly, in other words. A *mistake*, on the other hand, is less 'serious' since it is the retrieval that is faulty not the knowledge.[11] In other words the student knows the rule, but makes a 'slip' when producing it. The difference between errors and mistakes has important implications for the treatment of student incorrectness, as we shall see in 6.3.3.

The teacher will start a presentation stage by trying to *elicit* the new language from the students. Where this is unsuccessful he will then introduce the meaning and use of the new language and get the students to work with their new knowledge. As soon as possible he will encourage *immediate creativity* where the students use the grammar they have just learnt to create their own original sentences.

The presentation stage, then, in which the students receive finely-tuned input, is a time when the teacher is in firm control (in marked contrast to communication output, for example) of the accurate reproduction of pre-selected 'new' language. Students will be led through repetition stages, but as soon as possible be encouraged to create their own sentences using the new language form. We will look at ways of introducing new language in Chapter 6.

4.2.4
Signification and value

Henry Widdowson, in a 1972 article,[12] coined the used of the terms *signification* and *value* to describe two different ways of introducing and practising new language. Suppose that a teacher wishes to introduce the present continuous tense and does this walking to the door, opening it, and saying, 'Look, I'm opening the door': this is an example of signification. The teacher has clearly demonstrated one meaning of the present continuous (e.g. an action taking place in the present) by opening the door. But he has been misleading about the communicative value (or use) of such language. English people do not go around telling other people what they are doing in this way: they are not continually commenting on their actions (unless they are giving a cookery demonstration or defusing a bomb, for example). The teacher, in our example, is teaching the meaning of the present continuous, but not how it is used.

It is not difficult to think of other examples where teachers tend to omit the teaching of the communicative value of language: students are involved in drills in which they ask questions such as 'Where's the pen?' when they can all clearly see that the pen is, for example, on the table. Once again the meaning is being taught, but in real communication people rarely ask where something is unless they do not know the answer.

It may be, however, that such 'valueless' presentation and practice is not disastrous. In the two examples above students will probably not be misled about the communicative value of either the present continuous or the 'Where?' question. But it seems more sensible to try and teach value at the same time if this is possible. Thus we might introduce the present continuous in a lifelike context, where it is used to give real information about what is happening now. We could do this by showing a dialogue in which speaker *A* does not know what John is doing, whereas speaker *B* does, for example:

A: Where's John?
B: He's in the darkroom. He's developing a film.

The teaching of communicative value, then, means the teaching of language as it is used in real life, and we will try and ensure, during presentation and practice stages, that this value is clearly demonstrated. One of the ways of doing this is to introduce language in a real-life context. We have said (in 2.3.3) that situation and context are important in determining what language is used. By introducing new language in the context of, for example, a social situation, we will be giving students a clear idea not only of its signification, but also of its value.

**4.2.5
Practice output**

The teacher who has engaged his students in conscious learning – that is the controlled repetition and practice of language items – will want to ensure that students can use this language and he will do this by organising practice activities that prompt its use. The aim of such activities will be to get the students using language they have recently learnt in a context that is different from that used for presentation. As far as possible the use of the language will approximate real life and will be as much like genuine communication as the limitations of the activity permit.

Practice output marks a halfway stage between input and communication output. It will often be communicative in many ways, but the attempt to ensure that certain specific language is used will give it less communicative potential. In a teaching programme, however, there need be no linear relationship between practice and communication output. The latter is not necessarily an end product of input and practice. Indeed, it may often be the starting point for an accurate reproduction stage (see 5.4.4).

Practice output, then, is a way of encouraging students to use specific language they have recently learnt in a realistic way, and often in combination with other less recently learnt items. We will look at examples of practice in Chapter 7.

**4.2.6
Communication
output**

In 4.1.3. and 4.1.4 we examined the arguments for communication practice as part of a methodological approach, and stressed that it would have a significant role to play in the language programme.

Communication output refers to activities in which students use language as a vehicle of communication, and where the students' main purpose is to complete some kind of communication task. Because this task is of paramount importance the language used to perform it takes, as it were, second place. It becomes an instrument of communication rather than being an end in itself. In most communicative activities (which we examine in detail in Chapter 8) the students will be using any and/or all the language that they know: they will be forced to retrieve the English that they have in their language store, and they will gradually develop strategies for communication that an over-concentration on presentation and practice would almost certainly inhibit. It is when students are engaged in using language for communication, in other words, that they are responsible for their own learning: the very practice of communication encourages the ability to communicate!

Certain features of communication output will be exactly opposite to those we mentioned for the presentation of finely-tuned input. Instead of a concentration on accuracy, the focus will be on the success of the communication. The teacher's attitude to error and mistake will therefore be completely different. If, for example, he stops students every time they make a mistake and points this out, then he will be destroying the communication that he is supposed to be encouraging. Students will find it frustrating and de-motivating if the teacher's reaction to their ability to communicate *ideas* is focused solely on their ability to get the *grammar* right. This does not mean, of course, that teachers should not be interested in accuracy. But it does imply that there are stages when communicative efficiency (which can occur despite inaccuracy) must be the focus in the classroom.

This focus on communication implies, too, that the role of the teacher should change. If he continues to act as a controller then it is unlikely that any real communication can take place. Students must be allowed to take charge of their learning and their strategies for communication, and an over-dominant teacher will inhibit this. We will discuss the roles of a teacher in Chapter 10.

In our methodological approach, then, emphasis will be placed on activities in which students use language for communicative purposes since it is felt that this is an integral part of successful language learning.

4.3
A balanced
activities approach

We can now sum up a methodological approach to the teaching of languages which takes account of input (both roughly- and finely-tuned), practice, and communication output. It has been called by many writers the *communicative approach* to language teaching.[13] This is because its aims are overtly communicative and great emphasis, as we have seen, is placed on training students to use language for communication. The communicative approach is, then, an umbrella term to describe methodology which teaches students how to communicate efficiently and which also lays emphasis on the teaching of communicative value and, in some cases, the teaching of language functions.

Certainly the aim of all our teaching is to train students for communicative efficiency, but we have already seen components of the approach (e.g. finely-tuned input) which are not in themselves communicative at all. And the fact that communicative value is being taught does not necessarily make the methodology communicative if there is an emphasis on controlled accuracy work. It is, perhaps, better to see the methodology in terms of the activities which the students are involved in, and to assemble a balanced programme of such activities.[14]

A *balanced activities approach* sees the job of a teacher as that of ensuring that students get a variety of activities which foster acquisition and learning. The programme will be planned on the basis of achieving a balance between language input, practice and communication output. In other words our programme will stress the need for language input (of the two types we have mentioned) and practice while seeing the necessity for an emphasis on communicative activities.

We have said that input is an important component of language learning, and we will clearly, therefore, give a large amount of input activities to our students. But a programme based solely on input will not necessarily foster communicative efficiency. There is also a need for output activities of different types, the first (practice) in which students produce language under semi-controlled conditions, and the second (communicative) in which students engage in the very task of communicating in English in the classroom. The inclusion of activities designed to involve students in the different components of input and output will ensure that they are getting a good general programme in their language class. And we have seen the need for roughly-tuned input and communicative activities to predominate over (but not by any means to exclude) controlled language presentation and practice output. It is on this basis that we will effect our balance.

A balanced activities approach has a more human aspect, however, which is bound up with concerns of intrinsic motivation (see 1.2.3). By presenting students with a variety of activities we can ensure their continuing interest in the language programme. Classes which continually have the same activities are not likely to sustain interest, particularly where the students have no extrinsic motivation and do not perceive clear long-term goals. A programme, however, that presents a variety of activities is far more likely continually to engage the students' interest. The concern with a balanced activities approach will be reflected when we discuss planning in Chapter 11.

A final, but important, component of the balanced activities approach is the teacher's ability to be both *adaptable* and *flexible*. Adaptability refers to the teacher's ability to choose and adapt his programme on the basis of the different groups he finds himself teaching. We talked at length in 1.3 about motivational differences, and these should have a powerful influence on the teacher's use and choice of activities and materials. Flexibility refers to the behaviour of the teacher in the class and his ability to be sensitive to the changing needs of the group as the lesson progresses. In simple terms it means that his decisions, before the lesson, about what he is going to do, are not in some way sacred. He must be prepared to adapt and alter his plan if this proves to be necessary.

The concepts of adaptability and flexibility make the real difference between teaching and learning. The unadaptable teacher is the one who 'knows' how to teach and is oblivious to the effect his teaching is having on his students. The teacher who is flexible and is prepared to adapt, on the other hand, is the teacher who carefully assesses his beliefs and plans in the light of the particular situation he is faced with, and whose main concern is that acquisition and learning should take place.

The balanced activities approach, then, sees the methodology as being a balance between the components we wish to include in that approach, and it is an approach that sees the students' continuing interest and involvement in the learning process as being the dominating factor in language teaching.

4.4 Conclusions

In this chapter we have studied theories of teaching and learning languages in order to come to conclusions about a methodological approach to the subject.

We have seen that behaviourist philosophy saw the acquisition of language as the result of conditioning: cognitivism, on the other hand, saw language learning as the ability to be creative on the basis of acquired rules.

We studied the more recent methodological implications of approaches that stress the need for acquisition (rather than conscious learning) and communicative activities in the classroom. The suggestion was that these would be more effective than the conscious learning of language items.

We concluded that while students need a lot of input which is roughly-tuned, and while there must be an emphasis on communicative activities which improve the students' ability to communicate, there is also a place for controlled presentation of finely-tuned input and semi-controlled language practice.

Finally we advocated a balanced activities approach which sees the methodology as being a balance between the components of input and output. Both for pedagogical reasons and for our students' continuing interest in the language programme this balance (with the scales tipped in favour of roughly-tuned input and communication output) is the essential ingredient of the methodology.

Discussion   1 If you were learning a foreign language would you expect the teacher to involve you in conscious learning? If so, why?
2 Which do you think is more difficult for the teacher: organising communication output or presenting new language?
3 In your opinion, is conditioning an important part of learning either a first or second language?
4 What do you think the teacher should do about errors and mistakes that are made during a communicative activity?

Exercises   1 On page 36 one meaning (and use) of the present continuous is given. What other meanings and uses can you think of?
2 Make a list of activities that could be used in the classroom for communication output.
3 Look at an English language textbook and see if you can identify what activities it suggests. Say whether the activities/exercises give input or are designed for output practice. Decide if the input is roughly- or finely-tuned, and say if the output exercises are for practice or communication.

References   1 For more on the relative merits of behaviourism and cognitivism see J Lyons (1970) Chapter 3 and D A Wilkins (1972) Chapter 6.
2 See J B Watson and R Raynor (1920).
3 See B Skinner (1957).
4 See N Chomsky (1959).
5 See S Krashen (1977).
6 The concept of deep experience is expounded in E Stevick (1976).
7 See R Allwright (1977b).
8 See S Krashen (1981).
9 See R Ellis (1982) and E Stevick (1982) Chapter 3 on the need for learning as well as acquisition.
10 These terms are borrowed from Krashen (1981). In other articles (see, for example, Krashen (1982)) he prefers to refer to comprehensible input (e.g. input the students can comprehend without too much difficulty).
        One of the factors necessary for successful comprehensible input is that students should feel free from anxiety and this is of primary importance in the *natural approach* developed by Tracey Terell and detailed in S Krashen and T Terell (1982). The natural approach places heavy emphasis on a *pre-speaking phase* where students receive roughly-tuned input and react to it, but are not forced into immediate language production. The input gives them knowledge of the (vocabulary of the) language to be acquired, and the students only start producing language (output) when they feel like it. The natural approach is especially applicable to beginners.
11 For a detailed look at the meaning and treatment of error see S P Corder (1973) Chapter 11.
12 See H Widdowson (1972) and H Widdowson (1978) Chapter 1.
13 For more on the communicative approach see K Morrow (1981), W Littlewood (1981), C J Brumfit and K Johnson (eds.) (1979) Section 4 and J Revell (1979).
14 For a more detailed discussion of this point see J Harmer (1982).

5 Teaching the productive skills

PART B: PRACTICE

In this chapter we will discuss the nature of communication and its relevance to various stages of learning. We will emphasise the importance of integrating skills and we will also discuss the differences and similarities in learning to speak and write.

The main aim of this chapter is to preface Chapters 6, 7 and 8 which deal with specific techniques for the three major stages of learning the productive skills.

5.1 The nature of communication

Communication between humans is an extremely complex and ever-changing phenomenon, and it is not my intention to examine all the many variables that are involved. But there are certain characteristics that the great majority of communicative events share which have particular relevance for the learning and teaching of languages, and it is to these that we will address ourselves.

When two people are engaged in talking to each other we can be fairly sure that they are doing so for a reason. When one of these people speaks we can probably make the following generalisations:

1 *He wants to speak*: 'Want' is used here in a general way to suggest that a speaker makes a definite decision to address someone. Speaking may be forced on him in some way, but we can still say that he wants or intends to speak, otherwise he would keep silent.

2 *He has some communicative purpose*: Speakers say things because they want something to happen as a result of what they say. The speaker may want to charm his listener; he may want to give some information or to express pleasure. He may decide to be rude or to flatter, to agree or

41

complain. In each of these cases he is interested in achieving this communicative purpose – in other words being successful at what he wants to convey.

3 *He selects from his language store*: The speaker has an infinite capacity to create new sentences if he is a native speaker (see 2.2). In order to achieve his communicative purpose he will select (from the 'store' of language he possesses) the language he thinks is appropriate for this purpose.

These three generalisations apply equally to someone having a private conversation and to the politician giving a speech to thousands. They apply to the schoolteacher and the radio announcer, the judge and the shop assistant.

It is important, too, to realise that these generalisations do not only apply to the spoken word: they characterise written communication as well, and although a difference may be that the writer is not in immediate contact with the reader (whereas in a conversation two or more people are together), the same also applies to the example of the radio announcer, and, to some extent, the academic giving a lecture in a packed hall (although there is of course much greater contact here).

Assuming an effective piece of communication, we can also make some generalisations about a listener (or reader) of language. By effective communication we mean that there is a desire for the communication to be effective both from the point of view of the speaker and the listener. Of course there are many other characteristics that are necessary for effective communication (for example some communicative efficiency/competence on the part of the speakers – see 3.3), and there are many possible reasons for breakdown in communication, but once again three points can be made about the listener:

4 *He wants to listen to 'something'*: Once again 'want' is used in a general way. But in order for someone to understand what they are listening to (or reading) they must have some desire to do so.

5 *He is interested in the communicative purpose of what is being said*: In general people listen to language because they want to find out what the speaker is trying to say – in other words what ideas they are conveying, and what effect they wish the communication to have (see 2 above).

6 *He processes a variety of language*: Although the listener may have a good idea of what the speaker is going to say next, in general terms, he has to be prepared to process a great variety of grammar and vocabulary to understand exactly what is being said.

Once again these comments apply generally to all listeners, and are equally true of readers.

Whenever communication takes place, of course, there is a speaker (and/or writer) and a listener (and/or reader). This is the case even where a novelist writes a manuscript, for here the writer assumes that there will be a reader one day and that that reader will be performing a communicative act when reading the book.

In conversation and, for example, the exchange of letters, the speaker or writer quickly becomes a listener or reader as the communication progresses.

We can summarise our generalisations about the nature of communication in Figure 1:

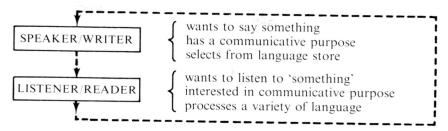

Figure 1 The nature of communication

When organising communicative activities (see Chapter 8) we will try to ensure that these activities share the characteristics we have mentioned here. We will discuss this further in 5.3.

**5.2
The information gap**

We have said that a speaker normally has a communicative purpose and that a listener is interested in discovering what that purpose is. However, even if our listener has some idea about the purpose, he must listen in order to be sure. He cannot be sure, in other words, what it is before he hears what the speaker says. We can illustrate this with a simple example. Consider the following example in which a man (*A*) speaks to a woman (*B*) at a bus stop:

A: Excuse me.
B: Yes?
A: Do you have a watch?
B: Yes . . . why?
A: I wonder if you could tell me what the time is?
B: Certainly . . . it's three o'clock.
A: Thank you.
B: Don't mention it.

The man who starts the conversation may have many reasons for speaking: he may want to get into conversation with the woman because he thinks she looks interesting, and the question about the time may simply be a pretext for this. On the other hand he may genuinely want to know the time. In both cases there exists an *information gap* between what *A* and *B* know. If the question about the time is a genuine one we can say that *B* has information that *A* doesn't have (the time) and *A* wants that information. In other words there is a gap between the two in the information they possess, and the conversation helps to close that gap so that now both speakers have the same information. But even if this were not the real purpose of the conversation there is still a gap between the speakers where *B* does not know what *A*'s purpose is before he speaks.

In the classroom we will want to create the same kind of information gap if we are to encourage real communication: the example in 4.2.4 of the question 'Where's the pen?' does not have this gap, and while it may be useful for purely manipulative practice during an accurate reproduction stage (see 6.3.2) it will not help students to practise English for real communication. Many of the activities in Chapters 7 and 8 will be designed so that there is an information gap between the participants, thus ensuring, to some extent, lifelike communication.

**5.3
The
communication
continuum[1]**

In 4.2.1 we considered the concepts of input and output and in 4.2.6 we said that there were stages where communication was more important than accuracy. Having discussed the nature of communication we can now suggest characteristics that are necessary for input and output stages.

Where students are working on an output stage with an emphasis on communication we can use our generalisations about the nature of communication to come to a number of conclusions. Whatever activity the students are involved in, if it is to be genuinely communicative and if it is really promoting language use, the students should have a desire to communicate (see points 1 and 4 in 5.1). If they do not want to be involved in communication then that communication will probably not be effective. The students should have some kind of communicative purpose (see points 2 and 5 in 5.1): in other words they should be using language in some way to achieve an objective, and this objective (or purpose) should be the most important part of the communication. If students do have a purpose of this kind then their attention should be centred on the content of what is being said or written and not the language form that is being used. The students, however, will have to deal with a variety of language (either receptively or productively) rather than just one grammatical construction, for example. While the students are engaged in the communicative activity the teacher should not intervene. By 'intervene' we mean telling students that they are making mistakes, insisting on accuracy and asking for repetition, etc. This would undermine the communicative purpose of the activity. The teacher may of course be involved in the activity as a participant, and will also be watching and listening very carefully in order to be able to conduct feedback. To these five characteristics of genuinely communicative activities we can add a sixth; no materials control (see Figure 2 below). Often students work with materials which force the use of certain language, or at least restrict the students' choice of what to say and how to say it (we will see examples of this in Chapter 7). But by restricting the students' options the materials are denying the language variety characteristic which we have said is important for genuine communication.

The six characteristics for communicative activities can be seen as forming one end of a continuum of classroom activity in language teaching, and they can be matched by opposite points at the other end of the continuum.

Thus for non-communicative activities there will be no desire to communicate on the part of the students and they will have no communicative purpose. In other words, where students are involved in a drill or in repetition, they will be motivated not by a desire to reach a communicative objective, but by the need to reach the objective of accuracy. The emphasis is on the form of the language, not its content. Often only one language item will be the focus of attention and the teacher will often intervene to correct mistakes, nominate students, and generally ensure accuracy. And of course the materials will be specially designed to focus on a restricted amount of language. A lot of language presentation techniques (see Chapter 6) have these characteristics.

We can summarise the points we have made in Figure 2:

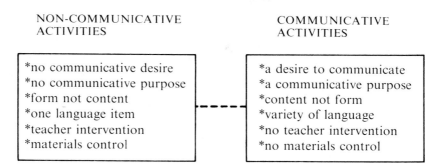

NON-COMMUNICATIVE
ACTIVITIES

COMMUNICATIVE
ACTIVITIES

*no communicative desire
*no communicative purpose
*form not content
*one language item
*teacher intervention
*materials control

*a desire to communicate
*a communicative purpose
*content not form
*variety of language
*no teacher intervention
*no materials control

Figure 2 The communication continuum

Of course not all classroom activities are either 'communicative' or 'non-communicative'. As we shall see in 5.4 there is a large amount of techniques that fall somewhere between our two extremes.

**5.4
Stages in language learning/ teaching[2]**

Based on the continuum in 5.3 we will divide work on the productive skills into three major stages, *introducing new language, practice,* and *communicative activities.*

5.4.1
Introducing new language

The introduction of new language is often an activity that falls at the 'non-communicative' end of our continuum. Often, here, the teacher will work with controlled techniques, asking students to repeat and perform in drills. At the same time he will insist on accuracy, correcting where students make mistakes. Although these introduction stages (often called *presentation*) should be kept short, and the drilling abandoned as soon as possible, they are nevertheless important in helping the student to assimilate facts about new language and in enabling him to produce the new language for the first time. We will concentrate on the introduction of new language in Chapter 6.

5.4.2
Practice

Practice activities are those which fall somewhere between the two extremes of our continuum. While, for example, students performing them may have a communicative purpose, and while they may be working in pairs, there may also be a lack of language variety, and the materials may determine what the students do or say. During practice stages the teacher may intervene very slightly to help guide and to point out inaccuracy (see the concept of gentle correction in 6.3.3 and 10.1.2).

Practice activities, then, often have features of both non-communicative and communicative activities and we will concentrate on such activities in Chapter 7.

5.4.3
Communicative activities

Communicative activities are those which exhibit the characteristics at the communicative end of our continuum. Students are somehow involved in activities that give them both the desire to communicate and a purpose which involves them in a varied use of language. Such activities are vital in a language classroom since here the students can do their best to use the language as individuals, arriving at a degree of language autonomy. We will look at activities of this kind in Chapter 8.

A point can be made here about the use of the students' own language (rather than English) during practice and communicative activities. Particularly where students working in pairs and groups share the same native language there is a tendency for them to revert to that language when they find a task hard. To some extent it will be their responsibility to make sure this does not happen, and the teacher will have to explain the importance of the activities and the use of English to the students. A committed class will use the native language rarely, if at all, but there is, of course, no reason why they should not do so occasionally – to help an activity along – if the native language does not predominate.

5.4.4
The relationship between the different stages

There is a clear relationship between the introduction and practice stages whereas the relationship between communicative activities and the introduction and practice stages is not so clear.

If a teacher introduces new language he will often want to practise it in a moderately controlled way. After an introduction stage, therefore, he may use one of the practice techniques we will look at in Chapter 7 to give the students a chance to use the new language in a controlled environment. However, the practice stage will often not follow the introduction stage immediately; other activities might intervene before students again work on the same language.

By the nature of communicative activities, they are not tied to the other stages since they are designed to elicit all and any language from the students. Two points can be made, though. Firstly, the teacher listening to a communicative activity may notice that a majority of students find it difficult to use the same language. By noting this fact he is in a position to design a subsequent class in which he introduces the language the students could not use.[3] There is, therefore, a natural progression from communicative activity to the introduction of new language.

Sometimes, of course, the teacher may have been working on a certain area of language which will be useful for a future communicative activity. Thus, for example, if students have been looking at ways of inviting they will then be able to use that knowledge in a communicative activity that asks students to write each other letters of invitation (see 8.2.2(a)).

It will of course be the case that while not all presentation activities fall exclusively at the 'non-communicative' end of the continuum, neither will all the activities in Chapter 8 have exactly the characteristics of communicative activities, although in general they will be followed.

It is probably true that at the very early stages of language learning there is more introduction of new language and practice than there are communicative activities. This balance should change dramatically, however, as the standard of students' English rises. Here one would expect there to be a heavier emphasis on practice and communicative activities than on presentation. However, this balance is often more the result of decisions about what the students need on a particular day in a particular situation (as we shall see when we discuss planning in Chapter 11) than it is a decision about the interrelation of stages. It should be remembered, too, that beginners should receive a large amount of roughly-tuned input (see 4.2.2)

5.5 Integrating skills

In 2.5 we discussed briefly the four main language 'skills' and it would seem clear that in a general class it is the teacher's responsibility to see that all the skills are practised. We have made a division between productive and receptive skills (see 2.5) so that Chapters 6, 7 and 8 deal with the former and Chapter 9 with the latter.

This suggests that in some way the skills are separate and should be treated as such; on one day students will concentrate on reading, and reading only, on the next speaking and only speaking, etc. In fact this position is clearly ridiculous for two reasons. Firstly it is very often true that one skill cannot be performed without another. It is impossible to speak in a conversation if you do not listen as well, and people seldom write without reading – even if they only read what they have just written. Secondly, though, people use different skills when dealing with the same subject for all sorts of reasons. Someone who listens to a lecture may take notes and then write a report of the lecture. The same person might also describe the lecture to his friends or colleagues, and follow it up by reading an article that the lecturer suggested. Another case would be that of a person who reads about a concert or play in the paper and invites a friend to go with him. The same person will probably read the programme for the concert/play and talk with his guest. Later he may well write a letter to someone telling of the experience.

In these cases, and in many more, the same experience or topic leads to the use of many different skills, and in our teaching we will try to reflect this. Where students practise reading we will use that reading as the basis for practising other skills. Students involved in an oral communicative activity will have to do some writing or reading in order to accomplish the task which the activity asks them to perform. Students will be asked to write, but on the basis of reading, listening or discussing.

Often our activities will have a focus on one particular skill, it is true, so that at a certain stage the students will concentrate on reading abilities. But the focus can later shift to one or more of the other skills.

In many of the examples in the next four chapters the principle of integrating skills – where focus on one skill leads to practise in another – will be followed, and although there are cases where individual skills may be treated individually the principle of integration is thought to be important.

5.6 Speaking and writing

The next three chapters in this book are concerned with focusing activities on speaking or writing – although promoting skill integration at the same time. In each chapter (Introducing new language, Practice, and Communicative activities) there will be sections on oral production and on written production, although in Chapter 6 there is less emphasis on writing as a separate skill since its function is often to reinforce new language learnt orally. This does not mean, however, that writing is considered in some ways to be a 'lesser' skill, and both Chapters 7 and 8 contain large sections on the learning of writing skills.

At this point it might be a good idea to make some comparisons between written and spoken English, since the differences imply different types of exercises which focus on different aspects of language.

A speaker has a great range of expressive possibilities at his command. Apart from the actual words he uses, he can vary his intonation and stress (see 2.1) which helps him to show which parts of what he is saying are more or less important, or whether, for example, he wishes to be taken seriously.

At any point while he is speaking he can re-phrase what he is saying or speed up (or slow down) depending on the feedback he gets from his listeners. People listening to him can show by a variety of means that they do or do not understand/approve of what is being said, and of course the speaker can use facial expression, gesture and body posture to help to convey his message.

Of course these points are especially true of a speaker involved in a conversation, where other participants can interrupt, ask for clarification or give other types of feedback. The speech maker, however, may not be asked for clarification, but he will still learn a lot from the attitude of his audience. Speaking on the telephone obviously does not allow for the use of facial expression or gesture, but intonation and stress are used to great effect as well as re-phrasing, etc.

Perhaps the single most important difference between writing and speaking, however, concerns the need for accuracy. Native speakers constantly make 'mistakes' when they are speaking. They hesitate and say the same thing in different ways and they often change the subject of what they are saying in mid-sentence. Clear examples of this are provided on page 176. Except in extremely formal situations this is considered normal and acceptable behaviour. A piece of writing, however, with mistakes and half-finished sentences, etc. would be judged by many native speakers as illiterate since it is expected that writing should be 'correct'. From the point of view of language teaching, therefore, there is often far greater pressure for written accuracy than there is for accuracy in speaking.

The writer also suffers from the disadvantage of not getting immediate feedback from the reader – and sometimes getting no feedback at all. He cannot use intonation or stress, and facial expression, gesture and body movement are denied him. These disadvantages have to be compensated for by greater clarity and by the use of grammatical and stylistic techniques for focusing attention on main points, etc. Perhaps most importantly there is a greater need for logical organisation in a piece of writing than there is in a conversation, for the reader has to understand what has been written without asking for clarification or relying on the writer's tone of voice or expression.

Lastly there are the twin problems of spelling and handwriting.[4] English spelling is notoriously difficult for speakers of other languages, and handwriting is particularly problematical for speakers of Arabic, Farsi, Chinese and other languages which do not have Roman script.

When teaching writing, therefore, there are special considerations to be taken into account which include the organising of sentences into paragraphs, how paragraphs are joined together, and the general organisation of ideas into a coherent piece of discourse. We will be looking at these areas in Chapter 7. There is also, of course, a need for communicative writing activities and we will look at these in Chapter 8.

Students need to see the difference between spoken and written English. In part this will happen as a result of exposure to listening and reading material, but it will also be necessary to provide exercises that deal specifically with features of spoken and written discourse.

5.7 Level

The three chapters dealing with the productive skills will give exercises at various levels. In general the emphasis will be on beginner and elementary materials, activities and techniques, but there will also be examples of more intermediate and advanced material.

5.8 Stages

Particularly with some communicative activities (see Chapter 8) the success of the exercise depends on a clear setting-up of the task. Students must be absolutely clear about what they are supposed to do and what the purpose of their activity is. For this reason the activities in Chapter 8 are described in terms of the stages the teacher would go through to initiate them. This should serve the dual purpose of explaining clearly how the activities work and also providing a clear teacher sequence for setting up such activities.

5.9 Conclusions

In this chapter we have studied the nature of communication in order to come to some conclusions about the type of activities our students should be involved in.

We have seen a need for activities that involve the students in having a communicative purpose, using language freely with no teacher intervention. We have also said, however, that students will need controlled exposure and practice of new language.

We have stressed the need for the integration of skills, showing how in real life people seldom work with one skill only when dealing with a topic, and we have shown how speaking and writing have some major differences which must be dealt with in a teaching programme.

Discussion

1 Which do you think are more important in a language learning programme; practice activities or communicative activities? Why?
2 Do you think that all speaking and writing has a 'purpose'?
3 If you were learning a foreign language would you like to work with your classmates with no teacher supervision? What advantages and disadvantages would there be in such an activity?
4 How important is the written skill for your students? How important would it be for you if you were learning a foreign language?
5 In what ways is writing 'more difficult' than speaking? Do all students find writing more difficult?

Exercises

1 Think of any conversation you have had in the last two days. What was your purpose in that conversation, and what purpose did the other participant in the conversation have?
2 Take an exercise from an English language textbook and say where it would occur on the communication continuum.
3 Take any piece of reading material from an English textbook and think of how it could be used for integrated practice of other skills.

4 Try and write down some English you have heard used by a native speaker exactly as he or she said it. Then note the number of 'mistakes', hesitations, re-phrasings, changes of subject, etc. that occur.

5 Take any piece of written English that explains how something works and then write down how you might explain the same thing orally to a friend. What differences would there be?

References

1 I am grateful to Jane Willis for her comments on an earlier version of this part of the chapter. I also found a transcript of a talk by John Sinclair entitled 'The Teaching of Oral Communication' (given in Singapore in April 1980) extremely useful.

2 W Littlewood (1981) divides the stages of learning into *pre-communicative* and *communicative* activities. Under *pre-communicative* he has *structural activities* (similar to 'introducing new language' in this chapter) and *quasi-communicative* activities (similar to the practice stage in 5.4.2).

3 This procedure as a general approach to language teaching is advocated by C J Brumfit (1978) and K Johnson (1980).

4 For comments on handwriting see D Byrne (1979), Appendix 2 and the references quoted there.

6 Introducing new language

In this chapter we will consider ways in which students can be introduced to new language. This is the conscious learning mentioned in 4.1.3 and 4.1.4 and which we called 'finely-tuned input' in 4.2.3. By 'new' language we mean language we think students have not seen before (or are unable to produce). This stage of the class is often called presentation.

6.1 What do we introduce?

The teacher's job at this stage of the lesson (aided by the materials he is using) is to present the students with clear information about the language they are learning. He must show students what the new language means and how it is used (see 4.2.4); he must also show them what the grammatical form of the new language is, and how it is said and/or written.

6.1.1 The presentation of meaning and use

We have frequently mentioned the idea of context and situation as being essential to an understanding of language use; in other words, real language occurs in real-life situations, or as a result of real information.

The presentation of meaning and use should take place in some context, either provided by the materials the class is using or created by the teacher. The teacher will want to check that the context provided in the materials he is using is appropriate for the language being introduced.

The context for introducing new language should have a number of characteristics. It should, for example, show what the new language means and how it is used. A lot of useful contexts, therefore, show the new language being used in a written text or in a dialogue. The students can thus see or hear the new language at the same time as they understand what it means and how it is used. A good context should also be interesting for the students. This doesn't mean that all the contexts that students see have to be wildly funny or incredibly inventive, but the students should at least want to see or hear the information. Ideally the context in which the language is introduced will be a reasonable model for students to imitate and then use as the basis for making their own sentences (see *immediate creativity* on pages 56 and 57).

Many contexts in textbooks have all the qualities that are mentioned here, and the teacher can confidently rely on the material to introduce the new language. Sometimes, however, the textbook context is inappropriate for your class. It may be uninteresting for the students, or too complicated; not all the students may have the book, or the quality of a dialogue on a tape may be insufficient. In such cases the teacher will want to create his own contexts for language use, and he should do so based on the principles we have outlined above.

6.1.2
Types of context

By *context* we mean the situation or the body of information that results in language being used. There are, of course, a number of different context types. In classroom terms we can divide context into three main areas, *the classroom, situations*, and *formulated information*.

The classroom can be a useful context for the introduction of meaning, although as we have seen it is difficult to show how language is used if we base our introduction of language on tables, chairs, blackboards and chalk, etc. (see 4.2.4). Nevertheless it is a fact that the classroom is full of objects and also students. The former may help the presentation of meaning of such items as prepositions, the latter such items as colours, size, comparatives, etc.

Situations are taken to mean events in which we list such things as participants and setting, etc. In other words the people, the places and the purpose of what is being said are important (see 2.3.2). Two major types of situation are *simulated real-life*, and *invented story. Simulated real-life* situations are particularly important for the introduction of more functional language. Thus it is important if introducing the language of invitation to show who the participants are (are they friends or acquaintances, is one speaker superior to the other?) and where the conversation is taking place. *Invented stories* have always been used by teachers and materials writers. A typical example of an invented story is that of the group of friends who were in a car crash and were injured. Thus '*Jane can't walk*' and '*Julia can't play tennis*', etc. Invented stories provide endless scope, but it is difficult to make them believable and they place great demands on a teacher's and materials writer's imaginative powers.

Formulated information is information presented in the form of charts, graphs, maps, etc. Here there is no 'situation' in that we do not introduce a setting and participants as we do in our simulated real-life scenes (see above). Formulated information can be either *simulated real-life* or *real-life*. Simulated real-life information is that of imaginary countries, statistics, or timetables. Teachers and materials writers are often attracted to the idea of presenting information in this way because they can then provide just that information they need for the introduction of the new language in a way that is clear and simple (unlike many real-life charts, graphs and maps, etc.). There is a danger, though, in asking students to say things that are not true, and it may be difficult to make such formulated information look authentic. In the case of real-life formulated information we do not have to worry so much about truth, but often the way in which such information is presented is less than ideal for the language classroom.

There are, of course, variations on these types of context, but in general we can represent them in the following way:

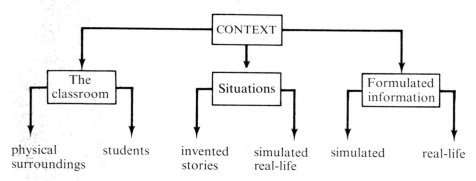

Figure 3 Contexts for language introduction

The context which is chosen will depend on the type of language being introduced. If the teacher is creating his own context he will consider the type of student to whom he will be presenting the language. It is possible to speculate that adolescents are less content with invented stories and happier with an information load that challenges them *per se*. Older students having difficulty, on the other hand, may prefer the less demanding story. But it is difficult to generalise, and teachers have to be sensitive to the varying degrees of motivation provided by different contexts.

Finally it should be pointed out that the language may be introduced in one context (e.g. a dialogue) and the accurate reproduction stage may take place in another (see for example 6.5.4 (b)).

**6.2
The presentation
of form**

It will be the teacher's job to show how the new language is formed and he may do this in a number of ways. He could do it by giving a grammatical explanation. This would seem to be difficult though for two reasons. Firstly many students may find grammatical concepts difficult – we have said that few people know about grammar rules and explanations (see 2.2) – and secondly it will be difficult unless the teacher is a fluent speaker of the students' native language. This clearly will not be the case in a group with students from different countries.

A more effective – and less frightening – way of presenting form orally is to let the students hear and/or see the new language, drawing their attention to the grammatical elements of which it is made.

These comments apply particularly to beginner and elementary students, whose language is limited. More advanced students may profit from more explicit explanations, although even in their case it should be remembered that few people are comfortable with grammatical explanations and terminology.

The presentation of form, then, can usefully take place without the need for complicated grammatical explanation: instead the teacher can give the students a clear oral model of the new language (with written backup if necessary) drawing their attention to important points.

6.2.1
Analysing the form

Before a teacher introduces any new language he should have analysed the form he is going to teach so that he understands its grammar and how it is said and written.

Suppose, for example, the new language to be introduced is the third person singular of the present simple tense (e.g. 'The President gets up at six o'clock'). The grammar point we wish to teach is the occurrence of the 's' on the verb stem. But we can use the third person singular of the present simple in many different constructions (e.g. 'He loves his wife', 'It never rains but it pours', 'He lives in Guadalajara', 'He goes to work by bus on Wednesdays', etc.). In the first sentence we have a subject + verb + object construction. The second sentence is, in fact, two clauses; the first one has an adverb of frequency, the second doesn't. The third sentence has a subject, a verb, and an adverbial ('in Guadalajara'). The last sentence has three adverbials ('to work', 'by bus' and 'on Wednesdays').

The materials writer or teacher will make a choice about the grammatical *pattern* in which he will introduce the new grammar point. In other words he might concentrate on a pattern of subject + verb + adverbial. This would produce such sentences as 'He lives in London', etc. The point about such a pattern is that it is made up of changeable units. In 2.2 we saw an interpretation of a sentence, and we saw how we could create different sentences with the same grammar (or pattern) simply by changing vocabulary items. We can demonstrate the principle of changeable units using our subject + verb + adverbial pattern in the following way:

PATTERN	SUBJECT	VERB	ADVERBIAL
Examples	He She It John	lives stays happens works	in London at home in the town at the airport

If, when we introduce the present simple (third person singular) for the first time, we stick rigidly to a pattern such as the one shown above it will help students to focus on the new grammar point (e.g. the 's' on the verb). Students will very soon, however, be able to use the new verb tense in different patterns. This can be tried at the immediate creativity stage, or even before with a good class.

The idea of changeable units is that they allow us to create *models* for the students to work with. A model is an example of the pattern. Thus the teacher who is introducing the present simple (third person singular) will ask the students to work with a number of sentences all of which conform to a pattern such as the subject + verb + adverbial sequence above. This will be during the accurate reproduction stage (see page 56). As soon as possible, however, students will be encouraged to use the present simple with other grammatical patterns.

So far we have considered the changeable units for a grammatical structure. Functional language, too, will often contain the same kind of units. If we are teaching students how to invite, for example, we might introduce the form *'Would you like to'* + *verb*. The latter part of this pattern is clearly changeable, so that we can introduce models such as 'Would you like to come to the cinema/have lunch/play tennis?', etc.

Certain phrases which teachers may introduce, or which may appear in the textbook, however, may not have such changeable units – or at least the choices may be very restricted. For the function of agreeing, for example, we can say 'I'd agree with you there'. The only real possibility for substitution would be to say 'I'd go along with you there'.

The teacher needs to be clear about how the language he is going to present is said and written. Thus the 's' of our present simple ending sometimes sounds like 's' (e.g. works, laughs, writes, etc.); sometimes it sounds like a 'z' (e.g. plays, says, lives, etc.) and sometimes it sounds like 'iz' (e.g. watches, closes, catches, etc.). The teacher may decide to introduce these verbs in a definite order depending on the different sounds of the ending. He will not do so, of course, if he thinks the different sounds will not cause problems.

The teacher must also work out how the models he is going to introduce are normally stressed so that in saying them to the students he will give a clear idea of correct spoken English.

6.3
A general model for introducing new language

We can now look at a general model for introducing new language which gives an overall picture of the procedure. All the examples we are going to show in 6.5 follow this model to some degree.

The model has five components: *lead-in, elicitation, explanation, accurate reproduction*, and *immediate creativity*.

During the *lead-in* the context is introduced and the meaning or use of the new language is demonstrated. This is the stage at which students may hear or see some language (including the new language) and during which students may become aware of certain *key concepts*. The key concepts are those pieces of information about the context that are vital if students are to understand the context and thus the meaning and use of the new language. If we are introducing a dialogue in which a visitor to a town is asking for directions from a local resident it will be necessary for the students to understand that:

1 The speaker is a stranger.
2 He doesn't know where something is.
3 He's talking to someone who lives in the town.

With this knowledge the students will understand what he is saying (and why) in the following dialogue:

VISITOR: Excuse me!
RESIDENT: Yes?
VISITOR: Where's the station?
RESIDENT: It's opposite the hospital at the end of this street.
VISITOR: Thank you very much.
RESIDENT: Don't mention it.

In the case of formulated information (such as the airline timetable in 6.5.4 (a)) it will be necessary for students to understand the concepts of *destination, via, departure* and *arrival*, for without these they will not understand the meaning of such sentences as 'Flight 309 goes to Paris'. During the lead-in stage the teacher can also demonstrate the probable course of an interaction (particularly at more advanced levels).[1] An example of this is 6.5.3 (e). During the lead-in stage, then, we introduce our context (making sure that key concepts are understood) and show the new language in use.

During the *elicitation* stage the teacher tries to see if the students can produce the new language (see 4.2.3). If they can it would clearly be wasteful and de-motivating for the students if a lot of time was spent practising the language that they already know. At the elicitation stage – depending on how well (and if) the students can produce the new language – the teacher can decide which of the stages he will go to next. If the students can't produce the new language at all, for example, the teacher will move to the explanation stage. If they can, but with minor mistakes, he may move to the accurate reproduction stage to clear up those problems. If they know the new language but need a bit more controlled practice in producing it he may move directly to the immediate creativity stage (this is indicated by the dotted lines in Figure 4). Elicitation is vitally important for it gives the teacher information upon which to act: it is also motivating for the students and actively involves their learning abilities. Elicitation techniques will be detailed in our examples in 6.5.

During the *explanation* stage the teacher shows how the new language is formed. It is here that he may give a listening drill or explain something in the students' own language; he may demonstrate grammatical form on the blackboard. This is where, in other words, the students learn how the new language is constructed, and we will look at explanation techniques in more detail in 6.3.1.

During the *accurate reproduction* stage students are asked to repeat and practise a certain number of models. The emphasis here will be on the accuracy of what the students say rather than meaning or use. Here the teacher makes sure that the students can form the new language correctly, getting the grammar right and perfecting, as far as is necessary, their pronunciation. We will look at accurate reproduction techniques in detail in 6.3.2.

When the students and teacher are confident that the students can form the new language correctly they will move to *immediate creativity*. Here they try to use what they have just learned to make sentences of their own, rather than sentences which the teacher or book has introduced as models. It is at this stage that both teacher and student can see if the students have really understood the meaning, use and form of the new language. If they are able to produce their own sentences they can feel confident that the presentation was a success. We will see many examples of immediate creativity in 6.5.

We can represent the model for introducing new language in diagram form:

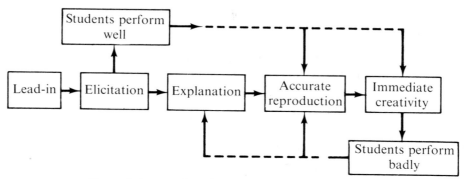

Figure 4 A general model for introducing new language

Notice again that if the students perform well during elicitation the teacher can move straight to immediate creativity. If at that stage they perform badly the teacher may find it necessary either to return to a short accurate reproduction stage or, in extreme cases, to re-explain the new language.

In 6.5 we will show how the model can be applied to a number of presentation situations, many of which are taken from published textbooks.

**6.3.1
Explanation
techniques**

We will look at two procedures for explaining the form of the new language. In both cases the intention is to demonstrate to the student what the grammar of the construction is.

(a) Explaining statements

In this case the teacher wishes to explain his first model based on the flight timetable on page 82. The model is:

Flight 309 goes to Paris.

The teacher will follow this procedure:

Stage 1 The teacher says the sentence in a normal way with a clear voice using correct stress and intonation. He may do this two or three times.
Stage 2 The teacher isolates a particular feature of the model.
Stage 3 The teacher distorts this feature showing how it is constructed.
Stage 4 The teacher returns to the isolated element.
Stage 5 The teacher gives the normal model again.

We can represent this procedure in Figure 5:

Figure 5

Sometimes, however, the teacher may not have to distort the isolated feature (where it is only a one syllable word).

Where there is more than one item that needs isolating the teacher goes through the procedure in Figure 5 with the first item to be isolated and then repeats the sequence with the second item.

The following example clearly shows the procedure in action. The teacher wishes to isolate both the verb form and the pronunciation of the flight number:

T: Listen . . . Flight 309 goes to Paris . . . flight 309 goes to Paris . . . listen . . . goes . . . goes . . . go . . . z . . . go . . . z . . . goes . . . flight 309 goes to Paris . . . listen . . . three-oh-nine . . . flight 309 goes to Paris . . . flight 309 goes to Paris.

The teacher may back up this oral explanation by writing the following on the blackboard:

Flight 309 goes to Paris.

The use of a box to highlight the main grammar points helps to focus the students' attention on that point.

(b) Explaining question forms

When the teacher has to do the same kind of explanation for a question form he may follow the same procedure as for (a) above. However, particularly where a question form is taught after the affirmative version of the same grammar point has already been the subject of practice, some extra techniques may help the students to understand the form of the question.

Unlike many languages English uses inversion to signal a question. Thus if we take an affirmative sentence such as 'He is running' we find that the equivalent question form has the subject and the auxiliary in a different order, e.g. 'Is he running?'. Even where we put a question word (such as 'which', 'what', 'how', 'when', etc.) at the beginning of the question this inversion is still used. Students of English frequently find this confusing.

When introducing a question the teacher will follow the same procedure as for (a) above. He will, however, isolate and distort in a slightly different way, and it will be advisable to use the blackboard and/or gesture to make the inversion clear.

Suppose the teacher wished to 'explain' the question model 'Is he running?' He might do it in the following way:

T: Listen . . . Is he running? Is he running? . . . listen . . . he is running? . . . no (*teacher shakes head and crosses his arms in an 'inversion' gesture*) . . . Is he running? . . . Is he running?

The teacher can write the following on the blackboard at the same time:

If the teacher wished to present the question 'Does flight 309 go to London?' he would follow the same procedure as for the previous example. On the blackboard, however, he might write the following:

Flight 309 goes to London .
Does Flight 309 go to London ?

The importance of visual demonstration for grammar cannot be exaggerated. Many students react far better to written stimuli, and in the examples we have shown the teacher's use of the blackboard (to highlight important features) helps students to understand the new point being taught.

Once the teacher has gone through an explanation phase he will then move to accurate reproduction.

6.3.2 Accurate reproduction[2]

As we said on page 56, the purpose of an accurate reproduction stage is to give students controlled practice in the form of the new language. We will look at three stages of this part of the lesson, *choral repetition, individual repetition* and *cue-response drills.*

(a) Choral repetition

When the teacher has explained a model as in 6.3.1 he asks the whole class to repeat the model together. This is choral repetition. The technique is useful because it gives all the students a chance to say the new language immediately, with the teacher controlling the speed and the stress. It gives students confidence (where immediate individual repetition might cause anxiety) and it gives the teacher a general idea of whether the students have grasped the model.

There are three things to remember about choral repetition:

1 The teacher should clearly indicate (by conducting) when the students should start the chorus.
2 The teacher should clearly indicate the correct stress during the chorus.
3 The teacher should stay silent during the chorus so that he can hear how well the students are performing.

If we take our model sentence from 6.3.1(a) the chorus might go something like this:

  T: (*finishing the explanation*) Fight 309 goes to Paris . . . flight 309 goes to Paris . . . everybody. (*T makes a gesture*).
SS: Flight 309 goes to Paris.
  T: Again. (*gesture*)
SS: Flight 309 goes to Paris.

The teacher will have to decide how many choruses he needs based on such factors as the difficulty of the model, the students, etc.

Choral repetition can also be used during correction (see 6.3.3(b)).

(b) Individual repetition

Individual repetition is conducted in three stages. The teacher nominates a student, the student responds, and the teacher gives feedback. Nomination (selecting the student) can be done by calling the student's name or by pointing, although the latter should be done with care so as to avoid causing offence.

We can summarise the procedure for individual repetition in Figure 6:

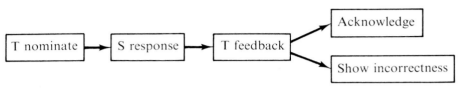

Figure 6 Individual repetition

If we continue with our sentence about flight 309 individual repetition might be something like this:

T: (*finishing choral repetition*) Again.
SS: Flight 309 goes to Paris.
T: Good . . . now Juan.
S1: Flight 309 goes to Paris.
T: Good . . . Myra.
S2: Flight 309 goes to Paris.
T: Yeah . . . (*T points to S3*)
S3: Flight 309 go to Paris.
T: Flight 309 go?
S3: Oh . . . flight 309 goes to Paris.   *etc.*

With the first two sentences the teacher gave feedback by acknowledging that the student's response was correct. This was done by saying 'good' and 'yeah'. The teacher might also say 'yes' or just nod his head. Some teachers say nothing at all, but pass on to another student. A lot depends on the individual students and the teacher. The main thing is that the students should be quite clear that the response was correct.

S3, however, made a mistake and so the teacher did not acknowledge a correct response, but rather showed incorrectness. We will discuss correction in more detail in 6.3.3.

When conducting individual repetition the teacher should be sure that he does not nominate students in a clearly discernible order, for this has the effect of making the drill less exciting. The students always know who is going to be nominated and when. A random order, however, keeps the interest level high since anyone could be nominated at any minute.

(c) Cue-response drills

Cue-response drilling takes place when the students are working with more than one model. When the teacher has presented the first model and organised choral and individual repetition he will elicit the second model. If the students can produce the model he might go straight to choral and individual repetition. If they cannot he may go through an explanation stage again. When there has been adequate repetition of the second model the teacher starts a cue-response drill in which he asks students to choose one of the two models based on a cue.

We can summarise this procedure in Figure 7:

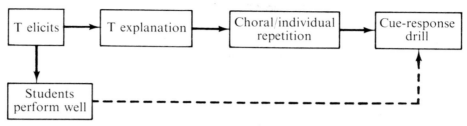

Figure 7 Introducing second and subsequent models

A cue-response drill is conducted in three stages:

Stage 1 Instruct: The teacher tells the students what he wants them to do. He might say 'tell me' to indicate that he wants a statement or 'question' to indicate that he wants a question. Often the instruction is not actually said, but is understood by the class.

Stage 2 Cue: The teacher then indicates which model he wishes the student to say. He might do this by giving a cue word. Thus he could say 'Paris' to get the response 'Flight 309 goes to Paris.' He might mime an action. Thus he could mime 'smoking' to get the student response 'John smokes three packets a day'. The teacher can also point to a particular picture or give a number (where he has previously assigned numbers to his models).

Stage 3 Nominate: The teacher selects the student he wishes to give the response (see (b) above).

We can now see the whole process described so far in operation:

   T: (*conducting individual repetition*) Juan.
S1: Flight 309 stops in Miami.
   T: Good . . . now can anyone tell me about flight 309 and Miami (*indicating the wallchart*) . . . anyone?
S2: Flight 309 stop in Miami.
   T: Yes . . . good . . . but listen . . . flight 309 stops in Miami . . . flight 309 stops in Miami . . . stops . . . stops . . . flight 309 stops in Miami . . . everybody.
SS: Flight 309 stops in Miami.
   T: Good . . . Myra.
S2: Flight 309 stops in Miami.
   T: OK . . . Keiko.
S4: Flight 309 stops in Miami.
      (*The teacher continues to conduct individual repetition and then says . . .*)
   T: OK . . . tell me . . . Paris . . . Juan.
S1: Er . . . flight 309 goes to Paris.
   T: Good . . . Miami . . . Myra.
S2: Flight 309 stops in Miami.　　　　　　*etc.*

Notice how the teacher does not distort the word 'stops' in his explanation, presumably because he thinks it is not necessary this time. Notice, too, how he elicited the second model.

When the teacher starts the cue-response drill he gives an instruction (tell me) but he drops this the next time because all the students understand that this is what is required of them.

As the teacher introduces subsequent models he will do less and less explanation, sometimes cutting it out completely.

As soon as the teacher is confident that the students can manage the cue-response drill, and when he has introduced all his models (usually between four and six examples) he should put the students in pairs. One student can now act as the teacher, giving the cue, and the other can give the response. Then the second student gives the cue and the first one responds, etc. It is important to include this stage so that as many students as possible get a chance to practise.

The teacher should make sure that this pair work stage does not last too long, for if it does the students will probably lose interest.

In general it must be emphasised that the accurate reproduction stage should be dealt with as quickly as possible. If it goes on for too long the students start to get bored and start making more and more mistakes: the drill is then completely counter-productive. The length of time will depend largely on the size of the class and the difficulty and number of models, but it is rarely advisable to continue the accurate reproduction stage for more than ten minutes, and even that will often be excessive.

6.3.3
Correction

During the accurate reproduction stage the correction procedure can consist of two basic stages: *showing incorrectness* (one way of giving feedback to a student response – see 6.3.2(b)), and *using correction techniques.*

(a) Showing incorrectness

Here the teacher simply indicates to the student that a mistake has been made. If the student understands this feedback he will be able to correct himself, and this self-correction will be helpful to him as part of his learning. It is probable that a student who can correct himself in this way has made a mistake rather than an error (see 4.2.3).

There are a number of techniques for showing incorrectness.

1 *Repeating:* The teacher simply asks the student to repeat what he has just said by using a word like 'again'. This will often indicate that the response was in some way unsatisfactory, but can also be mistaken as a signal that the teacher did not hear the response.

2 *Echoing:* The teacher may echo what the student has just said with a questioning intonation. This indicates that he is in some way doubting the accuracy or content of what is being said.

Sometimes the teacher may echo the complete student response, probably stressing the part of the utterance that was incorrect, for example:

Flight 309 GO to Paris?

Another possibility is to echo the student's response up to the point where the mistake was made, for example:

Flight 309 go?

This was the technique used in our example on page 60.

Echoing, in its various forms, is probably the most efficient way of showing incorrectness.

3 *Denial*: The teacher may simply tell the student that his response was incorrect and ask him to repeat it. This, of course, is potentially discouraging in a way that the previous techniques are not.

4 *Questioning:* The teacher may say 'Is that correct?' asking any student to answer his question. This has the advantage of focusing the students' attention on the mistake but could, of course, cause the student who made the mistake to feel exposed in front of his colleagues.

5 *Expression:* Many teachers indicate that a response was incorrect by their expression or by some gesture. This is very economical but can be dangerous if the student thinks that the teacher's expression or gesture is a form of mockery.

In general, showing incorrectness should be handled with tact and consideration. The process of student self-correction which it hopefully provokes is an important and useful part of the learning process. Showing incorrectness should be seen as a positive act, not as a reprimand.

It is often the case, however, that showing incorrectness is insufficient for the correction of a mistake or an error and the teacher may therefore have to use some correction techniques.

(b) Using correction techniques

If the student is unable to correct himself the teacher may resort to one of the following techniques.

1 *Student corrects student:* The teacher may ask if anyone else can give the correct response. He may, for example, ask if anyone can 'help' the student who has made a mistake. If another student can supply the correct information it will be good for his self-esteem.

However the student who originally made the mistake may feel humiliated if this technique is used insensitively.

2 *Teacher corrects student(s)*: Sometimes the teacher may feel that he should take care of the correction because the student is extremely mixed up about what the correct response should be. In this case the teacher can re-explain the new language to the student.

It is often the case that the teacher asks for student-student correction only to find that a number of students are having the same problem. In this case he may return to the explanation stage and then organise some choral repetition to make the point clear.

The object of using correction techniques, of course, is to give the student(s) a chance to get the new language right. It is important, therefore, that when the teacher has used one of the techniques suggested above, he asks the student who originally made the mistake to give him a correct response.

The stages of correction we have shown here are especially useful for accuracy work, where the main focus is grammatical correctness. Another possibility, however, for the immediate creativity stage and for practice activities (see Chapter 7) is *gentle* correction. This involves showing the student that something is wrong, but not asking for repetition (see also page 201).

6.3.4
The importance of meaning

It is undoubtedly important for the students to understand the meaning of the new language they are learning. This is conveyed during the lead-in stage where key concepts clearly demonstrate what is going on (see page 55). The teacher also needs to know whether the students have understood the new language so that he can organise his teaching accordingly. Not only is the lead-in stage vital, therefore, but it will also be necessary for the teacher to check frequently that the students have understood. If they have not he will have to re-present the key concepts.

Checking meaning can be done in three ways, *information checking, immediate creativity* and *translation*.

(a) Information checking
The teacher will often need to find out if students have understood the information in the lead-in, or whether students understand what a model means. He can do this in a number of ways. He might, for example, ask a question. An example of this would be 'Does Carlos like spaghetti?' (see page 67). If the students answer 'Yes' they clearly haven't understood the way the chart on page 67 is organised, or they haven't understood the meaning of the new language. Another way of checking is to say sentences which are incorrect, e.g. 'Carlos likes spaghetti but he doesn't like fish'. The students will then, if they have understood, correct this error. The same effect can be created by reading students' models and asking them to say whether they are true or false (see 6.5.4(a)).

(b) Immediate creativity and different settings
The immediate creativity stage is a good indicator of whether or not students have understood the meaning and use of the new language (as well, of course, as its form). The teacher may ask students to produce sentences of their own even before he gets to this stage in order to check that they have understood the new language.

Another good check of meaning is to ask the students something using the new language which is not part of the context that is being used for the presentation. Thus, for example, if the teacher introduces 'can' and 'can't' with the kind of invented story situation we mentioned on page 52 he may ask (at any stage during the presentation) 'Juan, can you run?'. Unless Juan has broken his leg or is in some way crippled he should answer 'Yes' to this question. If he does the teacher is confident that he has understood the meaning of 'can' that is being introduced.

(c) Translation
Where the teacher is teaching a monolingual class translation is obviously an

excellent technique if the teacher is fluent in the students' language. The main advantages are that it is quick and efficient.

There are, however, two disadvantages to the use of translation: the first is that it is not really possible with groups of different nationalities, although where there are two or more speakers of a language one student can translate for his classmates, and secondly it is not always possible to translate exactly. Not all languages have words for exactly the same concepts, and it is often the case that in a given language there is not really a word which means the same as a word in another language.

We have discussed the importance of checking meaning, and we will look at the presentation of vocabulary in 6.6.

6.4
The position of writing during presentation[3]

In this chapter we have been advocating a primarily oral approach in which the first thing students do with the language is to say it. At any stage, however, the teacher may ask the students to write the new language.

Often the teacher will use the writing as reinforcement for an oral presentation such as the type we have so far described. Thus either immediately before or after the immediate creativity stage the teacher asks students to write sentences using the new language. The sentences may be the original models the teacher used during the accurate reproduction stage, and the students might be asked to copy these sentences from the blackboard. They might see the same sentences, but the teacher might leave out certain words (this is commonly called a *fill-in* exercise).

The students might be shown model sentences and then asked to write similar sentences of their own. This is a written version of the immediate creativity stage. The students might see a short piece of connected writing using the new language and then be asked to write a similar piece. This is often called *parallel writing*.

All of these techniques have their merits, although copying is often unchallenging and boring. The main object, though, is to relate the spoken and written forms of the new language, and to enable the students to write the new pattern as well as say it.

Sometimes, of course, the teacher may want the students to write only the new language, not say it. In this case he might go through the explanation phase in the normal way, but then, after giving a clear written model he can ask students to write sentences using one of the techniques mentioned above.

Where students write in class as part of the introduction of new language it is often advantageous to 'correct' the written work in front of the whole class. One useful way of doing this is to ask the students to do the written work in their books. When the teacher sees that a student has finished (before the others) he asks him to write the first sentence on the blackboard. The second student writes the second sentence, and so on. When all the sentences are on the board the teacher goes through them one by one, asking the class if they are correct. If they are not the teacher can ask another student to write the correct sentence or correct the sentence himself. This technique is particularly useful since it gives the students feedback, and allows the teacher and the whole class to focus on grammar points if such focus is necessary.

We will see a number of different ways of introducing writing during the presentation stage in 6.5.

6.5
Introducing new
language:
examples

In this section we will look at a number of examples of language presentation. Many of the materials we will look at come from textbooks which are widely used all over the world. We will also include examples of more traditional teaching procedures which do not use published materials.

We will consider procedures for introducing new language under four headings: *the classroom, invented story situations, simulated real-life situations* and *formulated information*.

6.5.1
The classroom

In the two examples we are going to consider here the teacher uses information about the students in the classroom as the context for the introduction of new language. Particularly in the first example the procedure is extremely traditional and artificial and fails to demonstrate the communicative value of the new language. Nevertheless meaning and form are adequately conveyed, and most students (with this particular language) will be able to deduce the use of the language for themselves.

(a) Possessions[4]
The teacher wishes to introduce the statement 'It's ____'s ____' and the question 'Whose ____ is it?'.

The teacher selects a student and gets the class to say who he is. The teacher then selects something belonging to that student and holds it up. The class identifies the item (e.g. 'It's a pen'). The teacher then tries to elicit the sentence 'It's Maria's pen'. He can do this by saying 'Can anybody tell me . . . Maria . . . pen?'. The teacher then explains the model (if necessary) and gets choral and individual repetition. The teacher selects a small number of items from other students and thus has some models for the accurate reproduction stage (e.g. 'It's Celia's bag', 'It's Juan's book', etc.). The students can then work in pairs giving each other cues for the models in the following way:

S1: Bag.
S2: It's Celia's bag . . . pen.
S3: It's Maria's pen.   *etc.*

This follows the procedure laid down in 6.3.2(c).

The teacher now tries to elicit the question 'Whose pen is it?' by saying 'Can anybody ask the question . . . pen . . . whose . . . ?'. If necessary he gives a listening drill and gets choral and individual repetition and then conducts a cue-response drill with questions and answers, having pointed out that the answer to the question does not need the noun, for example:

T: Question . . . pen . . . Hans.
S1: Whose pen is it?
T: Answer . . . Keiko.
S2: It's Maria's.
T: Good.

The students then work again in pairs asking and answering questions. The teacher then elicits a number of questions and answers which he writes on the blackboard in the following way:

1 *Whose bag is it?*
2 *It's Celia's.*
3 _____ *pen is it?*
4 _____ *Maria's.*
5 _____ *book* _____ *?*
6 *It's* _____ *.(Juan)*

The teacher gets students to complete the sentences in their books. Then individuals come and fill in the blanks on the blackboard and the whole class checks to see that they are correct.

For the immediate creativity stage students collect more items from their colleagues and use them to ask and answer more questions.

The whole procedure is designed to last between ten and fifteen minutes at the very most.

(b) Likes and dislikes

This presentation will consist of two stages. In the first students will learn to say 'Do you like ____?' and in the second they will be presented with 'He likes/doesn't like ____'.

The teacher starts the sequence by asking students 'Do you like coffee?'. With mime and expression he will soon convey the meaning of the question and a student will answer 'Yes' or 'No'. The teacher then gets choral and individual repetition of the answers ('Yes I do/No, I don't') if this is necessary. For a very brief period the teacher asks students questions and they give their answers. Then the teacher elicits the question (which the students have heard him using). If necessary the question is explained and the teacher goes through the accurate reproduction stage, cueing students to ask and answer different questions. The students then work in pairs doing the same thing. This is a form of immediate creativity.

While the students are working in pairs the teacher puts the following on the blackboard:

NAME	FISH	CAVIAR	SPAGHETTI	LIVER	BANANAS

The teacher selects a student and puts his name in the name column. The other students now ask him whether he likes the items on the chart and the teacher puts a tick ($\checkmark$) if he does and a cross ($\times$) if he doesn't. The procedure is now repeated with other students until the chart looks like this:

NAME	FISH	CAVIAR	SPAGHETTI	LIVER	BANANAS
Carlos	$\checkmark$	$\checkmark$	$\times$	$\checkmark$	$\times$
Maria	$\checkmark$	$\times$	$\checkmark$	$\times$	$\checkmark$
Juan	$\times$	$\times$	$\checkmark$	$\checkmark$	$\checkmark$
Celia	$\checkmark$	$\checkmark$	$\checkmark$	$\checkmark$	$\checkmark$

The teacher then asks the students what they can say about Carlos and fish, hoping to elicit 'Carlos likes fish'. This new presentation (of the third person singular of the present simple with 'likes') now proceeds in the normal way using Carlos' likes and dislikes for the accurate reproduction stage and the others' preferences for immediate creativity, very like the flight timetable example on page 82. The teacher can later introduce the question 'Does Carlos like fish?', etc.

For the introduction of writing the teacher can use the fill-in idea (see (a) above) or the students can see the following model:

Carlos likes fish, caviar and liver, but he doesn't like spaghetti or bananas.

They can then be asked to write similar sentences about one of the other names on the list. This is a simple form of parallel writing.

This type of presentation seems enjoyable and motivating since it immediately involves the students in talking about themselves. The same type of procedure can be used when teaching such language as 'It looks/smells/tastes _____', 'Have you ever been to/visited/seen _____?', 'What do you do/Where do you live?', etc. We will see how questionnaires (which are similar) can be used in 7.1.5(c) and 8.2.6(d).

6.5.2
Invented story situations

In the following two examples we will see how two different types of invented stories provide the context for the introduction of verb tenses. In both cases there is considerable artificiality and it could be argued that little attention is being paid to communicative value. This is especially so since the text that provides the context for the first example is highly artificial and written very much in textbook style (see 9.2.2) and in the second the language consists of isolated sentences not linked to other language. Nevertheless, both examples effectively convey meaning and serve to teach students the form of the new language.

(a) Doctor Sowanso[5]
The textbook page opposite provides the context for the introduction of the 'will' future.

The teacher tells the students to cover the written text but to look at the picture at the bottom right-hand corner. He reads the text paragraph by paragraph, using the comprehension questions to check that the students have understood. After the reading of each paragraph students can uncover that part of the text and read for themselves. When the teacher has read paragraph three he can elicit sentences about what Doctor Sowanso will do tomorrow. If necessary he will then use these sentences for the explanation and accurate reproduction stages. The sentences from the last two paragraphs can also be used for accurate reproduction if necessary, and can form the basis for pair work where one student can cue the other as we saw in 6.5.1.

Doctor Sowanso is the Secretary General of the United Nations. He's one of the busiest men in the world. He's just arrived at New Delhi Airport now. The Indian Prime Minister is meeting him. Later they'll talk about Asian problems.

Yesterday he was in Moscow. He visited the Kremlin and had lunch with Soviet leaders. During lunch they discussed international politics.

Tomorrow he'll fly to Nairobi. He'll meet the President of Kenya and other African leaders. He'll be there for twelve hours.

The day after tomorrow he'll be in London. He'll meet the British Prime Minister and they'll talk about European economic problems.

Next week he'll be back at the United Nations in New York. Next Monday he'll speak to the General Assembly about his world tour. Then he'll need a short holiday.

Questions

Who is Doctor Sowanso?
Where's he just arrived?
Who's meeting him?
What'll they talk about?

Where was he yesterday?
Who did he have lunch with?
What did they discuss?
When did he leave Moscow?

Where will he fly tomorrow?
Who will he meet?
How long will he be there?

When will he be in London?
Who will he meet?
What will they talk about?

Where will he be next week?
What will he do on Monday?
Why will he need a holiday?

The teacher can then introduce the question forms and the students can again work in pairs asking and answering questions about Doctor Sowanso's schedule.

For immediate creativity the students can ask each other about schedules they have (maybe at their work or school or for a forthcoming holiday, etc.).

For the introduction of writing the teacher can ask the students to use one of the last three paragraphs as a model and then write about their own schedules.

(b) The homecoming[6]

The teacher puts up the following wall picture to introduce the past continuous:

He establishes that yesterday Mary (the lady in the doorway) went out, leaving her family in the house. She came back at eight o'clock in the evening. When she came back a number of things were happening.

The above form the key concepts, and the teacher now proceeds to give the various characters names (with the help of the class). If Mary's husband (John) is the man sitting in the chair, the teacher tries to elicit 'When Mary came home John was reading the newspaper/dropping ash on the floor'. These two models and some others (e.g. 'Jim was drawing on the wall', 'The dinner was burning', 'The dog was barking at the cat') form the basis for the explanation and accurate reproduction stages. The students can then make more sentences about the picture for the immediate creativity stage. The teacher can then ask for personalised sentences (students talking about themselves) where the students say 'When I got home/arrived at school my father was watching the television/the students were playing football', etc. Once again the teacher will put students in pairs to practise sentences about the picture and if he introduces a question (e.g. 'What was John doing when Mary came home?') students can practise questions and answers.

For the written stage the teacher can do a fill-in on the blackboard similar to the examples in 6.5.1.

6.5.3
Simulated real-life situations

We can now look at examples of presentation contexts where an attempt has been made to simulate real life. The language to be introduced has been placed in realistic situations and occurs in the context of other language – in other words, rather than isolated examples of the new language we see the new language occurring in conversations or written texts. This is superior in many ways to the examples we have seen so far since it demonstrates how the new language is used. We will look at six examples.

(a) Coffee time (1)[7]

The students read and/or listen to the following conversation between Neville and Jackie, characters they have already met at the beginning of the book:

The teacher checks that the students understand the conversation and especially that Neville offers Jackie a cup of coffee which she accepts and a biscuit that she refuses.

The teacher then tries to elicit the question 'Would you like a ____?' and using cues from the following picture teaches the question, going through the usual stages of explanation and accurate reproduction:

The teacher then elicits the answers ('Yes, please' and 'No, thanks') and teaches them in the same way. The students do a cue-response drill with questions and answers and then work in pairs.

The second question ('And a biscuit?') is then introduced – and taught if necessary – and the students then work together making conversations of their own based on the original model for the immediate creativity stage.

For a written stage students can write their own dialogues based on the relevant four lines of the original model.

(b) Coffee time (2)

In (a) above the students listened to the original dialogue and the context was clearly exemplified by the pictures. The teacher could equally well decide to teach the dialogue without the book in the following way.

The teacher draws two characters on the blackboard representing Neville and Jackie. He elicits the fact that they are in a cafeteria. He then tries to elicit the dialogue through gesture, cue words and mime. Thus he stands in front of the picture of Neville and (together with an appropriate gesture and/or expression) says 'Can anyone ask . . . cup of coffee?' and a student may be able to say 'Would you like a cup of coffee?' He continues with the next three lines of the dialogue in the same way until he has built up the exchange with the students' help. He then says the dialogue again using normal stress and intonation.

For the accurate reproduction stage the teacher gets choral and individual repetition line by line. As each line is added he cues students to ask and answer, so that after he has taught the first two lines, for example, the students say:

> *T*: Question . . . Juan.
> *S1*: Would you like a cup of coffee?
> *T*: Answer . . . Maria.
> *S2*: Yes, please.   *etc.*

When the students have learnt the complete dialogue they practise it in pairs for a very brief period. The teacher then asks them to think of other examples (e.g. something different from 'coffee' and 'biscuit'). They are then free to say 'Yes' or 'No' depending on their taste. This is an immediate creativity stage and students are now put in pairs again to make their own dialogues.

The teacher can then elicit the original dialogue and write it on the blackboard. Students write parallel dialogues as in (a) above.

The two different approaches we have seen to our 'Coffee time' dialogue both have advantages. In the first example, particularly where there is a tape of the conversation available, the students hear a 'real' conversation taking place and thanks to the visual material get adequate information about context. However the second approach is potentially more motivating because of the elicitation element (which also tells the teacher just how much students know). On the other hand the second approach only uses the teacher's voice as a model, which is a pity since different taped voices provide the students with vital information about how English is spoken.

We will now continue with more examples.

(c) Getting to know each other[8]

The students are going to learn how to ask for and give personal information. This is what they see and/or hear:

CHRISTINE:	That's good, Sam.
SAM:	Oh, thanks. I'm an art student.
CHRISTINE:	Are you? Where do you study?
SAM:	I'm at college in London. I work here in the holidays.

The class then learn and practise these three questions (and how to answer them) following our usual model:

Ask each other

What do you do?   *Example :*   I'm a sales assistant.
Where do you work/study?   I work in a shop.
Where do you live?   I live in London.

Writing is dealt with slightly differently here. The first stage involves the students in doing a simple fill-in:

Complete

I'm a ....

I { work in ....
   study at ....

I live in ....

The students are now asked to do some parallel writing and once again, as in our likes and dislikes example the language has changed to the third person singular:

Write sentences

Write three sentences about Sam (he) and three sentences about
a friend (she *or* he).

Example :
Christine Grant is a sales assistant. She works in a shop in
London. She lives in Hampstead, a suburb of London.

The teacher will have to explain how the third person singular is formed and the students can work in pairs to write their parallel sentences. This is a way of introducing a form without going through the oral stages of presentation. Only writing is required and the teacher can later return to the point for more practice and oral work.

In this example the students did not learn the dialogue, or use it as a model. It was used to show the new language ('Where do you work/study/ live?', etc.) in a normal language context. The same use of a dialogue to show language being used in context is apparent in our next example.

(d) Malcolm and the tent[9]
This is material designed for upper elementary/intermediate students. The aim is to introduce various teaching points in the context of a dialogue between characters the students already 'know' from earlier in the book.

The teacher tells the class that the group (who the students already know) are travelling in the van: two of them will sleep there, so where will the others sleep?

In order to get the students to listen for specific information (see 9.5.2) the teacher asks the students to write down (while they're listening to the tape) where each member of the group slept. The students then listen to the following introduction and dialogue:

① The group have arrived in Cambridge. They are staying at the house of Jane's parents – except for Steve. He has gone to stay with an old friend of his father's.

Jane and Lise slept in the house, in Jane's old room, and Bill and Nick spent the night in the van. Malc borrowed a tent from Jane's brother and camped in the garden. They are now sitting in the kitchen after breakfast.

JANE: You weren't cold in the van, were you, Bill?

BILL: No, it was really quite comfortable. Wasn't it, Nick? How about you and Lise?

JANE: Well, I slept well. But I'm afraid Lise wasn't very comfortable. She slept on the floor.

LISE: Oh, I was all right.

JANE: It would have been better if you'd slept in Sheila's room.

LISE: Yes, but then she would have had to sleep downstairs on the sofa. No, really, I slept very well.

MALC: I notice nobody asks about me!

LISE: Oh Malcolm! How did *you* sleep?

MALC: Huh! I hardly slept at all. It was really cold. And that tent's got a hole in it. If it'd rained, I would have got wet!

LISE: Poor Malc!

JANE: Has everyone finished? We'd better do the washing up. And *I* ought to help my mother upstairs.

LISE: *We'll* wash up, Jane. *You* go and help your mother.

The teacher conducts feedback on the specific information the students should have extracted. He can then ask other questions to check that the students have understood other parts of the dialogue.

The teacher then focuses on Malcolm and the tent. He can ask the students to look at the following pictorial explanation of the meaning of 'If it had rained I would have got wet'.

A Malc said:
'**If it had** rained,
I **would have got** wet!'

But it didn't rain, so Malc didn't get wet.

With a construction like this the teacher will probably want to use written explanation as well as giving the sort of listening drill we have suggested so far. The teacher could write the following on the board to show the grammar of the construction (DONE shows that a past participle is used):

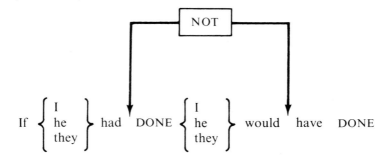

With their books open the students can now use the cues in Exercise 1 to make sentences for the accurate reproduction stage. The teacher might ask students to write one or two of the sentences and the students can work in pairs to do this or to do oral practice. The same procedure can be followed for Exercise 2:

1   *Complete these sentences in the same way:*

    a   STEVE: If I hadn't seen that notice, I ..... (know about the trip).

    b   STEVE: I would have had to sleep in the tent with Malc if I ..... (go to stay with friends).

    c   STEVE: If I ..... (phone my friend in York), I wouldn't have known about the house there.

    d   JANE: I ..... (know about my father's illness) if I ..... (speak to my mother).

    e   SHEILA: If Jane ..... (bring the group to Cambridge), I ..... (meet Malc)!

2   MALC: I'm glad it didn't rain! If it had, I'd have got wet!
    Continue in the same way, using the ideas in 1 above.

For the immediate creativity stage the teacher can ask the students to make similar sentences about things that happened in the past which they were glad they did or didn't do.

(e) Carla asks for directions[10]

In this material students learn how to ask for and give directions. A feature of the exercises, though, is that students are shown the predictable courses of the conversation. In other words, not only are they given language, but they are also given an understanding of when the language is used and what people say before and after it.

    The students listen to a tape and complete the following dialogue (the missing words are 'the coach station'):

4. CONVERSATION (2):   Listen to Carla and the man.

CARLA: Excuse me.

MAN: Yes?

CARLA: Could you tell me where _____ is, please?

MAN: I'm afraid I don't know. Sorry.

CARLA: Oh. All right. Never mind.

The teacher now teaches the dialogue using the procedure outlined in
6.5.3(b). Exercise 5 (below) forms a very basic immediate creativity stage:

5. PRACTICE
Ask for these places. Your friend answers like the man.

Fisherton Street	St Ann Street
Milford Street	South Western Road
New Canal	New Street
Castle Street	Queens Road

The students now listen to another dialogue (Conversation (3)) and complete
it (the missing words are 'the post office', 'the post office' and 'Castle Street'):

6. CONVERSATION (3):   Listen to Carla and the man.

CARLA: Excuse me. Could you tell me where _____ is, please?
MAN: Pardon?
CARLA: Could you tell me where _____ is?
MAN: Yes. It's in _____.
CARLA: Ah, Castle Street. Thanks.

Again they follow a similar procedure to that used in the first dialogue.
    The students are now in a position to work on an immediate creativity
stage since they have various conversational options which the writers of this
book represent in the following way:

7. PRACTICE
Have conversations like the ones below.

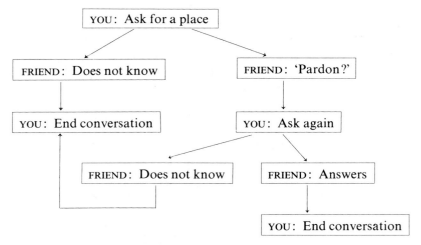

Look at the map of Salisbury. Ask for:

the hospital	the museum
the Red Lion Hotel	the railway station

In other words students can practise different conversations since they have a guide to the probable directions the interactions would take.[11] Students can now work in pairs using the following map:

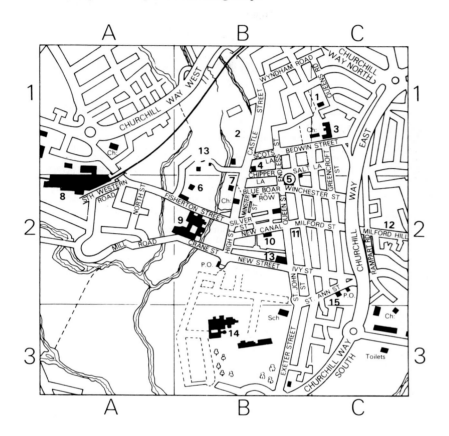

Key:

1	Swimming pool	**8**	Railway station
2	Coach station	**9**	Hospital
3	Council offices	**10**	Odeon Cinema
4	Post office	**11**	Red Lion Hotel
5	Bus station / Tourist information office	**12**	Youth hostel
		13	Car park
6	Playhouse Theatre	**14**	Cathedral
7	Library	**15**	Museum

(f) Pilots[12]

In this example students read a (simulated) newspaper article in which the language which is to be 'taught' occurs naturally in the context of the topic of the article and the language which comes before and after it. The material is designed for advanced students.

This is the text the students see:

Pilots – a special position?

BERNARD FOX looks at the high salary pilots receive

WHEN British Airways and Air France first put their brand new Concordes into service their pilots had undergone some months of special training, just as any
5 pilot now wishing to fly the supersonic plane must undergo a rigorous conversion course: flying Concorde is clearly not the same as flying a conventional airliner. There is, of course, nothing strange about
10 this, for every time an airline decides to use a new aircraft, the pilots must be taught to adapt to its special needs and characteristics, and every time pilots fly new aircraft they demand new rates of
15 pay. Many of us remember how British Airways were unable to use the new 747

until the Jumbo pilots were satisfied that they were getting adequate pay.

Both in the case of the Jumbo and the
20 Concorde, the airlines and the pilots eventually reached an agreement, but in the future pilots will no doubt continue to press for more money every time the airlines introduce new aircraft. As in the
25 past they can argue that new aircraft require extra skill and entail extra responsibility.

The whole question of how much pilots are paid was the subject of a television
30 programme last week when David Yeadon interviewed an airline captain who was also an active member of the pilots' union. Throughout the interview Yeadon insisted that pilots were overpaid; he even
35 said that they were in a position to force the airlines to pay them whatever they wanted. The threat of a long strike often was enough, he said, to frighten airlines into producing the required money. The
40 captain, naturally, argued that pilots deserved every penny they earned because of the responsibility they had, both in lives and money.

It is certainly true that the pilot's
45 position is a special one. By any standards, the training he has to go through is unusually tough. To get an air transport pilot's licence he has to do a course that is at least as difficult as a university
50 degree. Even then, the qualified pilot faces the constant risk of losing his licence just by failing one of the six-monthly medical and flying tests which he has to take to ensure that he is still fit,
55 and that his flying is still up to scratch.

In most other jobs, a man reaches retiring age at sixty or sixty-five years old, but this is not the case with pilots. Their career ends in their early fifties—
60 an age at which many other men are reaching the peak of their careers. It is difficult for a man of that age to find another job, and few pilots like the idea of being inactive so early, even if money
65 is no problem.

The main argument against the size of pilots' salaries is that there is nothing special about the responsibilities they bear. Some people would argue that a
70 train-driver is in the same position, and they would even go so far as to say that any bus-driver also deserves a much higher

salary than he gets at present. It is a fact of our society that we underpay many of 75 our most important workers. People have tended to think, for example, that nurses and teachers do their jobs because they feel a special 'calling'. The argument here is that if the type of job they are 80 doing satisfies them, they don't need to be highly paid. Here it is worth pointing out that most pilots take out a loss of licence insurance, and all of them receive a pension that is equal to half their pay. 85 Whatever the rights and wrongs of the situation it is undeniable that there is something special about a pilot's job. As we live our lives down here someone is in charge of a few hundred people thirty 90 thousand feet above the Atlantic Ocean; it is not a responsibility most of us would wish. The question we should ask ourselves is how much that kind of responsibility is worth.

After comprehension work the teacher asks the students what language was used to argue for or against the salary pilots receive. It should be noted that advanced students will often recognise the language used while at the same time having problems using it correctly and appropriately.

If necessary, then, the teacher will show the following chart to the students which demonstrates various ways of talking about arguments other people use.

(One of) the (main) argument(s) $\begin{Bmatrix} \text{against} \\ \text{in favour of} \end{Bmatrix}$ X is that . . .

It has been $\begin{Bmatrix} \text{said} \\ \text{argued} \end{Bmatrix}$ that . . .

Some people would argue that . . .

It can be argued that . . .

NOTE The writer may or may not agree with such arguments.

If an accurate reproduction stage is needed the following exercise can be used, and exercise **b.** can be used for immediate creativity:

a. Jet travel – particularly with planes like the Jumbo and Concorde – has always been a controversial subject. Below are statements about it which are, or have been, other people's arguments. Use the language from the chart to make these statements as if you were writing about/discussing the subject.

EXAMPLE   Jet aircraft are unnecessary.
It has been said that jet aircraft are unnecessary.

Now do the same with the following.

a) People need to get from place to place very quickly, and because of this we need jet transport.
b) All aircraft, and particularly Concorde, are too noisy.
c) Air travel helps to bring countries closer together.
d) Concorde should be banned.
e) Jets make a lot of people's lives intolerable.
f) Air transport is destroying our environment.

b. Using the language from the chart, can you give other people's arguments about
a) the amount of money paid to pop stars
b) learning classical languages like Latin and Greek

The material continues with other ways of arguing (using 'subjective' argument and the use of rhetorical questions) before asking students to use language they have studied in a free situation.

It is worth pointing out here that students are simultaneously working on more than one piece of language at a time (although the different exponents in our example have the same function). This will often be the case with intermediate and advanced students who will have seen the language before and will thus not be confused by having different realisations of the same function.

6.5.4 Formulated information

In this section we will look at two examples of formulated information – that is, where the information used for practice is formulated in chart, graph or tabular form. We have already seen an example of formulated information in 6.5.1(b) and we can now look at two more.

The advantage of charts and tables, etc. is that there is potential for a much greater quantity of information than in a picture or a dialogue.

(a) The flight timetable[13]

We have already used the following flight timetable for examples in 6.3. The flight timetable has the advantage of introducing a perfectly natural use of the present simple tense (presented here for the first time) but suffers from not showing that language being used in the context of other language. Nevertheless it adequately conveys one meaning and use of the new verb tense.

The students look at the following flight timetable:

Flight Number	Destination	Via	Departure	Arrival
714	New York	Dallas	08.15	11.45
603	Chicago	St. Louis	14.30	16.45
309	Paris	Miami	23.30	16.40
873	Montreal	Detroit	19.05	21.50
312	London	Bermuda	13.10	07.55

The teacher then ascertains that students understand what a flight timetable is, and what the words 'destination', 'via', 'departure' and 'arrival' mean.

The teacher now tells the students that they must listen to some sentences and circle the correct letter for each item. Here are the letters:

1 Listen, and put a circle round the correct letter for each item (D = destination; V = via; Dp = departure; A = arrival).

1 D	2 D	3 D	4 D	5 D
V	V	V	V	V
6 Dp	7 Dp	8 Dp	9 Dp	10 Dp
A	A	A	A	A

Here are the sentences the teacher reads:

1 Flight 309 goes to Paris.	D
2 Flight 873 stops in Detroit.	V
3 Flight 714 arrives in New York at 11.45.	D
4 Flight 312 stops in Bermuda.	V
5 Flight 603 goes to St. Louis.	V
6 Flight 873 leaves at five past seven.	Dp
7 Flight 603 departs at 2.30.	Dp
8 Flight 312 arrives in London at 7.55.	A
9 Flight 873 gets to Montreal at ten to ten.	A
10 Flight 603 reaches Chicago at a quarter to five.	A

This procedure has a double advantage: it gives the students ample listening practice and it tells both the teacher and the students (during the feedback session) whether the students understand the new language (see 6.3.4).

The teacher now proceeds to teach the new language using four models about, for example, 'flight 309' ('Flight 309 goes to/stops at/leaves at/arrives at . . .'). For the immediate creativity stage students can make more sentences of their own about the other flights.

The teacher can also introduce the two questions 'Where does flight 309 stop/go to?' and 'What time does flight 309 leave/arrive?'. Students can obviously work in pairs practising questions and answers.

For the written stage the students do the following exercise:

Read the following sentences and complete them appropriately, according to the departure board.

a Flight . . . . . goes to Paris. It stops in . . . . . .

b Flight . . . . . at 14.30 and it . . . . . in Chicago . . . . . 16.45.

c What time . . . . .? At 13.10.

d Does flight 309 . . . . . Miami? Yes, it does.

e Does flight 603 . . . . .? No, it stops in St. Louis.

Once again the teacher can write the exercise on the blackboard if he wants to and get students to fill in the blanks there after they have done so on a piece of paper.

(b) London Kid[14]

In this exercise the students are going to work on 'used to do' constructions.

The students have listened to a dialogue in which the following language has occurred:

My wife used to be keen on Abba.
She didn't use to like jazz very much.
Where did you use to live as a child?

After the teacher has made sure that the students understand how and why the language was used in the dialogue he asks them to look at the following notes:

London Kid

Growing up in the sixties by Patrick Cummings

Before writing his autobiography, Patrick Cummings noted down some memories of his childhood.

Family life
- lived in a tower block
- didn't get on with my father
- my brother played Elvis records all day

School
- went to a local comprehensive school
- swapped comics in the playground after school
- didn't wear a uniform like the other boys did

Holidays
- went to Blackpool every summer with my parents until I was 16
- never went abroad for a holiday

Clothes and appearance
- had short hair
- wore a green anorak (parka) and jeans and a hat most of the time
- didn't spend any money on clothes

Friends
- member of a street gang called 'The Tigers'
- didn't go out with girls until I was 14

Free time
- went to all the Rolling Stones concerts
- drove a moped
- sold second-hand records in the street market on Saturday mornings
- never watched TV (it was black and white)

The class then works with a small number of models (e.g. Patrick Cummings used to live in a tower block/go to a local comprehensive school, etc.). This language is handled in the usual way, including pair work.

The same procedure can be followed with the negative and question forms, and the students can work in pairs talking about Patrick Cummings. For the immediate creativity stage students can talk about what they did when they were children.

For a written stage the students can write sentences about what they used (and didn't use) to do.

Formulated information is especially useful, then, for conveying a great deal of information. Other possibilities include maps (e.g. for 'There's a cinema on Green Street', etc.), graphs (e.g. 'It's warmer in July than in September'), and diagrams (e.g. 'After the solution has been heated it is poured onto a wooden board').

**6.6
Presenting
vocabulary**

Frequently the teacher will find it necessary to explain the meaning of a word or short phrase. The teacher's aim here will be to explain the new word as quickly and as efficiently as possible and the following 'aids' can help to do this.

(a) Realia

This is the word we use to refer to the use of real objects in the classroom. Thus the words 'pen', 'ruler', 'ball', 'postcard', etc. can be easily explained by showing students a pen or a ball or a ruler, etc. This is clearly satisfactory for certain single words, but the use of realia is limited to things that can easily be taken into the classroom.

(b) Pictures

Pictures are clearly indispensable for the language teacher since they can be used in so many ways.

By pictures we mean *blackboard drawings, wall pictures* and *charts, flash-cards* and any other non-technical visual representation. Pictures can be used to explain the meaning of vocabulary items: the teacher might draw pens, rulers and balls on the blackboard, or have magazine pictures of cars, bicycles, and trains stuck onto cardboard. The teacher might bring in a wall picture showing three people in a room which could be used for introducing the meaning of the sentence 'There are three people in the room'. The same language could be introduced with a large street map (e.g. 'There's a church in Green Street') or a table of statistics (e.g. 'There are 3,000 women in Lower Archer'). A picture can also be used to create a situation or context.

(c) Mime, action and gesture

It is often impossible to explain the meaning of words and grammar either through the use of realia or in pictures. Actions, in particular, are probably better explained by mime. Thus concepts like running and smoking are easy concepts to explain if the teacher pretends to run, or takes a drag on an imaginary cigarette. Gesture is useful for explaining words like 'from', 'to', etc. or indicating that the past is being talked about (the teacher gestures backwards over his shoulder).

(d) Contrast

Sometimes a visual element (e.g. realia, picture, mime, etc.) may not be sufficient to explain meaning and contrast can be used. Thus the meaning of *'full'* is better understood in the context of *'empty'*, *'big'* in the context of *'small'*, etc. The meaning of the past continuous is often explained by contrasting it with the past simple, e.g. 'I was having a bath when the telephone rang'.

(e) Enumeration

The word *'vegetable'* is a difficult word to explain visually. If, however, the teacher rapidly lists (or enumerates) a number of vegetables the meaning will become clear. The same is true of a word like *'clothes'*.

(f) Explanation

Explaining the meaning of vocabulary items can be extremely difficult just as grammatical explanation can be (see 6.3.1), especially at elementary levels. It will be important, if giving such explanations, to make sure that the explanation includes information about when the item can be used. It would be unsatisfactory just to say that 'mate' was a word for 'friend' unless you also pointed out that it was colloquial informal English and only used in certain contexts. 'Do' means to perform, but information would have to be given about what words it is used with (as opposed to 'make').

(g) Translation

For many years translation went out of fashion and was considered as something of a sin. Clearly if the teacher is always translating this will impede students' learning since they want to hear and use the target language, not their own. But it seems silly not to translate if by doing so a lot of time can be saved. If the students don't understand a word and the teacher can't think how to explain it, he can quickly translate it; the same is true, in principle, of a piece of grammar. The big danger, though, is that not all words and phrases are easily translated from one language to the other, and it takes a communicatively efficient speaker of both languages to translate well. Translation, then, seems a useful measure if used sparingly, but it should be used with caution.

These aids and measures may be very useful for explaining the meaning of a word or sentence. (They may be used singly or in combination (e.g. pictures and mime, translation and enumeration, etc.)).

Exercises

1 What parts of the model *'John's taller than Mary'* would you isolate during an explanation stage? Why?
2 Design a context for introducing the meaning and use of the past continuous (e.g. *'John was playing the guitar'*).
3 Take a dialogue from any textbook and write down exactly the procedure you would follow when using it to introduce some new language.
4 What aids would you use to present the following vocabulary items?
tooth, tape recorder, charity, mammal

5 Design a context and presentation sequence which uses the students in the same way as our example in 6.5.1(b).

6 You have used a map of an imaginary town to teach 'There's a cinema on South Street/hospital on Green Street', etc. What could students do for an immediate creativity stage?

References

1 See R Scott (1981) and the reference cited in 11 (below) for an explanation and examples of how this can be done.

2 See J Willis (1981) Unit 15 for more on controlled oral drills.

3 See J Willis (1981) Unit 20 and D Byrne (1979) Chapter 4 for more on early controlled writing.

4 Examples of this traditional approach are given in P Davies et al. (1975), a book especially written for non-native-speaker teachers working in secondary schools.

5 Taken from B Hartley and P Viney (1979).

6 This situation has long been in use at the Instituto Anglo-Mexicano but I have been unable to trace its originator.

7 Taken from B Abbs and I Freebairn (1977). For the treatment of dialogues see also S Holden (1981) Chapter 8, M Long (1973) and J Willis (1981) Unit 14.

8 Taken from J Garton-Sprenger et al. (1979).

9 Taken from D Byrne and S Holden (1981).

10 Taken from R Scott and J Arnold (1978).

11 Similar 'guides' can be found in J Harmer and J W Arnold (1978). See also reference 1 (above).

12 Taken from J W Arnold and J Harmer (1978).

13 Taken from R Rossner et al. (1979a).

14 Taken from B Abbs and I Freebairn (1980).

7 Practice

In this chapter we will consider techniques and materials designed to give students practice in specific items or areas of language (see 4.2.5 'Practice output'). The activities will all fall somewhere between the two extremes on the communication continuum (see 5.3). We will look at *oral practice* and *written practice*.

7.1
Oral practice

In this section we will look at ways of getting students to practise oral English. We will consider *oral drills, information gap activities, games, personalisation and localisation* and *oral activities*.

7.1.1
Oral drills

In the following three examples we will consider drills whose main function is to encourage the practice of question forms. Since drills are usually very controlled they have a fairly limited potential and it is not suggested that they should be used either too frequently or for too long. However they do provide a controlled way of getting practice of certain language forms.

(a) Four-phase drills
Four-phase drills are so called because there are four phases or stages, i.e. Q-A-Q-A. The students are encouraged to ask a question and on the basis of the answer follow it up with another question, for example:

A: Is John English?
B: No, he isn't.
A: Where's he from, then?
B: He's Australian/from Australia.

In this case the drill has been designed to practise the question forms 'Is X + nationality?' and 'Where's he/she from?'.
The teacher will start by showing flashcards of people with some indication of their nationality. He then conducts a cue-response drill (see 6.3.2(c)) in which students ask questions such as 'Is John English?', for example:

T: Question . . . Maria . . . French?   (*Nominates S1*)
S1: Is Maria French?
T: Answer . . . Gloria.
S2: No she isn't.   *etc.*

He then moves on to the next question, adding the word 'then' if the answer to the first question is negative, for example:

T: Question . . . Maria . . . French?   (*Nominates S1*)
S1: Is Maria French?
T: Answer . . . anyone.
S3: No she isn't.
T: Good . . . ask somebody a question with 'where' . . .
S4: Where's she from?
T: Good . . . but you can say 'Where's she from, then?' so . . . ask again Jorge . . .
S4: Where's she from, then?
T: Answer, Gloria.
S2: She's from Mexico.   *etc.*

The teacher then conducts this drill with the whole class for a short space of time and the students then practise the drill in pairs. The teacher can give them flashcards or they can think of famous people to ask about.

In our example the drill depended on a negative answer to the first question. But of course four-phase drills can be constructed with any question sequence, for example:

A: What's your favourite hobby?
B: Tennis.
A: How often do you play?
B: Once a week.

Four-phase drills are useful for practice and revision of specific question forms and can be successfully used for quick five-minute sessions after these questions have been introduced, perhaps in a previous class.

(b) Mixed question and answer drills

The difference between mixed question and answer drills and four-phase drills is that the former have more questions than the latter and they can be asked in any order.

In the following example the teacher works with the whole class who see the following wall picture:

The teacher then elicits
the following questions:

– What's his/her name?
– Where's he/she from?
– What's his/her job?
– What does he/she do?
– How old is she/he?

He does this by conducting
a cue-response drill:

T: OK. Ask me about Pierre's age, Hans.
S1: How old is Pierre?
T: Answer . . . Heidi.
S2: He's thirty-one.   *etc.*

Pierre   Maria   John

b.1952   b.1930   b.1947

Students are then put in pairs to work with similar pictures and they might use the answers to write short paragraphs, for example:

Jean-Paul's from France. He's a pilot and he's forty-six years old.

Mixed question and answer drills provide a good opportunity for quick revision of language the students have previously studied. Like four-phase drills they are suitable for short practice sessions.

(c) Talking about frequency of activities[1]

In this drill students work with a specially prepared set of flashcards. The cards show various activities taking place.

Students are put in groups of four and a set of flashcards is placed in front of them, face downwards. A student picks up a card and has to ask another student how often a relative of that student performs the activity shown on the card. The drill might go in the following way:

S1: (*Picks up a card showing a man brushing his teeth.*)
How often does your brother brush his teeth, Tomiko?
S2: Twice a day, I should think. (*Picks up a card showing someone playing tennis.*) How often does your mother play tennis, Monica?
S3: She doesn't play at all! (*Picks up a card showing a person getting on a bus.*) How often does your sister travel by bus, Tarek?
S4: Never . . . she always gets me to drive her everywhere!

This is a simple cue-response drill, but the students are conducting the drill themselves rather than being controlled by the teacher. The random selection of the cards makes the drill enjoyable and quite challenging, and the use of group work means that many students get a chance to participate in a co-operative and friendly way.

Cards of this kind have a use in many kinds of drill activities where students can practise specific items of language without being inhibited by the teacher.

Drill work, then, if used sparingly and for short periods of time, can be very effective in the language classroom. It should be noted, however, that in all three examples students work in pairs or groups as soon as possible. This maximises student practice and enables the students to work at their own pace.

7.1.2
Information gap activities

Information gap activities are those in which students are given different bits of information. By sharing this separate information they can complete a task.

In 5.2 we saw that an information gap was an ingredient in most real-life communication, and the majority of the activities in Chapter 8, both oral and written, will have some kind of information gap built into them. The three examples we are going to show here, however, use the information gap principle to prompt the practice of specific items of language, and the purpose of each activity is to close the information gap, usually by writing information down.

The following examples will show, then, how practice of specific language can be made enjoyable and fairly communicative since there is both an information gap and a purpose to the activity.

(a) The store inventory

Students are put into pairs in which one student is *A*, the other *B*. They are given the following cards, but told not to show their cards to their partners:

STORE INVENTORY : A	
apples	15 kilos
bananas	
pears	10 kilos
cheese	
sugar	36 kilos
coffee	
oranges	15 kilos
butter	

STORE INVENTORY: B	
apples	
bananas	5 kilos
pears	
cheese	3 kilos
sugar	
coffee	12 kilos
oranges	
butter	4 kilos

The students then ask questions using 'How much/How many' and write down the missing information on their cards. The activity finishes when both students have full inventories. They then check their cards to make sure the information is right.

In their pairs the students might work like this:

A: How many bananas are there?
B: 5 kilos (*A writes 5 kilos on his list*) . . . How much sugar is there?
A: 36 kilos . . .   *etc.*

This is the simplest version of an information gap activity and is very much like a drill. Nevertheless the students have been provided with a purpose for engaging in this drill. In real life the list would need to be considerably longer if the activity is not to finish in 30 seconds!

(b) Geographical information[2]

In this activity students ask and answer questions about various towns and cities, their location, population, climate, etc.

Once again students are put in pairs where one student is *A* and one is *B*. Once again they are told not to show their paper to the other students.

This is what the students receive:

STUDENT A

	BATH	SYDNEY	NEW ORLEANS	DUNDEE
country?	England		the U.S.A.	
which part?	the west			the east coast
population?		3 million		180,000
weather?		hot and dry		windy and cold
what/like?		modern busy	lively commercial	
famous for?	the Roman Baths		Jazz music	

STUDENT B

	BATH	SYDNEY	NEW ORLEANS	DUNDEE
country?		Australia		Scotland
which part?		the east coast	the south-east	
population?	85,000		600,000	
weather?	mild and rainy		hot and dry	
what/like?	quiet attractive			very old traditional
famous for?		the Opera House		cakes

They will then ask each other questions such as 'What's the weather like in Sydney?', 'What's the population of Bath?', 'What's New Orleans famous for?', etc. The activity is finished when students have charts which are completely filled in.

This is a useful activity for practising a variety of information questions, and has the advantage (over (a) above) that the information itself is somewhat interesting. In a very basic way it also uses the skill of note-taking.

(c) Immigrant in Britain[3]

This information gap activity is designed for intermediate students and shows how such an activity can be used not only for oral practice but also for reading and form-filling, etc.

Students are again divided into pairs with the usual restriction about not looking at each other's papers. They are told that they must each complete the paper in front of them.

This is what student *A* receives:

By asking Student B questions, fill in the missing information in the Immigrant Survey Sheet below in pencil. (Student B will also ask you questions.)

IMMIGRANT SURVEY SHEET   July 19

Name: .... Abraham Jacobs ......   Nationality: ....

Occupation: ... Bus driver ....   Married/Single

Number of children: ....

Length of time in Britain: .... – years ....

Date of arrival: ...... June 17th 1970 ....

Reason for coming to Britain: ....
....

Present address (town/village only): ... Birmingham ....

Length of time in present town/village: ....

Other towns/villages where person has lived: ... London ....
... Bradford, Liverpool ....

Knowledge of English:
1 on arrival: Good/quite good/fairly good/poor
2 now: Good/quite good/fairly good/poor

Number of English courses attended: ....

Language(s) spoken at home: ....

Problems/difficulties living in Britain:
1 ... Difficult to get a good job ....
2 ... Difficult to find decent accommodation ....
3 ... Colour prejudice ....
4 ... Not considered to be English ....

Contact with English people:
1 at work: ....
2 outside work: ....

When you have finished, compare books to check that you have filled in the missing information correctly.

And this is what student *B* receives:

By asking Student A questions, fill in the missing information in the
passage below in pencil. (Student A will also ask you questions.)

IMMIGRANT IN BRITAIN

Abraham Jacobs lives in . . . . with his wife and six children.

But he is not English. He was born in Kingston and came to Britain in

. . . . 1970 – mainly because it was impossible to get a job in

Jamaica. He lived in . . . . with relatives when he first arrived, then

moved to Wolverhampton, ... and Liverpool before finally

moving to . . . . where he has been living since 1975.

He spoke English fairly well on arrival, so he did not bother to attend any

special English courses. His English is . . . . now and since three of

his children were born in Britain, English is the only language spoken at

home.

He likes England, but thinks there are three main problems facing immigrants.

To begin with, it is difficult to get . . . . Secondly, there is the

problem of finding . . . . and finally, there is still a lot of colour

prejudice in Britain. In fact his children are still considered to be foreigners,

even though three of them were born in England.

He works as a . . . . but has very little contact with English people

since 95 per cent of his workmates are West Indians. And even outside work,

the only contact he has with English people are one or two he meets when he

goes to the local club.

July 19—

When you have finished, compare books to check that you have filled
in the missing information correctly.

The material makes students ask a large number of questions in order to
complete their task. In order to ask these questions both students have to
read their material and work out what questions to ask.

This is an impressive example of an information gap exercise which
integrates skills.

Information gap tasks, then, provide students with a reason to
communicate with each other, and can be designed to practise more or less
specific language.

If students have not done an exercise of this type before the teacher
would be well advised to demonstrate the technique before putting the
students in pairs. Thus for the first example the teacher could write up a
similar (but different) store inventory on the blackboard with different
information. He then gets a student up to the front of the class. The student
asks the teacher the questions; the teacher gives answers and the student has
to fill in the inventory on the blackboard.

When an activity of this type is over the teacher can conduct feedback by
getting students to ask and answer the questions. This serves to check not

only the students' language production, but also whether they have got the information right.

7.1.3 Games[4]

Games are a vital part of a teacher's equipment, not only for the language practice they provide, but also for the therapeutic effect they have. They can be used at any stage of a class to provide an amusing and challenging respite from other classroom activity, and are especially useful at the end of a long day to send the students away feeling cheerful about their English class. We will look at four well-known examples.

(a) Ask the right question[5]

Students are divided into pairs in which there is A and B. Student A in each pair is given cards such as the following:

Student A then has to ask B questions so that B gives exactly the answer written on A's card. If B fails to give the exact answer A has to ask the question again until B gets it exactly right.

This game, suitable for all levels (although the teacher would choose more difficult answers for more advanced students) is great fun and quite difficult since A has to think of exactly the right question to get exactly the right answer.

(b) Twenty questions

This is a team game which originated from a popular BBC programme. Students are divided into two teams. Each team must think of a number of objects. The game commences when one person from team A answers any questions from any of the team B members. The questions may only be answered by the words 'Yes' or 'No'.

If team B finds out what the object is after only a maximum of fifteen questions they get two points. If it takes them between sixteen and twenty questions they get one point. They get no points if they do not discover what the object is after asking 20 questions.

The game can be made more fun if each team is given a pile of cards (showing various objects) placed face downwards.[6] The member of the team who is answering the questions picks up a card and has to answer questions depending on what the card shows.

(c) Noughts and crosses

This popular children's game can be easily adapted for the English classroom enabling the teacher to ensure practice of specific language in an amusing context.

The class is divided into two teams; one represents noughts (O) and the other crosses (X). The teacher puts the following up on the blackboard:

this	never	running
their	can't	are
isn't	play	can

The team selects the square it wishes to play for, and a member of the team has to say a sentence using the word on that square. If his sentence is correct the square is filled with a nought or a cross, depending on the team the player comes from.

The game can be adapted to any language the teacher wishes to have practised. The squares could all contain question words, for example, or modal auxiliaries, frequency adverbs, etc. More fun can be added if the teacher brings in the game on a card and the squares are all covered. The students select a square which the teacher uncovers, and the team have to make a sentence with whatever is underneath.

(d) Quizzes

Quizzes can always be used to practise specific language items in an enjoyable and motivating way. In this example students will be practising the use of the 'was/were' past.

The students are divided into two teams. Each team is given time to write a number of general knowledge questions using the 'was/were' past. Their questions might be like the following:

Who was the first man on the moon?
What was the name of the last American President?
Where was the 1982 World Cup?
When were the Moscow Olympics?   *etc.*

In the game a member of team *A* asks a question to a member of team *B*. If the question is said correctly team *A* get one point. If the member of team *B* gets the answer immediately the team gets two points. If he has to confer with his team mates to get the answer the team get one point.

Games like these have been widely used for many years. They are great fun and provide practice in an amusing context.

7.1.4
Personalisation and localisation

Personalisation and localisation refer to those stages of practice where students use language they have recently learnt to say things about themselves or about things they know. The use of personalisation and localisation can be extremely controlled or extremely free.

Before we look at examples of these techniques we can make a few general comments.

1 *The truth factor in personalisation*: The aim of personalisation and localisation is to get students to use recently learnt language to make their own, real sentences. In other words it is not just accuracy that we are after, but the use of grammatical/functional knowledge to say things that have genuine meaning for the students. One way of doing this is to ensure (within limits) that the students make true statements, for if they do they will be forced to select language which is appropriate for the satisfying of this condition. Students who make true statements about their lives or about, for example, the place they live in, will thus not simply be constructing grammatically correct sentences. They will be conveying real meaning.

Of course it is not being suggested that we should insist on truth where students are reluctant to talk about themselves.

95

2 *Follow-up questions and real answers*: Language teaching materials in general tend to give students a highly grammatical (and not very real) idea of how questions are asked and answered. Students practise questions such as 'Do you smoke?' and are expected to answer 'Yes I do/No I don't'. Even worse are textbook drills such as the following, 'Where's John?', 'John's in the kitchen'.

Research[7] has suggested, however, that answers to questions in real life are seldom grammatically parallel to the questions. The answer to a question such as 'Are you happy?' is seldom 'Yes I am/No I'm not'. Much more likely are responses such as 'More or less', 'Can't complain' or even 'Why do you ask?'.

Teachers should encourage this type of response and a way of doing so is to insist on an additional remark being made. This means that where a student gives a yes/no type answer he must then add a comment to it. The following example shows such a remark being prompted:

S2: Do you like swimming?
S1: Yes.
 T: Yes . . . and?
S1: Yes . . . I go every Sunday.

Another feature of conversation is that people rarely ask a question, get an answer, and then finish the conversation (although many textbook drills are like this). The following exchange therefore is unlikely:

JOHN: Hello, Mary. Have you been to the movies recently?
MARY: Yes I have.
        (*John walks away*)

The conversation would be more likely to run in one of the following ways:

JOHN: Have you been to the movies recently?

MARY: Yes, actually.	*or*	No...no I haven't.
JOHN: What did you see?		Really. Don't you like films?
MARY: Oh...I saw *Raiders of the Lost Ark*!		Yes, but I don't have the time to go to the cinema.
JOHN: Hadn't you seen it before? It's been out for ages.		Why?
etc.		*etc.*

In other words John's original question starts a conversation which he continues by asking questions which follow up the answer to the original conversation starter.

Particularly during personalisation and localisation stages the teacher can prompt the use of additional remarks and follow-up questions in order to encourage realistic communication.

We can now look at three examples of personalisation and localisation stages, bearing in mind the truth factor and the need for the teacher to prompt the use of additional remarks and follow-up questions, etc.

(a) Personalisation plans

In this case students have recently been learning the use of the present continuous to express future plans (e.g. 'He's going to Rome tomorrow').

The teacher then asks students what they are doing, for example, at the weekend and they give sentences using the present continuous, for example:

T: What are you doing this weekend, Gunter?
S1: I'm visiting Scotland.
T: Oh really . . . When are you leaving?
S1: Early on Saturday morning.   *etc.*

The teacher then gets students to ask each other questions of the same type (making sure they use, for example, follow-up questions in the same way as he did). They can work in pairs or groups to do this.

This type of personalisation may form an immediate creativity stage (see 6.3) or it may be used at some stage after students have learnt the new item of language.

(b) Localisation: Guadalajara

Students are learning English in Guadalajara, Mexico. They have recently learnt how to talk about the location of places (e.g. 'There's a cinema in South Street', etc.).

The teacher then gets students to ask and answer questions about Guadalajara in a similar way:

T: OK . . . well . . . is there an airport in Guadalajara?
S1: Yes . . . of course.
T: Where is it exactly?
S1: It's on the road to Chapala . . . about 11 kilometres from here.   *etc.*

Students are then encouraged to ask and answer questions of the same type, and they will be put in pairs to do so. Once again this activity could be used as an immediate creativity stage, but it would also be suitable for language practice sometime after the new language has been originally introduced.

(c) Social talk

This describes a stage at which the students discuss themselves and/or topics of current interest in a relaxed way. Originally it may be teacher-directed, but students who are used to this kind of activity in English will soon be eager to handle it on their own.

A way of organising this activity is to single out a student for 'questioning'! The idea is to get students to ask him or her as many questions as they know, for example:

   T: OK Juan . . . ask Maria about yesterday evening.
   S1: What did you do yesterday evening, Maria?
   S2: I went to the supermarket.
      (*Pause*)
   T: Well Juan . . .
   S1: Oh . . . why?
   S2: Because I needed some things.
   S3: What did you buy?
   S2: Eggs . . . meat . . . that kind of thing.   *etc.*

Supermarkets may not be very exciting as a topic for social conversation of this type, but of course the topic will depend on the students. In this example the teacher was controlling the proceedings, even to the extent of encouraging Juan to use a follow-up question. But the advantage of this kind of whole-class conversation is that the teacher may, if he thinks it is necessary, intrude with prompting and gentle correction (see page 201) at the same time as getting a good idea of how the students are progressing with language that has recently been used for conscious learning.

    Any subject of current interest can be used for such a session and it will be suitable for the beginning of classes, particularly, where it will serve to 'warm the class up'.

    A much freer version of the same activity will be shown in 8.1.5(a).

Personalisation and localisation, then, are techniques for getting students to practise language in a way that ensures appropriate language use. Students have to be able to make the connection between grammar, etc. that they have learnt and the way to apply it to things that have real meaning for them. Personalisation and localisation are useful for various stages of practice as well as the immediate creativity stage that we looked at in Chapter 6.

7.1.5
Oral activities

We will look at three activities designed to encourage practice of specific language in an enjoyable and active way.

(a) Find someone who
This activity is designed to get the students asking a number of different questions in an active way.

    Each student is given the following card:

```
FIND SOMEONE WHO

1  likes chocolate _____

2  often goes to the cinema _____

3  has three brothers _____

4  went to bed late last night _____

5  plays the guitar _____
                                      (etc.)
```

All the students then stand up and circulate, asking each other questions such as 'Do you like chocolate?'. If they get the answer 'yes' they write that person's name in the space provided. They can only ask someone a question once. The activity ends when a student has got names for each question.

The activity is obviously noisy but it is great fun. The teacher can ensure practice of whatever questions he likes by altering the items on the card. The activity is particularly suitable for a group that has only recently met since it helps students to get to know about each other.

It is a good idea to check that the 'winning' student has written down the names correctly.

(b) Likes and dislikes

This activity starts as a way of practising like/dislike language and the language of agreement and disagreement. If it is successful it may well develop into a free conversation.

The teacher and the students decide on a topic. The teacher then asks the students to write down two reasons why they like or dislike the topic, using the following formula:

I like/don't like (*the topic*) because ———— .

Before the activity starts the teacher will introduce agreement and disagreement language. In a fairly elementary class the following language might be introduced:

Agree	I agree, and + additional remark
Disagree	I'm afraid I don't agree. (I think) + opinion

The teacher now asks a student to read one of his sentences and asks another student to agree or disagree with it. The opinion or additional remark consists of what the second student had originally written down for that topic.

Suppose the topic were bullfighting, the session might start like this:

T: Read one of your sentences Juan.
S1: I like bull fighting because it's very exciting.
T: Agree or disagree, Maria.
S2: I'm afraid I don't agree . . .
T: I think . . .
S2: I think it's cruel because the bull always dies.
T: (*Nominates S3*)
S3: I'm afraid I don't agree. The bull sometimes wins.
S2: But he doesn't receive the ears of the matador!

The teacher starts the activity by cueing students and treating it like a drill. Thus he has to prompt *S2* to add an opinion to her disagreement. *S2*'s final contribution shows how the conversation is 'taking off'. If this happens (and it will probably not happen as quickly as in our example) the teacher will stop treating it as a drill, and cease prompting or correcting. He might then join the discussion as a participant (see 10.1.5).

This activity is equally suitable for group work. Once the students understand the procedure they can be put into groups to continue the activity.

(c) Questionnaires

Questionnaires are a useful way of encouraging practice of specific language items in an interesting and motivating way. In this example students will ask each other about films they have (or have not) seen and what their opinions of the film were.

The teacher and the students discuss some of the most recent films that have been shown. The students are then given the following form:

NAME OF FILM	Tick if seen	tick if		
		good	satisfactory	bad

Students then question each other asking questions such as 'Have you seen *The French Lieutenant's Woman*?', 'What did you think of it?/Did you like it?', etc. As the form suggests they put ticks (√) where indicated.

When they have filled in their questionnaires they will then write a short paragraph such as the following:

> More people have seen *The French Lieutenant's Woman* than any other film, but most of them did not like it very much. The film that everybody thought was good was *The Stunt Man*.   *etc.*

The activity thus provides practice of the present perfect and past simple tenses and shows how oral and written skills can be integrated. The writing also encourages the use of comparatives.

The questionnaire, then, is a useful practice technique. We have already seen its use in presentation (see 6.5.1(b)) and we will see how the idea can be considerably extended in 8.2.6(d).

7.2
Written practice[8]

In this section we will consider ways of encouraging written practice. We will look at *sentence writing, parallel writing, cohesion and coherence* and *oral compositions.*

7.2.1
Sentence writing

We will look at three examples of sentence writing which aim to give students practice in specific written language.

(a) Sentence completion

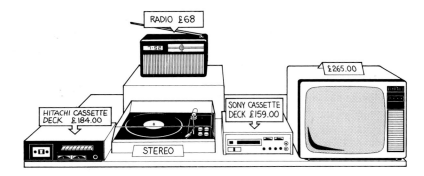

In this example the students look at a picture and then complete the sentences that follow it. This is the picture.

These are the sentences:

1 The _____ is on the shelf above the stereo.
2 The _____ cassette deck _____ £159.
3 _____ the television _____ ? £265.
4 _____ £68.

This is clearly a very controlled exercise designed to get the students to practise the use of the present simple for stating prices, etc. It resembles the fill-in type of exercises we saw in Chapter 6.

Exercises of this type are useful in that they force students to use specific verb tenses/vocabulary items, etc. They should be short and not too frequently used. They may, however, form the basis for useful homework.

(b) What are they doing?

In this example students are asked to look at a picture and write four sentences about what the people in the picture are doing. This is the picture:

This exercise has the advantage of getting the students to use specific language (in this case the present continuous) to make their own sentences. It is thus slightly more challenging than the first example.

(c) Christmas

In this example students use personalisation (see 7.1.4) to write sentences using time clauses.

The students have recently learnt how to make time clauses using words such as 'before', 'after', 'when', 'while', etc. To start this sentence-writing activity the teacher might proceed in the following way:

  T: What happens on December the 25th?
 S1: Christmas.
  T: Right . . . do you do the same thing every
      Christmas?

S1: Yes . . . more or less.

T: OK . . . do you go to church Juan?

S1: Yes.

T: OK . . . and what happens after you've been to church?

S1: After we've been to church we open the presents.

T: Good . . . now I want you to write me four sentences using 'after', 'when', 'before' and 'while' about what you will do this Christmas.

Clearly this topic will only be suitable in Christian countries, and is probably appropriate for use near December the 25th. Any routine activity that is about to take place would do, however.

This exercise has all the advantages of oral personalisation since it is asking students to use specific language in what is, for them, a meaningful way. Topics such as this can, of course, serve as the basis for composition work.

The three examples we have considered have all been concerned with the production of accurate written sentences. They have not, however, asked the students to write connected prose since their concern has been specific language items in isolation. Clearly connected written discourse is necessary, however, and in the next three sections we will look at ways of encouraging students to write in this way.

7.2.2
Parallel writing

The concept of parallel writing is central to the teaching of connected discourse since it suggests that students should have a model from which to work. In other words students will first see a piece of writing and then use it as a basis for their own work. The original piece that they look at will show them how English is written and guide them towards their own ability to express themselves in written English.

We have already discussed parallel writing during the presentation stage (see 6.4) and seen examples (see 6.5.2(a), 6.5.3(c)) of how parallel writing can be used in that context. We can now look at three practice examples using the same technique.

(a) Hotels[9]

With this stimulating material students have to write descriptions of hotels based on a guide book after first seeing how the symbols are used in a written model. On the page opposite is the material the students see.

The teacher starts by getting the students to look at the 'Key to symbols' either singly or in pairs. He then finds out if there is any vocabulary the students do not understand. When he is confident that the students understand all the symbols he asks them to study the entry for the Hotel Concorde. He will then ask them comprehension questions to check they have understood the text. If he feels it is necessary he can then elicit similar sentences about, for example, the Castille Hotel as a further check that they can apply the symbols to the model. Students are then asked to write

This is a page from a hotel GUIDE BOOK.

(1) Read the symbols and their meanings:

INTERNATIONAL TRAVEL GUIDE: HOTELS: KEY TO SYMBOLS	
★ ★ ★ ★ good hotel	**B** breakfast
★ ★ ★ average hotel	✗ lunch
★ ★ simple hotel	▽ dinner
☏ telephone number	⌣ bathrooms
◉ city centre	▨ swimming pool
♣♠ countryside	⋔ showers
○ time of opening	▰ railway station
⛏ bedrooms	✖ no station
▥ central heating	

(2) Here is the entry for the Hotel Concorde, Paris.

HOTEL CONCORDE: PARIS, FRANCE

★ ★ ★ ★ ☏ 88-66-21 ◉   ○ all year

40 ⛏ ▥ **B** 7-9 ✗ 11-3 ▽ 8-11

25 ⌣ 15 ⋔ ▨ in hotel ▰ 2km

It means:

The Hotel Concorde in Paris is a good hotel. The telephone number is 88-66-21. It is in the city centre.

The hotel is open all year and there are forty bedrooms. There is central heating in the hotel.

Breakfast is from seven to nine, lunch is from eleven to three, and dinner is from eight until eleven. There are twenty-five bathrooms and fifteen showers. There is also a swimming pool in the hotel. The nearest railway station is two kilometres away.

Now read these symbols, and describe the hotels in the same way:

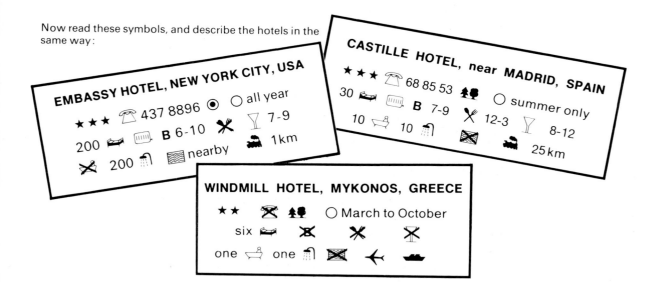

EMBASSY HOTEL, NEW YORK CITY, USA

★ ★ ★ ☏ 437 8896 ◉   ○ all year

200 ⛏ ▥ **B** 6-10 ✗ ▽ 7-9

✗ 200 ⋔ ▨ nearby ▰ 1km

CASTILLE HOTEL, near MADRID, SPAIN

★ ★ ★ ☏ 68 85 53 ♣♠   ○ summer only

30 ⛏ ▥ **B** 7-9 ✗ 12-3 ▽ 8-12

10 ⌣ 10 ⋔ ✖ 25km

WINDMILL HOTEL, MYKONOS, GREECE

★ ★   ✖ ♣♠   ○ March to October

six ⛏   ✖   ✗   ▽

one ⌣ one ⋔   ✖ ✈ ⛵

(either singly, or in pairs or groups) a similar paragraph about one of the other hotels. They might write something like the following:

> The Windmill Hotel in Mykonos is a simple hotel. It has no telephone. It is in the countryside.

The writing in this example is extremely controlled, but the activity is sufficiently challenging since the students have to interpret the symbols in order to complete their paragraph.

(b) Focus magazine[10]

This example, designed for beginner students, works on the same principle as the hotel material above, but because there is a degree of personalisation involved the students have the opportunity to be slightly more creative.

The students see the following material:

1. **FOCUS MAGAZINE** NEW STAFF

Meet our new secretary, Jackie Young. Here's Jackie.

"Hello! My name's Jackie Young. I'm 20. I'm a secretary at Focus Films. I'm Australian but I live in England now. I live with my parents in Trafford, a suburb west of Manchester. But I want a flat near Focus Films".

2. **Imagine that you are a new student in your class. Write a few lines like this about yourself for a class magazine (give the magazine a name).**

Before asking the students to complete Exercise 2 (the parallel writing) the teacher may check that students have understood the text and get students to produce oral sentences about themselves before doing the writing task. However these stages may be unnecessary and the students can move straight to the parallel writing.

The teacher can then collect the students' pieces and hand them round to other students in the class. This would be a good activity at the beginning of a course to help students to get to know each other.

(c) The Ingrams[11]

This example of parallel writing is freer than the two previous ones. The original text gives the students a model that they are free to imitate as closely as they wish. But once again, since there is an element of personalisation involved, the students can be fairly creative. This is the material the students see:

1. Last summer, the Ingrams exchanged houses with some friends who live on the south coast of England. Joan Ingram left a note to say where to find things.

Dear Anne,

Just a short note to say where things are in the house. The sheets and towels are in the cupboard at the top of the stairs. Extra blankets are in the yellow wardrobe in the small bedroom.

The vacuum cleaner is in the cupboard under the stairs. There's a spare front door key on the shelf above the sink in the kitchen.

One more thing. Could you feed the cats?* Don't feed them more than once a day as they're on a diet! Also could you give them some water in their bowl outside the back door every day? Don't give them milk – they don't like it!

Hope you have a good time.

Love,

Joan.

* The cat food is in the small cupboard under the sink in the kitchen.

Imagine someone is going to stay in your room/flat/house.
Write a note to say where things are.
Give any instructions you think are necessary.

The teacher gets the students to read the text and may do comprehension checking, or at least give the students a chance to clarify the meaning of vocabulary, etc. that they are unsure of. They can then write their own parallel note. The teacher should be prepared to help with vocabulary the students are unclear about.

The three examples of parallel writing have shown how a text can form the basis for the writing of connected discourse in a way that gives the students considerable help and guidance. At the same time, particularly with the first two examples, the written practice of specific items has been assured by the use of those items in the original model.

**7.2.3
Cohesion and
coherence**

In 5.6 we discussed some of the differences between speaking and writing and in particular saw the need for coherent organisation and logical thought. We saw how this was in some ways more difficult in writing than in speaking, particularly since the reader is often not in a position to clarify points he does not understand with the writer, in the way that a participant in a conversation can stop the speaker and ask for repetition and re-explanation.

In this section we will look at a number of exercises designed to help students to organise their writing clearly and coherently. This involves not only the ordering of sentences, but also the use of cohesive devices (e.g. language that is used to join sentences together). We will look at four examples of exercises designed to teach students about coherence and cohesion.

(a) Co-ordinators: Concorde

In this example we will look at a simple exercise for beginner students designed to teach them how to join sentences with 'and' or 'but'.

After the teacher has ascertained that students know the meaning of the two co-ordinators and how they are used he gives them the following exercise:

Join the following pairs of sentences using 'and' or 'but':

1 Concorde is an ideal way to travel. Concorde is expensive.
2 Concorde is fast. Concorde is comfortable.
3 Travellers like Concorde. People living near airports don't like Concorde.

Not only will the students have to select the correct sentence co-ordinator, but they will also have to decide where to change 'Concorde' for 'it'. The use of words like 'it', 'they', 'she', etc. to refer back to subjects mentioned earlier will be discussed in more detail in (c) below.

When the students have done the short exercise the teacher will ask them to write more sentences about Concorde (or a related topic) using 'and' or 'but'.

(b) Concession: The fridge[12]

The aim of this exercise (designed for advanced students) is to train them in the use of concessive devices such as 'in spite of', 'although', etc. It also has the advantage of showing students how informal spoken language can be formalised for written style.

After the students have seen the concessive devices in use in a text they are shown the following:

Read the following story:
Two months ago I bought this fridge. Very expensive it was too. But I've had nothing but trouble from it. For a start the 'COLD CONTROL' didn't work. I set it at 'medium' and it froze everything – I had to put my butter on the stove to thaw it out. I phoned the company, but nobody came. After I'd waited a week I wrote them a letter, but still nobody came. After phoning again (with no result) I went round to see them, and they sent a man round. He said he'd fixed it, but it still didn't work. The fridge has got a guarantee, but they still sent me a bill.

Now imagine that it was you telling the story and make sentences in written style using 'in spite of (the fact that)', 'although' and 'despite'.

Although this exercise is designed for advanced students the principle can easily be used at more elementary levels with elements like 'although', 'because', relative clauses, etc.

(c) Babar[13]

In this example we will look at a lesson sequence designed to train students how to write more coherent discourse using cohesive devices such as 'it', 'she', 'they' etc. (see (a) above). We will train students to recognise topic sentences (i.e. sentences that introduce a topic) and how connected discourse follows on from such sentences.

The teacher writes the following on the blackboard:

a It will give her more time to wash all the clothes so she's very happy now.
b John and Mary have six children.
c It takes Mary three hours to clean it.
d They live in a large flat.
e Luckily she was given a vacuum cleaner for her birthday this morning.

The students are asked to re-order the sentences by putting the letter of the sentence against the following numbers:

1 _____

2 _____

3 _____

4 _____

5 _____

When the students have done this individually the teacher asks them what order they have chosen and asks them why. He can point out that sentence b has to be the topic sentence because it introduces the subject matter of the paragraph. Sentence d follows, and the clue to this is clearly the use of 'they' which refers to 'John', 'Mary' and 'the six children'. The sentence ends with the information about the flat which is then picked up by the second 'it' in sentence c, etc. This is the point at which students are actually made aware of elements of cohesion and how a paragraph is organised. (The rather sarcastic tone of this domestic tale might also provoke comment or discussion!)

The teacher then organises students into groups and tells them they are going to be given sentences from a story for children. The groups are then given individual sentences on pieces of card which they have to put in what they think is the correct order.

Here are the sentences from one of the paragraphs given to one of the groups:

Babar grew bigger.

He killed Babar's mother.

Then the hunter ran up to catch poor Babar too.

In the great forest a little elephant was born.

Soon he was playing with the other baby elephants.

His name was Babar.

He was one of the nicest of them.

After some days, tired and footsore, he came to a town.

His mother loved him very much, and used to rock him to sleep with her trunk.

One day, Babar was riding happily on his mother's back, when a wicked hunter, hiding behind a tree, shot at them.

Babar ran away because he was afraid of him.

(The choice of the story clearly depends on the type of students being taught.)

After each group has put its paragraphs in order, the teacher shows them the correct paragraphs so that they can compare and see if they were correct.

Next the teacher might give students sentences followed by, for example, pronouns which they have to use to make new sentences based on the first. Continuing with the story of Babar the teacher might give the students the following:

Babar was amazed, because this was the first time he had ever seen so many houses.

1 They ──

2 He ──

The students are now putting into effect what they have learnt from the previous sentence-ordering tasks.

Another exercise that could be used is the following:

Where you think it necessary replace the words 'Babar', 'the rich old lady' and 'the two gentlemen' with 'he', 'she', and 'they'.

Babar was amazed because this was the first time he had ever seen so many houses. So many things were new to Babar! The beautiful avenues! The cars and buses! But what interested Babar most of all was two gentlemen Babar met in the street. The two gentlemen were wearing smart suits. Luckily Babar was seen by a very rich old lady who understood little elephants, and knew at once that Babar wanted a smart suit. The rich old lady liked making others happy, so she gave him her purse. 'Thank you madam', said Babar politely. Without wasting time Babar went into a big store. Babar got into the lift. Babar had such fun riding up and down, Babar did not want to stop.

Once again, when students have decided where to replace words with 'he', 'she' and 'they', the teacher will show them the original for them to compare with their own versions.

This lesson sequence clearly shows students how sentences are ordered and joined together with cohesive devices. The variety of exercises in the sequence gives students practice not only in working out the logic of such organisation but also in putting their newly acquired understanding into practice.

(d) Logical organisation: The faulty projector

The examples we have so far looked at concern the use of linguistic devices for coherence and cohesion. Students also seem to have trouble, however, with the logical organisation of the ideas they wish to include in written discourse. In the following example the teacher elicits the 'ideas' the students wish to include in a complaint letter and then gets the students to order these general ideas into a logical sequence before asking them to put the ideas into writing.

The students are told that they are going to write a letter of complaint to the manager of British Airways about the fact that on a recent flight they paid for the hire of headphones to watch an in-flight movie. Unfortunately, however, the film projector broke down so that the film was never shown. They want their money back.

The teacher then asks the students what 'ideas' they will include in their letter and writes their answers on the blackboard in the order they are given, for example:

a The film projector broke down.
b The headphones were paid for.
c The traveller wanted to watch the film.
d The date, destination, flight number, etc.
e The traveller wants his money back.
f Reason for writing.
g Salutation.
h Signing off.

The students are then told to work in pairs to put these ideas into a logical order which will be the following:

1 *g*	5 *b*
2 *f*	6 *a*
3 *d*	7 *e*
4 *c*	8 *h*

They can then work on the letter itself which will be something like this:

```
Dear Sir,

I am writing to complain about the malfunction
of a projector on one of your flights.

On July 3rd I travelled from Mexico City to
London on a British Airways flight, number BA 301.
I particularly wanted to watch the in-flight
movie (The Stunt Man) and so I paid $3.00 for
the hire of a pair of headphones. Unfortunately,
however, the projector broke just as the film
started and I was unable to see the film.

In view of the failure of the projector I would
ask you to return the amount of $3.00 which I
paid for the hire of the headphones.

Yours sincerely,
```

This type of exercise can be adapted for many kinds of writing (e.g. narrative, description, instructions, etc.) and helps the students to see the need for logical organisation and try it out.

The four examples in this section have been aimed at getting students to organise written discourse in a logical way, using a variety of linguistic devices to do so. The logical organisation of written English is vitally important and students need a lot of this kind of exercise to help them practise this skill.

7.2.4
Oral compositions

Oral compositions have been very popular in English language teaching for some time. The idea is for the teacher and students working together to build up a narrative orally before writing it. The process of building up the composition with the whole class allows the teacher and students to focus in on a variety of language items from tense usage to cohesive elements, etc.

Oral compositions can be handled with visual[14] or aural[15] stimuli. In other words the teacher can show the students a series of pictures, mime a story, or play them a tape with a series of sounds. The example we are going to look at uses pictures.

(a) The rich man and the pauper

The teacher starts the procedure by showing the students a picture and eliciting the information from them using the language he and they want.

This is the first picture that the students see:

The teacher has prepared the following text for this picture:

Yesterday John Smith left his home at eight o'clock. As usual he said goodbye to his wife and got into his Rolls Royce. It was raining heavily.

The teacher introduces the key concepts (e.g. that the story is about yesterday, that the man's name is John Smith, etc.). He might then continue in the following way:

> T: So . . . yesterday John Smith . . . (*mimes 'leaving' and points to picture*) . . . anybody?
> S1: Yesterday John Smith go away.
> T: Go . . . yesterday?
> S1: uh . . . went . . . went away.
> T: Yes . . . that's OK. But can we say anything else? . . . John Smith . . . his house . . .
> S2: Yesterday John Smith left his house . . .
> T: Good . . . at? (*T points to time*)
> S3: Eight o'clock.
> T: Good . . . so can anybody give me the whole sentence?
> S1: Yesterday John Smith left his house at eight o'clock.

The teacher builds up the story with four more pictures (showing John Smith picking up a tramp, the tramp at John Smith's home, the tramp and Mrs Smith kicking John Smith out of the house, and the tramp at the wheel of the Rolls passing John Smith in rags).

When the teacher and the students have built up the whole story the teacher will write up key words from it, for example:

Yesterday John Smith _____ at eight o'clock. As usual _____ and _____ Rolls Royce. It _____ heavily.   *etc.*

Working in pairs the students complete the story which is then checked with the whole class on the blackboard.

The finished story may form a useful model for a parallel writing task where the teacher brings in a similar picture sequence and the students write their own narrative either singly or in pairs or groups.

Oral compositions are useful, then, for the teaching of narrative style and thus the use of various past tenses. However, they take a long time and should therefore be used sparingly!

Exercises

1 Select a language item or language items that you are going to teach and then design an information gap activity to practise that language.
2 Take a unit from a textbook that you are using (or are familiar with) and design the following activities to practise language from that unit:
   (a) A noughts and crosses game.
   (b) A personalisation/localisation stage.
   (c) A 'find someone who' activity.
3 Look at your textbook (or one that you are familiar with) and say what kinds of written practice the book contains.
4 Take any English written text, from any source, and identify cohesive devices used in that text.
5 You wish to teach students how to write descriptions. Design an activity for logical organisation practice followed by some actual writing.

References

1 This idea is taken directly from J Kerr (1979) Teacher's Book page 74. Kerr's cue cards are ideal for this kind of activity (see also reference 6 below).
2 Taken from A Matthews and C Read (1981).
3 Taken from P Watcyn-Jones (1981).
4 For more on games see especially A Wright et al. (1979) and W R Lee (new edition 1980).
5 A slightly different version of this game can be found in J Willis (1981) page 122.
6 Kerr's cue cards would be extremely useful for this (see 1 above).
7 See J Richards (1977). An excellent comparison of textbook 'short answers' and real-life exchanges was made by W Plumb (1979).
8 For more on controlled writing see D Byrne (1979) especially Chapter 4 and J Willis (1981) Unit 20.
9 The material is taken from E Davies and N Whitney (1979).
10 Taken from B Abbs and I Freebairn (1977).
11 Taken from B Abbs and I Freebairn (1979).
12 The material is taken from J W Arnold and J Harmer (1978).
13 This class sequence was planned by Anita Harmer, and the story, adapted by her, is from *The Story of Babar* by Jean de Brunhoff (Magnet books 1978). For a demonstration of a sentence re-ordering exercise see the British Council film *Pair and Group Work in a Language Programme.*
14 For examples of picture composition material see L Hill (1960), J Heaton (1966), D Byrne (1967) and especially L Markstein and D Grunbaum (1981).
15 Examples of aural stimuli for composition can be found in A Maley and A Duff (1977).

8

Communicative activities

In this chapter we will consider activities for communication output (see 4.2.6) which comply as far as possible with the characteristics we said were necessary for communicative activities (see Figure 2 on page 45).

In the first part of the chapter we will look at activities with a largely oral focus (although it will be necessary to remember the discussion concerning skill integration in 5.5) and in the second half we will concentrate on written communication.

**8.1
Oral communicative activities**

8.1.1 Reaching a consensus

We will look at various ways of promoting oral communication in the classroom. We will divide our examples into seven areas: *reaching a consensus, relaying instructions, communication games, problem solving, interpersonal exchange, story construction* and *simulation and role play*.

In these examples students have to agree with each other after a certain amount of discussion. The task is not complete until they do.

Consensus activities have been very successful in promoting free and spontaneous use and we can now look at three examples.

(a) Going to New York[1]
In this activity students are told that they are going on holiday and have to decide what ten objects to take with them. They will have to reach a consensus on these objects.

Stage 1 All the students are asked to write down the ten items they would choose to have in their luggage if they were going to stay in New York for two weeks.

Stage 2 When all the students have completed their lists they are put into pairs. Each pair has to negotiate a new list of ten items. This will involve each member of the pair changing his original list to some extent.

Stage 3 When the pairs have completed their lists two pairs are joined together to negotiate a new list that all four students can agree to.

Stage 4 Groups can now be joined together and the lists re-negotiated.

Stage 5 When the teacher thinks the activity has gone on for long enough a feedback session is conducted with the whole class in which each group explains and justifies its choices.

This activity, which can be used from the elementary level upwards, is great fun and produces a lot of English. Of course there is no reason for selecting New York as the destination. Other places can be used.

(b) Moral dilemmas

Students are given a situation and alternative suggestions for acting in such a situation are given. The following is an example:

Stage 1 Students are told that they are invigilating an important school/university exam. They see a student cheating with notes he has illegally brought into the exam room. They have four possible courses of action:
  – Ignore the incident.
  – Warn the student that if he cheats again he will be reported to the authorities.
  – Ask the student to leave the exam, tear up his exam and mark him as absent.
  – Report the student to the authorities, in which case he will have to leave the school/university.

Stage 2 Students are put in small groups to reach a consensus on this issue.

Stage 3 Pairs of groups are combined and have to reach a consensus on which alternative to adopt.

Stage 4 The procedure can be repeated with groups joining each other. Alternatively after Stage 3 the teacher can conduct a feedback session in front of the whole class in which groups justify their choices.

(c) Reading tasks

Where students are asked to decide the answers to reading comprehension exercises (see the many examples in 9.4) it is often a good idea to put them in pairs or groups and ask them to reach a consensus on the correct answers. This involves a considerable amount of skill integration.

A lot of successful simulations and role plays are based on the need of the participants to reach a consensus, and we shall see examples of these in 8.1.7.

8.1.2
Relaying
instructions

In this type of activity a group of students has the necessary information for the performance of a task. Without showing them these instructions they have to enable another group or groups of students to perform the same task. We will look at two examples.

(a) The traditional dance[2]

Stage 1 A small group of students are given the following instructions for an English traditional dance.

Example 1
TRADITIONAL DANCE

Holding hands, form a circle facing inwards with males and females placed alternately.

(1) When the music starts, skip in a clockwise direction keeping hands held.
(2) Do the same in the opposite direction.
(3) Drop hands and skip slowly to the middle of the circle, jump up in the air (all dancers at the same time) and clap your hands. Return to your place slowly skipping backwards.
(4) Repeat instruction (3).
(5) Men turn to face the lady on the left. Ladies turn to face the man on the right. Linking left arms turn together twice on the same spot in an anticlockwise direction.
(6) Do the same as (5) but with right arms linked turning twice in the opposite direction. Return to your place.
(7) Walk to the middle. All dancers raise their left arms and touch hands, and with all hands linked together turn in a complete circle anticlockwise.
(8) Immediately turn round and do the same as (7) with right hands linked. Return to your place and repeat the whole sequence.

Stage 2 The group is told to get other members of the class to perform the dance without showing them the instructions. If it is a small class the small group can simply join the rest of the class so that all the students work together. Otherwise the original group can split up and organise different groups of dancer-students.

The only drawback of this activity of course is the need for space.

(b) Making models

Stage 1 A small group of students are given material to make models with (e.g. building bricks, Lego, etc.) and are told to make a model.

Stage 2 The original group now have to instruct another group or groups so that they can duplicate the original model. It is, of course, necessary for the original model to be hidden from the second group or other groups at this stage.

This type of activity can also, of course, be used for written communication activities (see 8.2.1).

8.1.3
Communication
games

Communication games are based on the principle of the information gap (see 5.2).[3] Students are put into situations which are 'game-like' and have to use all and any language they possess to complete the game.

We will look at three examples.[4]

(a) Describe and draw

One student has a picture which the other student cannot see. The second student has to draw an identical picture (in content, but not style!) by listening to his partner's instructions and/or asking questions.

Stage 1 Students are told that they are going to work in pairs.

Stage 2 Students in each pair are given the letters *A* and *B*.

Stage 3 Each student *A* is given a picture which he is told not to show to student *B* until the end of the game.

Stage 4 Students are told that *B* must draw the same picture as *A*: *A* should give instructions and *B* should ask questions where necessary.

Stage 5 When *B* thinks that he has completed the picture he should compare his work of art with the original to see how successful the activity was.

(b) Find the similarities

Students are put in pairs and given two pictures which are different but which contain a certain number of similarities. Without looking at each others' pictures they must discover what these similarities are:

Stage 1 Students are told that they are going to work in pairs.

Stage 2 Students are told that each person of each pair will be given a picture which he must not show to his neighbour.

Stage 3 After handing out the pictures the teacher tells the class that there are a certain number of similarities between the pictures that each pair has. Without looking at the pictures students must find out (by discussion) what these similarities are.

Stage 4 When the pair thinks it has discovered all the similarities the two students may show each other their pictures to see how well they did.

This technique is, of course, equally successful with pictures that are basically similar. In this case students have to find the differences.

(c) Describe and arrange

Once again students work in pairs: one member of the pair has a picture with items in a certain order, for example:

The other student has the same items, but they have been separated and are loose.

The second student has to put his items in the same order as the first without looking at his partner's picture.

Stage 1 Students are told they are going to work in pairs.

Stage 2 Students in each pair are given the letters *A* and *B*.

Stage 3 Each student *A* is given a picture which he is told not to show to student *B* until the end of the game.

Stage 4 Each student *B* is given an envelope containing a number of separate items. He is told not to show them to *A*.

Stage 5 Students are told that *B* must order his items in the same way as *A*: he should do this by discussing the items with *A*.

Stage 6 When *A* and *B* in each pair think that *B* has got the items in the correct order they may look at *A*'s picture to check if they are right.

There are many communication games of this type. Readers should refer to the references at the end of this chapter for more ideas.

8.1.4
Problem solving

Problem-solving activities are very much like 'consensus' activities (see 8.1.1). The difference is that students are faced with a problem to which there is a solution. We will look at two examples.

(a) Desert dilemma[5]

Students are given a considerable amount of information and told to make a decision. Since the information is all written down students are left very much on their own for the completion of the task.

Stage 1 Students are told that they are going to work in small groups.

Stage 2 Students are given the following information. They are told to study it and then follow the instructions. This is what they receive:

THE SITUATION

It is about ten o'clock in the morning in July, and you have just crashed in a small aeroplane in the Sonora desert in Northern Mexico. The pilot and co-pilot are dead and the aeroplane is a burnt-out shell. One of the passengers is injured.

The aeroplane had no radio, and the survivors think that they were about 100 kilometres off course when they crashed. Just before the crash the pilot told the passengers that they were 120 kilometres south of a small mining camp.

From experience you know that daytime temperatures can reach 43° centigrade (110° Fahrenheit) and night-time temperatures reach freezing. All the passengers are dressed in light clothes. The area is flat and arid as far as the eye can see.

Instructions

The following is a list of items that came out of the crash in good order:
— Flashlight with four batteries
— Jack knife
— Detailed pilot's chart of the area
— Large plastic poncho
— Compass
— Instrument to measure blood pressure
— Loaded .45 pistol
— One red and white parachute
— Bottle of 1000 salt tablets
— One quart of water per person
— Book *Edible Desert Animals*
— One pair of sunglasses per person
— Two bottles of vodka
— One overcoat per person
— One pocket mirror

Now do the following:
(a) Individually write down a list of the seven most important items on this list to ensure survival and/or rescue.
(b) Agree with the other members of the group what these items are.

Stage 3 When the groups have reached a decision the teacher and class can conduct a feedback session. The proposed solution to this problem is the following:

The seven most important items are:
mirror, flashlight, one quart of water per person, plastic poncho, sunglasses, overcoats, parachute

Given that walking (e.g. to the mining camp) is inadvisable due to the heat and the injured passenger, the best chance of survival is to use the mirror to signal search planes by day and the flashlight by night. The parachute can be used as a shelter and for searchers/planes to see. Sunglasses may stop blindness and the overcoats keep the survivors warm at night. The water is clearly important, and the plastic poncho can be used to create more water, for example:

This exercise involves the students in a considerable amount of reading and discussion. The fact that the instructions are written down means that the teacher's role is confined to organising the groups and conducting feedback: there is really no teacher 'intervention' here!

(b) Shops in Kingston[6]

Students are given the following 'logical problem' to solve:

Stage 1 The teacher arranges the class into pairs or groups.

Stage 2 The teacher gives each pair (or group) the following information:

> Kingston has a grocery, a bakery and a bookshop. When I went to Kingston last week, the bookshop was open.
>
> 1 Those three shops are not open together on any day of the week.
> 2 The bakery is open 4 days a week.
> 3 The grocery is open 5 days a week.
> 4 All three places are closed on Sunday and Wednesday.
> 5 On three consecutive days:
>   the bakery was closed on the first day
>   the bookshop was closed on the second day
>   the grocery was closed on the third day
> 6 On three consecutive days:
>   the bookshop was closed on the first day
>   the grocery was closed on the second day
>   the bakery was closed on the third day
>
> On which one of the days of last week did I go to Kingston?

Stage 3 After a given time, and supposing the students have not got near a solution, the teacher can give or tell the students the following clue:

> Draw up a grid with the shops and the days marked on it:

	Sunday	Monday	Tuesday	Wednesday	Thursday	Friday	Saturday
Grocer	Closed	Open	Open	Closed	Open	Open	Open
Baker	Closed			Closed			
Bookshop	Closed			Closed			

> Fill it in with the information given, and use the conditions to work out the rest.

Stage 4 The teacher and the class engage in a feedback session to see what solutions they have arrived at. The real solution is the following:

	Sunday	Monday	Tuesday	Wednesday	Thursday	Friday	Saturday
Grocer	Closed	Open	Open	Closed	Open	Open	Open
Baker	Closed	Closed	Open	Closed	Open	Open	Open
Bookshop	Closed	Open	Closed	Closed	Closed	Closed	Closed

When completing the grid we first of all fill in closed for all shops on Sundays and Wednesdays. The grocer must also be open for the five remaining days (3). The baker must also be closed on Mondays to comply with (5) and (6). (Baker closed Monday, bookshop Tuesday, and grocer Wednesday: bookshop closed Saturday, grocer Sunday and baker Monday.) We know from (2) that the baker must remain open on Tuesday, Thursday, Friday and Saturday. But since all three shops cannot be open on one day, the bookshop must be closed on Thursday and Friday too. In fact it only opens on Mondays – and that was the day I went to Kingston.

This kind of puzzle again involves the students in reading and discussing and is highly enjoyable.

8.1.5 Interpersonal exchange

We will look at two examples where the stimulus for conversation comes from the students themselves.

(a) Finding out

Here the students are put in pairs and they have to find out about experiences that each other has had. In our example we will talk about films:

Stage 1 Students are told they will work in pairs.
Stage 2 Students in each pair are given the letters *A* and *B*.
Stage 3 The students are told that *A* should find out from his partner about any film *B* has seen, and what it was about, what *B* thought of it, etc. The teacher may suggest that *B* then asks *A* for the same information.
Stage 4 When the pairs have finished their conversations the teacher may lead a feedback session by finding out what was interesting about the conversations each pair had.

The same procedure may be followed with many other topics, such as what students did last weekend, what food they have eaten, where they have been on holiday, etc.

(b) Your favourite food[7]

Students are put in pairs or small groups to find out things about each other's childhood, and what each student liked best when he was a child.

Stage 1 Students are put into pairs or small groups.

Stage 2 The teacher tells them that he is going to give each student a questionnaire which he should fill in. This he does by asking the other person in his pair, or another person in the group, the questions.

Stage 3 The teacher hands out the following questionnaire:

```
              QUESTIONNAIRE
    Fill in the following questionnaire about
    another student in your class.

    When he or she was a child, what was
    his/her favourite food?
    Why?                                   _____

    When he or she was a child, what was
    his/her favourite song?
    Why?                                   _____

    When he or she was a child, what was
    his/her favourite person?
    Why?                                   _____

    etc.
```

Stage 4 When students have completed this task the teacher leads a feedback session by asking, for example, 'Did anyone have a really strange favourite food?' or 'Did anybody hear anything interesting?'.

Exercises such as these, based on Gertrude Moskowitz's concept of 'humanistic techniques' are often incredibly productive in terms of the amount of language students use.

8.1.6
Story construction

The aim of these activities is to give students only partial information and then ask them, for example, to use that information as part of a story which they must complete by asking other students (who have other bits of information) for other parts of the story. We will examine the concept again when we consider 'jigsaw listening' (see page 187). We can look at one example.

(a) The hospital case[8]

After dividing the class into groups each group is given part of a story (in this case a picture sequence). When they have absorbed the information in their picture, groups are re-combined so that each member of the new group has seen a different picture. By telling each other what their picture contained, the group can build up the complete story. For the sake of convenience we will imagine that we are teaching a group of twenty-four students.

Stage 1 Students are put into groups (of six, for example).

Stage 2 Each member of each group is given a letter: *A*, *B*, *C*, *D*, *E*, and *F* (vitally important).

Stage 3 Each group is given one of the following pictures and told to study it for a short while:

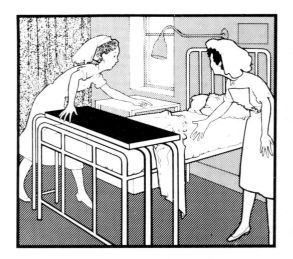 

Stage 4 The teacher collects the pictures. The teacher then asks the students to form new groups. He tells all those students with the letter *A* (there will be four) to form a new group, all those students with the letter *B* to form a different group, and the same for students with the letters *C, D*, etc.

Stage 5 The teacher tells each group to try and piece together the whole story (since each student was originally in a group which saw a different picture).

Stage 6 The teacher then asks the different groups to say what their stories are. Very often (and particularly with a sequence like the one shown here) the stories will differ to a large extent! The teacher finally shows all the students all the pictures.

This technique is very enjoyable and produces a great deal of discussion and interaction. It has many variations. Instead of pictures, the original groups may be given parts of a written story. This has the advantage of involving some reading as well. Another alternative is to ask students to write two sentences about their original pictures. When the new groups are formed students have to produce a written version of the story (see 8.2.5(a)).

8.1.7 Simulation and role play

The idea of simulation and role play is to create the pretence of a real-life situation in the classroom: students 'simulate' the real world. Thus, for example, we ask our students to pretend that they are at an airport, or we ask them to get together to organise a reunion. What we are trying to do – very artificially – is give the students practice in real-world English, as it should be used in English-speaking environments.

In the two examples (mentioned above) we say to the students that they are in this situation as themselves. Sometimes, however, we may ask them either to be someone else or to express views that are not necessarily their own: we may ask them to be a travel agent, a police inspector trying to get information, or a television 'anchor man'. In each of these cases we will be asking them to play a role.

Whether or not students are taking part in a simulation as themselves or whether they are playing a role they will need to do a certain amount of 'acting'. But this is not acting in the classical sense, of course. It simply means that students are prepared to enter into the activity with enthusiasm and conviction.

There is some controversy about the usefulness of role plays, but many teachers feel that they have certain advantages because students do not have to take responsibility for their own actions and words – in other words it's the character they are playing who speaks, not themselves. It has certainly been noticed that some shy students are more talkative when playing roles. With the right kind of class involvement and teacher encouragement, simulations with or without role playing are highly productive of language and extremely enjoyable for both students and teacher.

During a simulation the teacher may act as a participant, that is to say as one of the people involved. The advantage of this is that it enables him to 'help the simulation along' if it gets into difficulty. The teacher can also help to organise the direction of the simulation, particularly where he takes the part of the chairman of a meeting, etc. Of course it would be preferable to have a well-prepared student in this role if possible.

Where simulations get off to a shaky start the teacher may want to act as a prompter. He can make suggestions about what students might say or do next, and supply them with information if it is necessary. But this must be done as unobtrusively as possible and only when absolutely necessary for the success of the activity. Otherwise the simulation becomes teacher-dominated and this restricts students from communicating among themselves.

After the simulation has finished the teacher will want to conduct feedback with the students. The object here is to discuss with them whether the activity was successful, why certain decisions were reached, etc. If the teacher has been recording the proceedings (either by writing down good and bad points, or by using a tape recorder or a video) this will be a good opportunity to show where students performed particularly well (they may have used a convincing argument or a particularly effective piece of English) and to point out where poor English, for example, made communication less effective.

It is important for the teacher to conduct feedback about the content of an activity such as simulation as well as discussing the use of English. If only the latter is focused on the students will perceive the object of the exercise as being concerned only with linguistic accuracy rather than the ability to communicate efficiently – which is the main motive for this kind of activity.

We will now look at five examples of simulations.

(a) The travel agent

In this example students are divided into pairs in which they play the roles of a travel agent and a customer. The latter wants to book a holiday in a hotel, but insists that the hotel should have a number of qualities (such as the right price, good food, etc.). The travel agent has all the information about the hotels.

Stage 1 Students are told that they are going to work in pairs.
Stage 2 Students in each pair are given the letters A and B.
Stage 3 Students are told that A is a travel agent and B is a customer who wants to book a holiday in Miami.
Stage 4 The teacher tells the students not to show each other the information he is going to give them, and then gives the following piece of paper to B:

B. CUSTOMER

You want: (a) to go to a hotel in Miami for a week and you can spend up to $450 on a hotel

(b) to be as near as possible to the town centre

(c) to go to a hotel with a good discotheque

(d) there to be a children's swimming pool for your small son

(e) there to be someone to look after your son at the hotel

(f) the hotel to serve good food

(g) a comfortable room (with a good view)

Get all the information from the travel agent and then write down the hotel of your choice.

A gets the following hotel list:

A. TRAVEL AGENT

Study the following information carefully so that you can answer B (the customer).

	HILTON	HYATT REGENCY	HOLIDAY INN	FLORIDA
COST (double) per night	$40	$60	$75	$35
DISTANCE FROM CENTRE	10 kms.	12 kms.	20 kms.	3 kms.
DISCO	2*	1**	3***	-
RESTAURANT	3**	2***	4*	1**
VIEW	***	*	**	*
SWIMMING POOL				
Adults	1***	2*	1**	1*
Children	1*	1**	1***	-
CHILDCARE FACILITIES	-	**	*	-

<u>Note</u>: Various features (e.g. view, discos, restaurants, etc.) have been given stars to indicate quality. *** = very good, ** = good, * = fair. As an example we can say that you get a better view if you're staying at the Holiday Inn than if you're staying at the Hyatt Regency.

The students are told to study their information for a short period.

Stage 5 B is told to select the hotel of his choice based as far as possible on the six qualities he is looking for. The activity commences.

Stage 6 When all the pairs have completed the activity (or when the majority have finished) the students and the teacher will discuss what choices have been made. Clearly, in this simulation, the Hyatt Regency is the logical choice since it has most of the qualities that *B* is looking for.

(b) Arranging to meet

In this simulation groups of students are going to arrange a reunion to celebrate some event (a birthday, anniversary, etc.). They have to agree when and where the reunion will take place.

Stage 1 The teacher tells the class that they are going to work in groups of five, and that they are going to arrange to meet in honour of . . . (here the teacher can invent a reason based on the members of the class).

Stage 2 The teacher explains that each group must decide where they should meet and when, based on the information that they will be given.

Stage 3 The teacher tells the students he is going to give them some pieces of paper, and that they should not show them to each other. The teacher then distributes the following:

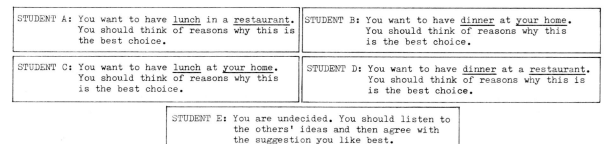

```
STUDENT A: You want to have lunch in a restaurant.    STUDENT B: You want to have dinner at your home.
           You should think of reasons why this is               You should think of reasons why this
           the best choice.                                      is the best choice.

STUDENT C: You want to have lunch at your home.        STUDENT D: You want to have dinner at a restaurant.
           You should think of reasons why this                  You should think of reasons why this is
           is the best choice.                                   is the best choice.

                        STUDENT E: You are undecided. You should listen to
                                   the others' ideas and then agree with
                                   the suggestion you like best.
```

Stage 4 The teacher tells the students to think about their instructions for a short time. Then he tells them to start the activity.

This activity is very successful and produces a great deal of spoken English. The teacher will need to keep an eye on each group and perhaps act as a prompter to make sure that they realise there are two variables – where they are going to meet and when.

c) The job interview[9]

In this simulation students are involved in interviewing and being interviewed for a job. The aim of the simulation is to select the successful candidate.

Stage 1 The teacher puts the students in pairs and asks them to consider ideal questions for interviewers in job interviews.

Stage 2 The teacher and the class discuss what such questions might be, and what interviewers will look for in a successful candidate.

Stage 3 The same process is then repeated, this time considering the best way an applicant can approach a job interview.

Stage 4 The teacher tells the class they are going to work in groups of five (or six). In each group there will be one (or two) interviewer(s) and four candidates. Each candidate will get a role card that he should study carefully. He should use that information to answer the questions, and may add any other appropriate facts. Applicants should not show their role cards to each other or to the interviewer. Each applicant and interviewer will also have a rating sheet. They should give each applicant (except themselves) a score from 0 (= very poor) to 5 (= excellent) based on their suitability.

Stage 5 The teacher gives the following rating sheet to the interviewer(s):

Garry Johnson	0	1	2	3	4	5
Paul Smith	0	1	2	3	4	5
Sheila Daze	0	1	2	3	4	5
John Murray	0	1	2	3	4	5

The applicants are given the following role cards:

Shop Manager: A

NAME: John Murray

AGE: 32

CIVIL STATUS: Married

CHILDREN: 1 girl

EDUCATION: High School
Business Administration
University degree

WORK EXPERIENCE: 3 years as accountant for Sears-Roebuck 5 years as business manager for tyre factory

HOBBIES/INTERESTS: Football, squash

Garry Johnson	0	1	2	3	4	5
Paul Smith	0	1	2	3	4	5
Sheila Daze	0	1	2	3	4	5

Shop Manager: B

NAME: Garry Johnson

AGE: 40

CIVIL STATUS: Single

CHILDREN: —

EDUCATION: High School

WORK EXPERIENCE: 20 years as accountant / Junior Executive Manager of hardware store.

HOBBIES/INTERESTS: Classical guitar; books; theatre

John Murray	0	1	2	3	4	5
Paul Smith	0	1	2	3	4	5
Sheila Daze	0	1	2	3	4	5

Shop Manager: C

NAME: Paul Smith

AGE: 25

CIVIL STATUS: Married

CHILDREN: 3 girls

EDUCATION: High School

WORK EXPERIENCE: 5 years shop assistant at sports centre shop. 2 years as junior manager at supermarket

HOBBIES/INTERESTS: Films; bowling

John Murray	0	1	2	3	4	5
Garry Johnson	0	1	2	3	4	5
Sheila Daze	0	1	2	3	4	5

Shop Manager: D

NAME: Sheila Daze

AGE: 30

CIVIL STATUS: Single

CHILDREN:

EDUCATION: High School; business administration at Sheen Polytechnic

WORK EXPERIENCE: 5 years as an executive secretary at Kodak. 5 years as restaurant manageress

HOBBIES/INTERESTS: Dogs, plants

John Murray	0	1	2	3	4	5
Garry Johnson	0	1	2	3	4	5
Paul Smith	0	1	2	3	4	5

Stage 6 When all the applicants have been interviewed a member of the group adds up the scores and selects the successful candidate (the one who scored the most points).

Stage 7 The class and teacher discuss the reasons for the success of the winning student. Often each group will select a different person and the class can discuss the reasons for this.

This activity can be extremely motivating and puts the students in a realistic situation. It is clearly appropriate for a more intermediate class.

(d) The Loch Ness monster[10]

The monster, who is supposed to inhabit Loch Ness in Scotland, has long been the object of interest and speculation. In this simulation, which forms part of a unit about 'Nessie' four people have seen the monster and describe it to a police inspector who has to build up an 'identikit' picture.

Stage 1 The class discusses the Loch Ness monster and the teacher tells them they are going to take part in an activity about it. Students are told that the monster has been seen by a number of people who are going to describe it to the local police in Scotland.

Stage 2 Students are told they are going to work in groups of five. One student in each group will be the police inspector who should question the other students (witnesses) about what they saw and then fill in the following identikit form and draw a picture of the monster in the space provided.

Form PK IR4	IDENTIKIT PICTURE
Age : Sex : Height : Weight : Distinguishing features :	

Stage 3 The students in each group are given the following role cards:

1ST WITNESS

You were having a stroll along the shore and you distinctly saw a small, flat thing moving on the surface of the water. You believe it was the head of the monster. It had a large mouth, two bulging red eyes and two small horns.

2ND WITNESS

You were having a nap in the grass when you were woken up by loud tramping noises. When you got up you had just enough time to see a very large greenish animal diving into the water.

3RD WITNESS

As you were fishing early one morning, you saw the monster splashing on the surface of the water. You estimated its overall length to be perhaps between 20 and 30 feet and it had a very small head in comparison with the size of its body.

4TH WITNESS

You were surveying the loch from the top of the hill with a pair of binoculars. You saw a large animal with a stout body, two humps on its back, four legs and a long neck, grazing on the shore of the loch.

INSPECTOR CAMERON

Ask each witness how and when he saw the monster. Draw up an identikit picture by putting together the various accounts you get.

The activity can start after each 'witness' has had a chance to study the role card.

Stage 4 The different groups study the final identikit picture of the monster to compare their versions.

This simulation is highly amusing, and although designed for intermediate groups could also be suitable for elementary students since it mixes the best elements of simulation with the describe and draw technique we discussed in 8.1.3(a).

(e) The Tyne Art Gallery[11]

In this simulation, designed for advanced students, a decision has to be taken about how a public art gallery should spend £70,000.

Stage 1 Students are given the following information and told to read it:

The Situation

The Tyne Art Gallery, in the North of England, is a public gallery run for the people of that area and paid for by the government. In other words money for the gallery comes from the taxes that ordinary people pay.

The gallery at present has £70,000 to spend on a work, or works, for its modern art section. Because the director of the gallery, Cyril Forbes, is sensitive about public opinion, he has asked a number of people to come to a meeting and to express their likes, dislikes and preferences for the five works of art from which the gallery will have to choose.

The five works being considered by the gallery are:

Sheet by Carlos Begonyou.
Price: £35,000.
This is simply a nylon sheet
purchased at a London supermarket.

Test Card by Charles Footley.
Price: £42,000.
This is a 6ft high painting of a
television colour test card.

Appetites by Alexandra Glassman.
Price: £32,000.
This is a painting of a young girl
eating an apple.

Interior Landscape by Derek Carriage.
Price: £49,000.
This is a semi-naturalistic painting of
a typical suburban sitting room.

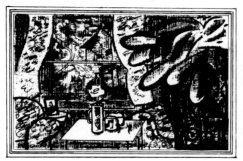

Contrasts by Caroline Snow.
Price £39,500.
This is a series of concentric circles.

Stage 2 The following roles are given to various students in the class:

The students are told that they should read their roles and prepare their arguments to support the point of view their characters have.

Where a group of people agree (e.g. Elizabeth Cutts, Peter Hunt and Denise Clifford) they should get together to plan their arguments.

At the meeting CYRIL FORBES will ask all those present to express their likes, dislikes and preferences for the various works.
The following people are present at the meeting:
CYRIL FORBES, the director of the gallery. He will ask everyone what they think of the works, and try to get everyone to agree.
MARY PROSSER, the director of the modern art section. She likes all the works except for 'Sheet', which she dislikes intensely. Nevertheless she must try at all times to be polite.
PATRICIA CUNTHORPE, personnel officer of the gallery. She particularly likes Caroline Snow's work and dislikes all of the others, especially 'Appetite'. Nevertheless she will have to try to be fairly polite.
DAN POPE, the director of the town council's department. He is very traditional, and strongly against most modern art. None of the works shown at the meeting appeal to him at all, and he is strongly against any money being spent.
CAROL PRESTWICK, the art critic on the 'Evening Post', the local paper. She particularly likes 'Appetite', but she thinks all the works have something to recommend them. She especially dislikes Dan Pope's attitude to art.
ROGER KANE, the art critic from the national paper 'The Sunday Star'. He is a great fan of Carlos Begonyou's work, and also the artist's friend.

The following members of the public like 'Test Card':

ELIZABETH CUTTS, a housewife	They should be prepared to say why
PETER HUNT, a doctor	they like the work, and what they
DENISE CLIFFORD, a dentist	do not like about the others.

The following members of the public like 'Interior Landscape':

TOM CREED, a bookshop owner	They should be prepared to say why
RAY ALLSOP, a butcher	they like the work, and what they
LEO TANKARD, a librarian	do not like about the others.

The following members of the public have not yet made up their minds about the works, or indeed whether they think the gallery should purchase any of them:

RUTH POWER, a secretary	They should study the works and see
GORDON MORGAN, a baker	if they like any of them or if they
VIVIAN GODDARD, a teacher	think it would be irresponsible of the
IVOR WALSH, a bank employee	gallery to spend its money in this way.

Stage 3 The teacher rearranges the classroom in the form best suited to the public meeting that Cyril Forbes has called. Each student should have in front of him a large card with the name of the role he is playing written on it. When everyone is ready, the simulation can begin.

Stage 4 The meeting should end with the participants taking a decision about which paintings to buy. The teacher then conducts feedback.

This simulation has the advantage of involving a large number of students at the same time. It produces fierce controversy and a lot therefore depends on the conduct of Cyril Forbes, the chairman. This is one case where the teacher might decide to act as a participant, taking the Forbes role (see 8.1.7).

With a simulation on this scale it may well be advisable to leave a day (or days) between Stages 1 and 2 and Stage 3 so that students can absorb the situation and have ample time to prepare their roles and arguments.

8.2 Written communicative activities

We will look at various ways of promoting written communication in the classroom. We will consider examples under six headings: *relaying instructions, exchanging letters, writing games, fluency writing, story construction* and *writing reports and advertisements*.

8.2.1 Relaying instructions

Just as in 8.1.2, one group of students has information for the performance of a task, and they have to get another group to perform the same task by giving them written instructions. We will look at four examples.

(a) Making models

This is the same as the activity in 8.1.2(b) except that instead of passing on oral instructions the original group of students have to write directions.

Stage 1 A small group of students is given material to make a model with (e.g. building bricks, Lego, etc.) and are told to make a model.

Stage 2 The group now writes instructions which will enable other people to duplicate the model.

Stage 3 Other students are given the instructions and told to build the model by reading the instructions.

There is, of course, immediate feedback. The original group can see how well they have written instructions by watching the efforts of the other students to duplicate their model.

(b) Giving directions

In this activity students write directions which other students have to follow.

Stage 1 Students are told to write directions from the place where they are studying to some other place in the same town or city. They are told not to mention the destination by name.

Stage 2 Students give their directions to a partner who has to guess what the destination is by following the directions.

The same effect can be created by letting the students work from a street plan of a town with clearly marked buildings, etc.

(c) Writing commands[12]

Students write each other messages which contain commands.

Stage 1 The teacher tells students to write a command for one of their classmates on a piece of paper. The student might write something like this:

Maria:
Take off your left shoe!

Stage 2 The written messages are then passed to the students who have to obey the commands.

This activity is especially appropriate for beginner students and is most enjoyable.

(d) Writing messages

As in (c) above students write to each other. This time they will write a 'message' that needs an answer.

Stage 1 Students are told to write a message to another member of the group which demands an answer.

Stage 2 The completed messages are then given to the student who has been written to.

Stage 3 The student who has received the message then writes a reply which is passed back to the original writer.

The original message might be something like this:

To Maria
What kind of house do you live in?
from José

and the reply might be:

To José
My house has three bedrooms,
and a small garden at the front.
from Maria

Once again, this activity is especially useful for beginner students.

8.2.2
Exchanging letters

In this type of activity students write each other letters and then receive a reply. In the four examples we will consider, the writing is based on simulation and role play.

(a) Inviting[13]

Students write each other letters of invitation which they give to each other. The letters are then answered depending on what the recipient's plans are.

Stage 1 The teacher asks students in his class to fill in a diary for the following week in which they should have at least three definite arrangements.

Stage 2 The teacher puts students in pairs and asks each student to write a letter to his partner inviting him to do something next week.

Stage 3 The letters are exchanged and the teacher asks students to write replies to the invitations depending on their diaries and their inclinations.

This activity is particularly suitable, of course, if students have recently been working on the language of invitation.

(b) The agony column

This activity has long been a favourite with both teachers and students. It involves students writing letters to 'agony columns' – those parts of newspapers and magazines where supposed experts give advice on everything from marital problems to trouble with the neighbours. In this activity students invent some problem and then have it answered by other members of the class.

Stage 1 The class and the teacher discuss 'agony columns', getting examples from the students' knowledge of their own countries. Where students say there is no such thing in their newspapers and magazines the teacher will show them examples from English or American agony columns.

Stage 2 The teacher arranges the class into small groups and asks each group to think of a problem and then write a letter.

Stage 3 The letters from each group are then given to another group who have to consider the best answer and then write a reply.

Stage 4 The replies are then given to the original groups to consider. The teacher can put them into a folder which can be passed round the class. If there is a notice board the best and/or most amusing letters can be pinned up for all to see.

This activity is particularly suitable, of course, after the students have been working on the language of advice. It can be used at a fairly elementary level, but is even more successful with intermediate and advanced students.

(c) The complaining customer

In this activity students write complaining letters about goods they have bought after seeing an advertisement. The students representing the company who make the goods then have to reply to these letters.

Stage 1 Students are divided into small groups. Each group is given an advertisement. It would be ideal if they could be given advertisements prepared by their classmates (see 8.2.6(c)).

Stage 2 The groups are told to imagine they have bought the item that is advertised but are not satisfied with it for some reason. They should write a letter of complaint to the company.

Stage 3 The letters are then given to different groups. The new group has to study the letter of complaint and decide what to do about it. When

the decision has been reached they can write a reply to the original
letter.

Stage 4 The letters are then returned to the original groups who read them
and discuss what they have been sent.

This is an enjoyable and useful activity involving a number of different skills.
It is particularly suitable for intermediate and advanced classes.

(d) The job application

Just as in 8.1.7(c) this activity involves applying for a job. The application will
then be judged and a decision taken about whether it should be successful.
There is no reason why students should not be given role cards as they were
in the job interview. In this example, however, we will ask them to create
their own roles.

Stage 1 Students are shown the following advertisement:

GREAT FUTURE: GREAT PAY

Work in Public Relations for A Major Airline.

Experience in transport not necessary, but good personality and bright ideas
are essential.

Applications in writing are requested, giving any information about yourself
you think might be relevant.

Write to: The Manager, Box 247.

Stage 2 Students are asked to apply for the job in writing, making their
applications as attractive as possible.

Stage 3 The teacher divides the class into small groups. The groups are then
given some of the letters (which must not be the work of anyone in
the group).

Stage 4 Each member of the group must read each letter, giving the applicant
a score of 0 (= very poor) to 5 (= excellent) depending on his
suitability for the job.

Stage 5 The scores are added together and the winning applicant chosen.

Stage 6 The group writes two letters. One is to the successful applicant asking
him to come to a meeting. The other is the letter they will send the
applicants who were not successful.

Stage 7 The letters of the winning applicants can be read to the whole class
and comments made on them.

This is a good exercise for skill integration and forces the students to write for
a purpose. It is particularly suitable for intermediate and advanced classes.

8.2.3
Writing games

These are somewhat similar to the oral games we looked at in 8.1.3. We will
look at two examples.

(a) Describe and identify (1)

Students write descriptions of people or places and the rest of the class has to guess who the people are or what the places are. In this example we will show how the activity can be used as a team game:

Stage 1 The teacher divides the class into two teams.
Stage 2 The students are all instructed to write a description of a famous person (or a member of the class) without mentioning that person's name.
Stage 3 A member of one of the teams reads his description. If someone from the opposing team can identify the person the team scores a point. If not there is no score. The teacher may take away a point from the team reading the description if (a) the information about the person is wrong or misleading, or (b) the English is totally indecipherable.

This game is enjoyable at all levels, but especially for beginner students.

(b) Describe and identify (2)

Based on the same principle as our example above students are this time asked to describe a famous event in history without saying what it was. They should give as much background information as possible. In this example we will show how the activity can be used for pair work:

Stage 1 The teacher divides the students into pairs.
Stage 2 The teacher tells all the students to describe an 'event' in history, giving as much detail as possible without saying what the event was.
Stage 3 Students exchange papers with their partners. Now they have to guess what the event was from the written description.
Stage 4 The teacher selects some of the better descriptions and the students who wrote them read them to the whole class, who try to guess the historical event.

This game is useful at all levels, particularly where students have recently been working on past tenses.

8.2.4
Fluency writing

The aims of the activity we are going to describe are quite simple: to get students to write as much as possible in a definite period of time. Research has suggested[14] that if this is done frequently students are able not only to write greater quantities, but the quality improves as well.

(a) The picture story

Students are given a series of pictures just as they were for oral composition (see 7.2.4(a)). They are given a time limit and told to write as much as they can about the pictures.

Stage 1 Students are told that they are going to do some free writing, and that the objective is to write as much as they can within a certain time limit.
Stage 2 Students are shown a picture sequence and told to write about it.
Stage 3 When the time limit expires the teacher stops the students and collects the work.

This activity is especially useful at the beginning of a class if some late arrivals can be expected. Unlike other written work there is no need to correct the 'compositions', although a sample could very well be used for student-student correction (see 8.3).

The time limit suggested is between six and twelve minutes. If this procedure is followed regularly over a period of time, students will find that they can write more in the time limit (with fewer errors) when the term or semester is over, than they could at the beginning.

Of course the activity can be done with topics rather than picture stories. The teacher can simply say 'Write about dogs' or something similar.

8.2.5
Story construction

Once again, as in 8.1.6, the aim is to give individual students partial information which they must 'pool' with other students in order to piece together a narrative. In the second example below, however, students simply add to the story that has been created so far.

(a) The hospital case

This picture sequence is being used again (see 8.1.6(a)) to show how the oral technique of story construction can be adapted to writing. Once again we will assume that there are twenty-four students in the class.

Stage 1 Students are put into groups of six.

Stage 2 Each member of the group is given a letter (A–F) as in 8.1.6(a).

Stage 3 Each group is given one of the pictures from the sequence we showed in 8.1.6(a). All the members of the group should write two sentences about their picture together, using past tenses (to avoid the eventual story being written in, for example, the present continuous). Each member of the group now has the same two sentences.

Stage 4 The teacher now collects the four pictures, and re-forms groups so that all the A's are together, all the B's and so on. The new groups must now put their sentences together to form a coherent story. They should be reminded that they will probably have to make changes from the original sentences, especially in terms of tense and the use of cohesive devices, etc.

Stage 5 The groups now read out their stories and the class compares them. In the event of any confusion the teacher can show the original picture sequence.

This is an excellent activity for the practice of narrative writing, and has the advantage over the oral version of the exercise (in 8.1.6(a)) that students are using all four skills to complete the activity.

(b) The fairy story

In this activity students are put into groups and they then write joint stories. In this example we will show how a fairy story can be used for this purpose.

Stage 1 Students are put into groups. Where possible, they should be of equal numbers.

Stage 2 Students are told to tear a page from their exercise books and write the following sentence on it:

Once upon a time there was a beautiful princess who lived in a large castle at the edge of a forest.

Stage 3 The students are then instructed to continue the story by writing the next sentence.

Stage 4 The students are then told to give their piece of paper to the student on their left. They should now continue the (new) story they have in front of them by writing the next sentence. The procedure is repeated until the papers have gone round the whole group but one. The teacher then tells the students to write the concluding sentence.

Stage 5 The stories are now returned to their originators (by passing the papers to the student on the left). Students can read the resulting tales to the rest of the class.

This activity can be immensely enjoyable, and often produces wildly differing stories. Of course there is no reason why the activity should concern a fairy story. Another alternative is not to supply the original sentence.

8.2.6
Writing reports and advertisements

We will look at four activities in which students write reports or advertisements.

(a) The news broadcast[15]

Students write items for a news broadcast which they then organise for 'transmission'.

Stage 1 The teacher asks all the students in the class to write two news items on a piece of paper.

Stage 2 The teacher then collects all the pieces of paper and forms the class into small groups.

Stage 3 The teacher then distributes the pieces of paper equally between the groups in no special order. The students are asked to combine the items (making changes where necessary) to make up a complete news broadcast.

Stage 4 Each group then reads its broadcast to the rest of the class. Ideally, of course, each group could record their broadcast to make it more realistic.

This activity is attractive because it involves all the skills, as well as the ability to order and organise ideas. It also involves current events and is thus interesting and motivating.

(b) The tourist brochure

In much the same way as the news broadcast, students can be asked to join together to write a brochure about the place they live in or are studying in.

Stage 1 The students are all told to write two sentences (or more) about the attractions of the place they live or study in.

Stage 2 The class is then divided into small groups.

Stage 3 In each group the students pool their sentences and use them to devise a short brochure about the place they live or study in for a tourist magazine.

Stage 4 Students from each group may read out their final version. A better alternative, however, is to put the texts in a folder which can be passed round the class or to stick them to a notice board in the classroom (see 8.2.2(b)).

(c) The advertisement

After discussing what successful advertisements contain students can write and design their own.

Stage 1 The class discusses (together and/or in pairs/groups) what makes a successful advertisement.

Stage 2 The class is divided into groups. They are told that their task is to select a product and write an advertisement for it which will appear in a magazine.

Stage 3 When they have completed their advertisements they can pass them round the class. Alternatively they can be given a period of time (e.g. a weekend) to design the artwork for their text. The advertisements can then be pinned to the class notice board.

This activity is ideal as a starter for the letters of complaint activity (see 8.2.2(c).

(d) The smoking questionnaire

This activity has the status of a project. Students will devise a questionnaire and then write a report based on the results they obtain (See also 6.5.1(b) and 7.1.5(c).) In this example the topic selected is 'smoking'.

Stage 1 Students are told that they are going to work in groups to write a report on society's attitudes to smoking based on a questionnaire that they will design.

Stage 2 The teacher discusses with the class what kind of information they might want to obtain and the kind of questions they could use to get it. For example the following areas might be selected:

Smokers:	– their smoking habits (how many? when?, etc.)
	– their reasons for smoking
	– their feelings about smoking in public places
	– their attitude to non-smokers who complain
Non-smokers:	– their reasons for not smoking
	– their reasons for having given up (in some cases)
	– their attitude to smoking in public places
	– their suggestions for change

Stage 3 The groups write their different questionnaires. The teacher can act as a resource or prompter if necessary (see 10.1.4 and 10.1.6).

Stage 4 The groups then administer their questionnaire. If they are in an English-speaking country they can ask people in the street. If they are studying in a non-English-speaking community they can administer the questionnaire to other classes in their school, etc.

Stage 5 The groups study the information that they have managed to collect and write a report in which they reach conclusions about the results of their investigations. The reports can then be compared. Groups can read the finished reports that other groups have written and discuss why they are different from or similar to their own.

This activity involves considerable commitment from the students and is more suitable for intermediate and advanced classes. Nevertheless it involves the use of a great deal of English and is a perfect example of skill integration (see 5.5). It may take two weeks at least to complete, with a certain amount of class time devoted to the project, and the rest done outside class hours. A successful project of this type is well worth the effort and students feel satisfied at having used their English to put together a substantial piece of work (and find out interesting information).

8.3 Correcting written work[16]

The correction of written work can be organised on much the same basis as the correction of oral work (see 4.2.3, 6.3.3, and 10.1.2). In other words there may well be times when the teacher is concerned with accuracy and other times when the main concern is the content of the writing. Certainly the tendency is for teachers to be over-preoccupied with accuracy. This means that the student's work is often covered with red ink and no comment is made about whether the work was interesting or succeeded in its purposes.

Correction of written work can be done by both teacher and student. If the teacher is correcting written work he must always remember to react to the content of the work, showing the student where the work was effective and where it was not.

Where the teacher wishes to correct the English in the written work, he may wish to use a variety of symbols. Thus he underlines the mistake in the written work and puts a mark in the margin to show what kind of mistake it was. The following example shows how the teacher can indicate that the student has made an error in word order:

WO   I like <u>very much tennis</u>.

The teacher will need symbols for spelling, wrong tense usage, concord (the agreements between subject and verb), wrong word order, inappropriate language, punctuation, a word missing and unclear meaning, among others. Whatever the symbols are the students should understand clearly what they mean.

When the teacher first uses the system of symbols he may underline the word in the text and put the symbol in the margin. Later it will only be necessary to put the symbol in the margin for the students to identify the error. When students correct each other's work (see below) no symbols will be necessary.

When the teacher hands back written work with his comments on content and the correction symbols in the margin, he should allow the students time, during the class, to identify their mistakes and correct them. In this activity the teacher is acting as a resource, and can help where students do not know what is wrong. If this kind of stage is not gone through, however, students may not be able to take advantage of the system of correction symbols.

Ideally written work can form the basis for student-student correction, which in itself can be classed as a communicative activity. Students work in pairs, exchanging their work. They then look for mistakes in each other's writing and attempt to correct them.

Where a piece of student writing contains a number of common errors, the teacher may want to photocopy the work (erasing the writer's name) and show it to the whole class, asking them to identify problems. In this way the attention of the class can be drawn to common mistakes and the photocopied document can form the basis for remedial work.

Exercises

1 Design your own oral communicative activity for a beginners' class based on the ideas in this chapter.
2 Design your own written communicative activity for an elementary class based on the ideas in this chapter.
3 Take any simulation activity from a coursebook that you are familiar with and write out a procedure for using that activity using the stages described in this chapter. Then give your 'stages' and the material to a colleague and ask him or her to try the activity following your instructions.
4 If possible consult the references below on the correction of written work and then design your own symbols based on the ideas in 8.3.

References

1 I first saw this activity demonstrated by Peter Taylor.
2 Taken from N Bullard (1981).
3 For the use of the information gap in this type of exercise see S Rixon (1979) and M Geddes and J McAlpin (1978).
4 The examples are taken from M Geddes and J McAlpin (1978). Other examples can be found in D Byrne (1978) and the British Council film *Activity days in language learning*. B Baddock (1981), however, feels that too much attention has been given to games and that students should be given more chance to speculate rather than complete tasks.
5 I have been unable to trace the original author of this exercise.
6 This problem-solving activity is taken from A Maley and F Grellet (1981). A good article on problem-solving activities and their uses is A Maley (1981).
7 This is one of several 'humanistic' techniques to be found in G Moskowitz (1978). See also the activity in 7.1.5(a). Some of the activities are very successful, although her insistence on only stressing the positive aspects of our students' lives seems to me a bit exaggerated.
8 I first saw this technique demonstrated by Alan Maley. The picture sequence is from D Byrne and S Holden (1978).
9 See also R M Turnbull (1981) on a slightly different application of the interview role play.
10 Taken from D Hicks et al. (1979).
11 Taken from J Harmer and J W Arnold (1978).
12 See D Byrne (1979) pages 46–49.
13 For a demonstration of this exercise see the British Council film *Pair and Group Work in a Language Programme*.
14 See E. Brière (1966).
15 For this and other ideas in 8.2.6 see D Byrne (1979) Chapter 5 although I have often adapted his descriptions of these exercises.
16 For more on correcting written work see J Willis (1981) pages 172–4, R V White (1980) pages 106–109, C J Brumfit (1977) and D Byrne (1979) pages 132–4. Both Willis and Brumfit encourage the use of student-student correction and both give symbols for use at this stage.

9 Receptive skills

In this chapter we will look at material designed to teach students how to deal with written and spoken text – how to practise reading and listening skills. In 2.5 we called these receptive skills but we made the point that reading and listening involved active participation on the part of the reader or listener (see also 2.4 on interaction with context). We called the material that students are asked to read and listen to roughly-tuned input (see 4.2.2) making the point that students could cope with a higher level in receptive skills than they could with language production (see 9.2.1).

We can start by looking at some basic principles.

9.1 Basic principles

We will look at some basic principles that apply to both reading and listening, for despite the fact that these skills are performed with different mediums (written and spoken text) there are underlying characteristics and skills that apply to both when being practised by native speakers. We will look at *content, purpose and expectations* and *receptive skills*.

9.1.1 Content

In our daily lives we read and listen to a great deal of language, and it is possible to divide this language into two broad categories: *interest* and *usefulness*.

Very often we read or listen to something because it interests us – or at least we think it will interest us. A magazine reader, for example, chooses to read the article on page 35 rather than the story on page 66 because he thinks the former will be interesting whereas the latter will not. The buyer in a bookshop often selects a book to buy because he thinks it will interest him, and the discerning radio listener tunes in especially to programmes that he expects will be stimulating. The category of interest, then, includes reading and listening for enjoyment, pleasure and intellectual stimulation, etc.

Sometimes, however, it is not the fact that a text may be interesting that causes the reader or listener to pay attention to it; it is, rather, the usefulness of the text. If you wish to operate a hot-drinks machine for the first time you will have to read the instructions so that you can be sure of getting the kind of coffee you want rather than tea or hot chocolate. No-one would suggest that the instructions you read are in any way interesting, and the same would be true of instructions for operating a telephone, directories, rules and regulations and maintenance manuals, among others.

These two categories are not, however, always independent of each other. The student may well read something that he needs for his studies (and which we would therefore categorise as 'useful') and find it interesting at the same time. We would certainly hope that this were the case! And the person who listens on the radio to instructions on how to design solar heating panels, may do so with mixed motives. The instructions may have the joint characteristics of usefulness and interest. Nevertheless the two broad characteristics of usefulness and interest are important when making decisions about the kind of texts students should be exposed to, as we shall see in 9.2.2.

9.1.2
Purpose and expectations[1]

The suggestion that people read and listen to language out of interest or for the usefulness of the information they are reading or listening to brings us to the concept of purpose which is similar to the communicative purpose we described in 5.1 and 5.3.

In real life people read or listen to language because they want to (in the same sense as we used 'want' in 5.1) and because they have a purpose for doing so. The purpose may be to discover how to operate a hot-drinks machine or to have a pleasurable read. The purpose may be to find out what has been happening in the world (for the listener to the news) or to discover the latest trends in language teaching (for the listener to a talk at a language teaching convention). In real life, therefore, readers and listeners have a purpose that is more fundamental than the typical language learners' comprehension exercises that often concentrate only on details of language.

Another characteristic of a language user's reading and listening is that he will have expectations about what he is going to read or hear before he does so. If you tune in to a radio comedy programme, in other words, you expect to hear something funny (although this is sadly not always the case!) and the Englishman who picks up a newspaper and sees the headlines 'STORM IN THE COMMONS' expects to read about a heated political debate in the House of Commons, the British Parliament. The reader who picks up a book will have expectations about the content of the book as a result of the description on the book jacket or even simply because of the design of the cover or the words in the title.

People read and listen to language, then, because they have a desire to do so and a purpose to achieve. Usually (except when they turn on the radio at random, for example,) they will have expectations about the content of the text before they start the task of reading or listening. The concepts of purpose and expectations will have important methodological implications in language learning as we shall see in 9.2.3 and in the methodological model in 9.3.

**9.1.3
Receptive skills[2]**

The reader or listener employs a number of specialist skills when reading or listening and his success at understanding the content of what he sees or hears depends to a large extent on his expertise in these specialist skills. We can look at six of these skills which we will be focusing on in this chapter.

(a) Predictive skills

The efficient listener or reader predicts what he is going to hear or read and the process of understanding the text is the process of seeing how the content of the text matches up to these predictions. In the first instance his predictions will be the result of the expectations he has – which we discussed above. As he continues to listen and read, however, his predictions will change as he receives more information from the text. It is precisely this skill that is involved in the language user's interaction with context that we discussed in 2.4. One of the main functions of the lead-in stage when teaching receptive skills (see 9.3) will be to encourage predictive skills, and the examples of materials and techniques in 9.4.1 and 9.5.1 are especially designed for this purpose.

(b) Extracting specific information

Very often the listener or reader is involved in the use of receptive skills for the sole purpose of extracting specific information. In other words the reader, for example, may look at a piece of written language not in order to understand it all, but for the purpose of finding out only one or two facts. He may quickly read a film revue only to find out the name of the star. The listener may turn on the radio and listen only for a particular item of news that he wants to hear. In both cases the reader/listener will disregard everything except the information he is interested in. This skill when applied to reading is often called *scanning* and we will concentrate on the skill of extracting specific information in 9.4.2 and 9.5.2.

(c) Getting the general picture

Readers and listeners often read or listen to something because they want to 'get the general picture'. In other words they want to read something, for example, and as a result of their reading have a general idea of the main points of what they have read: it is the main points that they are interested in, not the detail. Indeed the skill of reading in order to get the general picture (often called *skimming*) presupposes the reader's ability to pick out the main points and discard what is irrelevant, or what is only detail. The reader is able to skim rapidly over information that is repeated more than once. The skill of getting the general picture, then, is concerned with rapidly assessing the main points of a text and not paying attention to irrelevance or detail. In listening, too, this skill is necessary and widely practised, particularly since speakers often include language which is not relevant to the main points they are making or which is redundant (i.e. they have already said the same thing in a different way).

The ability to discard redundant, irrelevant or over-detailed information when reading or listening is a vital one and we will be looking at material designed to promote this skill in 9.4.4 and 9.5.4.

(d) Inferring opinion and attitude

A reader or listener often has to be able to work out what the writer or speaker's opinions and attitudes are, particularly since they are not always directly stated. The experienced reader or listener will know, from various clues he receives while reading and listening, whether the writer or speaker approves of the topic he is discussing, or whether his opinion of the personality he is describing is favourable or not. The ability to infer opinion and attitude is largely based on the recognition of linguistic style and its use to achieve appropriate purposes. We will look at material designed to train students in this ability in 9.5.7.

(e) Deducing meaning from context

Even native speakers often come across words in written and spoken texts that they do not understand. Most usually, however, the fact that a word is unknown to them does not cause any particular problem. Based on the context in which the word occurs (the sentences, information and grammar that surround it) the native speaker guesses its meaning. Usually, too, his guess will be right. The point is that the deducing of meaning is important for a language user who will often meet unknown words and we will try to train students in the same way to guess the meaning of unknown words (see 9.4.5 and 9.5.6). It should be said, of course, that for a native speaker or a foreign language user there is a point at which they are not able to deduce meaning from context where there are a great number of words that they do not understand.

(f) Recognising function and discourse patterns and markers

Native speakers know that when they read or hear someone say 'for example' this phrase will be followed by an example. When they read 'in other words' a concept will be explained in a different way. Recognising such discourse markers is an important part of understanding how a text is constructed. It is important to know, for example, which sentence in a paragraph is a generalisation and which sentence then backs up that generalisation with evidence. It is also important to be able to recognise devices for cohesion and understand how a text is organised coherently. We have already looked at exercises that train students in the understanding and use of cohesive devices and coherent organisation (see 7.2.3) and we will see more examples of materials designed to train students in the recognition of function and discourse patterning in 9.4.6 and 9.5.5.

The skills we have been discussing fall into two main categories which we will call *type 1* and *type 2*. Type 1 skills are (a), (b) and (c) above and type 2 skills are (d), (e) and (f) above. The difference between type 1 and type 2 skills will be discussed in 9.2.5 where the methodological implications of these differences will be assessed. The place of type 1 and type 2 skills in a methodological model will be demonstrated in 9.3.

9.2 Methodological principles for teaching receptive skills

The discussion in 9.1 has important implications for the teaching of receptive skills which we can now consider. We will look at *receptive and productive skills, types of text, purpose, desire and expectations, receiving and doing,* and *teaching receptive skills.*

9.2.1 Receptive and productive skills

We have already said in the introduction to this chapter that students can generally deal with a higher level of language in receptive skills than with productive skills. This, after all, is the point of roughly-tuned input (see 4.2.2): the language learner (and the child) can process and understand language that is above their own level of production. Despite the fact that receptive skills demand considerable involvement and activity on the part of the receiver (see 2.4) the process does not necessarily involve the encoding of language into speech or writing (but see 9.2.4). Rather the student's job will be to interact with the text in order to understand the message, and this seems possible even where the text contains language the students are not themselves able to produce. All over the world there are students who can read English (often for scientific or academic purposes) but who are unable to speak it.

Receptive skill work, then, should involve students in roughly-tuned input which means language that the students can work with and process even though it is (sometimes considerably) above their productive level.

9.2.2 Types of text

Clearly a major consideration in teaching English will be the selection of materials and this will be particularly true of texts for receptive skills work.

A first distinction must be drawn between *authentic* and *non-authentic* material. Authentic texts (either written or spoken) are those which are designed for native speakers: they are real texts designed not for language students, but for the speakers of the language in question. Any English newspaper is composed of what we would call authentic English, and so is an English radio programme. An English advertisement is an example of authentic English, so is a chapter from a book on teaching methodology written by an Englishman for English-speaking readers.

A non-authentic text, in language teaching terms, is one that has been written especially for language students, but here again there is a distinction to be made between texts written to illustrate particular language points for presentation (see for example 6.5.2(a)) and those written to appear authentic, even though there has been some language control of the 'rough-tuning' type. The justification for the latter is that beginner students will probably not be able to handle genuinely authentic texts, but should nevertheless be given practice in reading and listening to texts that look authentic (even if there has been some language control). The reading of such texts, in other words, will help students to acquire the necessary receptive skills they will need when they eventually come to tackle authentic material.

Some examples may help to clarify the point. In the following text[3] from an elementary textbook the intention is clearly to present new language structures.

The Next Morning

The flat is very untidy. There are dirty glasses, cups and saucers all over the room, on the table, on the shelves, under the chairs and on the floor. All the ashtrays are full. Penny and Kate have got to clean the flat quickly. Their new friend, Rodney Johnson, is coming for the guitar. Joyce Franklin left it here last night and he is going to take it to her.

The two girls are drinking coffee. It is very good and very black. Kate is a bad cook but she can make good coffee.

Outside it is raining hard. There are a lot of clouds in the sky. It is a dull, wet day. The girls are very tired but they have got to tidy the flat. Kate is going to wash the plates and the glasses and Penny is going to clean the room and put everything back in its place. Kate is walking slowly into the kitchen. She didn't have much sleep last night.

The text has a number of features that show it to be artificial; it does not even appear authentic. For example, we can see the same structures repeated a number of times in an obviously contrived way (e.g. 'Penny and Kate have got to clean the flat quickly . . . they have got to tidy the flat . . . he is going to take it to her . . . Kate is going to wash the plates and the glasses and Penny is going to clean the room . . . the two girls are drinking coffee . . . outside it is raining hard . . . Kate is walking slowly to the kitchen'). The repetition of these structures is clearly unnatural.

The text is also very elementary in terms of cohesive devices. '*And*' and '*but*' are used, and so are words like '*they*' and '*their*' (see 7.2.3) but the text sounds remarkably awkward.

Lastly, a description of 'the next morning' would probably not be in the present tense in an authentic text.

The text, then, is obviously written with considerable language control and is artificially written in the present so that the '*going to*' future can be introduced. Such texts, however, will not be useful in the teaching of reading skills precisely because they are so unlike authentic language. The intention behind the text is to show the meaning of a structure, not to train students in receptive skills.

The following text,[4] however, designed for students at roughly the same level, does appear to be more real:

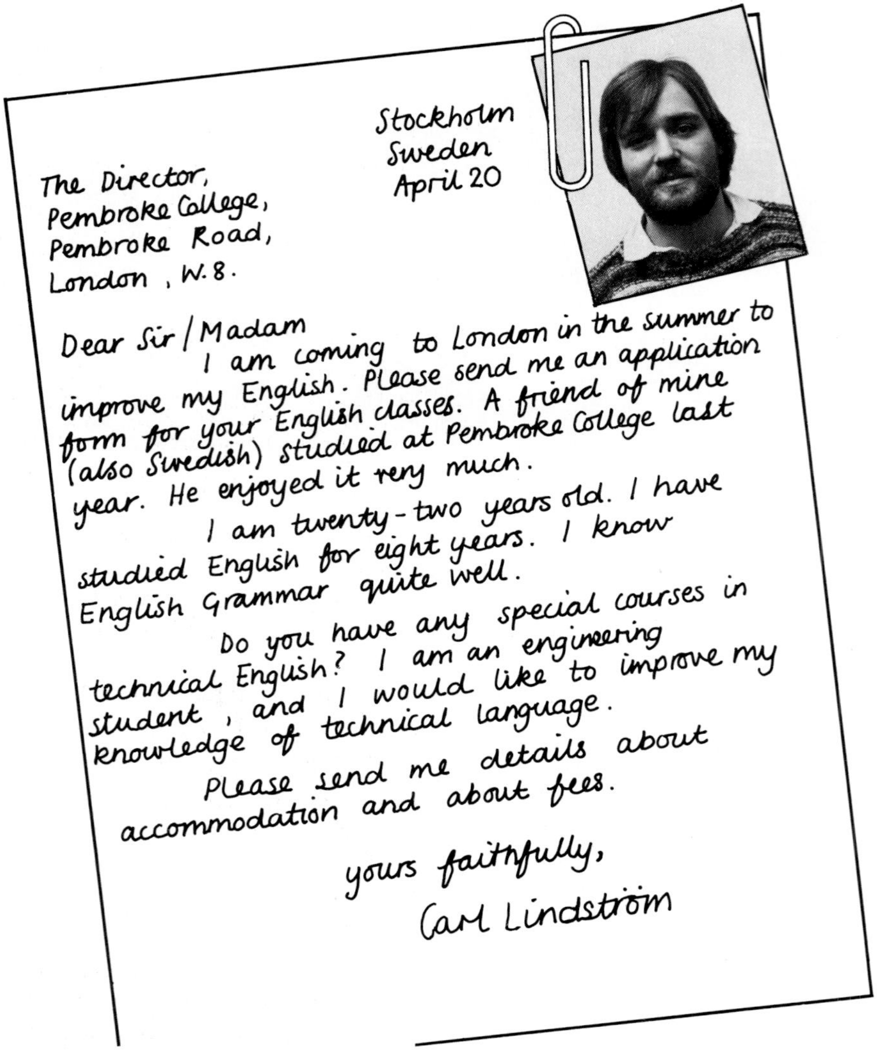

Stockholm
Sweden
April 20

The Director,
Pembroke College,
Pembroke Road,
London , W. 8.

Dear Sir / Madam
I am coming to London in the summer to improve my English. Please send me an application form for your English classes. A friend of mine (also Swedish) studied at Pembroke College last year. He enjoyed it very much.
I am twenty-two years old. I have studied English for eight years. I know English Grammar quite well.
Do you have any special courses in technical English? I am an engineering student, and I would like to improve my knowledge of technical language.
Please send me details about accommodation and about fees.

yours faithfully,
Carl Lindström

Certainly the English is fairly simple here, but then it would be in real life: a letter asking for an application form usually employs fairly straightforward language. There does seem to be some point in getting students to read this kind of text, then, as a means of training them to be able to read English.

The same point about non-authentic and *simulated-authentic* texts (the latter, as we have discussed, are those that are written to appear real) can be illustrated with dialogue material – where people are supposed to be talking to each other. In the first example[5] two people are talking to each other about their sun-glasses, but we could safely say that the conversation sounds completely unreal:

Two pairs of sun-glasses

TOM   What are those in your hand, Martin?

MARTIN   They are my sun-glasses, my new pair of sun-glasses.

TOM   Oh, yes. They are smart.

MARTIN   Your sun-glasses are very smart, too.

TOM   Thank you. They are very expensive.

MARTIN   Oh, these aren't expensive. They are made of plastic. They are very cheap.

TOM   What! Oh, yes. Your sun-glasses are made of plastic and my pair is made of glass. Plastic is not as smart as glass.

MARTIN   And plastic is not as expensive as glass.

TOM   Plastic is not as heavy as glass. Your sun-glasses are not as heavy as these.

MARTIN   No, but glass is not as strong as plastic. These plastic sun-glasses are very strong. Look! They are under this chair leg.

TOM   Oh, yes. They are very strong. But they are not as smart as my pair. Oh, here's your friend, Jillian.

JILLIAN   Hello, Tom. Hello, Martin.

TOM   Jillian, there are two pairs of sun-glasses here. These are his glasses and this is my pair. What are they made of?

People speaking to each other do not do so perfectly grammatically in the same way as Tom and Martin. Neither would it be usual to find so many examples of '*not as . . . . . as*' in such a short conversation. Once again the dialogue was written for language presentation (and would seem to be teaching signification, not value – see 4.2.4), not as an example of realistic spoken English. It would not be suitable, therefore, for listening skill training.

The following example,[6] though, designed for students at the same level, does sound authentic:

LISTENING TEXT
S1: Excuse me. How can I get to the station please?
S2: The station, the station, the station . . . let me see. Ah, yes. You can go down . . . no. Go straight on until you come to a cinema. Let's see now – that's the second turning on your right. The cinema's on the corner. Turn right at the cinema and you'll be in Bridge Street. I think it's Bridge Street. Go along Bridge Street for a few minutes and then take the second – no, not the second, the first, that's right, the first turning on your left. The station is straight ahead, right in front of you.
S1: So that's second right and first left. Thank you very much. That's very kind of you.
S2: Don't mention it.

The speaker (S2) sounds like any native speaker and behaves in the same way. He pauses, changes his mind, and gives his directions realistically.

What is being suggested, therefore, is that material designed to foster the acquisition of receptive skills must be at least simulated-authentic. In other words, despite a certain amount of language control, texts for reading and listening must be useful for the acquiring of receptive skills. If they are as artificial as two of the examples shown here they will not serve this purpose since students will be unlikely to encounter anything like them in real life. The artificial texts have a presentation function, but are not particularly useful for receptive skills training.

In 9.1.1 we divided the content of reading and listening texts into two main categories; interest and usefulness. Both these categories should be reflected in the teaching of receptive skills. While we clearly wish our students to be interested in what they are going to read or hear we will also train them to read or listen to texts that are 'useful' in a not necessarily interesting way.

9.2.3
Purpose, desire and expectations

In 9.1.2 we said that people usually read or listen to something because they have a desire to do so and some purpose to achieve. Furthermore they generally have some expectations about what they are going to read or hear before they actually tackle the text.

The methodology for teaching receptive skills must reflect these facts about real life, and the tasks we ask students to perform must be sufficiently realistic and motivating for the students to perceive a useful purpose for text study. This is true not only for interesting texts, but also for material which is designed to teach students to handle 'useful' input. Our methodological model in 9.3 will reflect our points about creating a desire to read and allowing students to have expectations, and the material in 9.4 and 9.5 will be designed to get students to read and listen for a purpose.

9.2.4
Receiving and doing

The purposes for which people read and listen are, of course, extremely varied, but we can say that when people read or listen they *do something* with what they have just seen or heard. We discussed this point in some detail in 5.5 where we saw how skills are not performed in isolation but are integrated with other skills. As a general methodological principle, therefore, we would expect students to use what they have read or heard in order to perform some task. When they have done work on comprehension skills, in other words, we would expect them to react to, or do something with, the text. This might take the form of giving opinions about what they have just read, following instructions, writing a postcard, summarising the content of the text or having a conversation based on the text.

Many of the materials we will look at in 9.4 and 9.5 will have just such a follow-up task which is called in 9.3 a *text-related task*.

Sometimes of course the task the students perform is an integral part of the initial type 1 skill exercises which the students work on with the text. Even here, however, we would expect there to be some follow-up activity.

**9.2.5
Teaching receptive skills**

The job of the teacher, then, is to train students in a number of skills they will need for the understanding of reading and listening texts. In 9.1.3 we divided these skills into *type 1* and *type 2* skills. Type 1 skills are those operations that students perform on a text when they tackle it for the first time. The first thing students are asked to do with a text concerns the treatment of the text as a whole. Thus students may be asked to look at a text and extract specific information. They might read or listen to get the general picture. They might read or listen to perform a task, or they might be attempting to confirm expectations they have about the text. Type 1 skills are those that we detailed in 9.1.3, (a), (b) and (c), and it is suggested that such tasks form the basis for the first activities that students are asked to perform when learning receptive skills. Type 2 skills are those that are subsequently used when studying reading or listening material and they involve detailed comprehension of the text (after students have performed type 1 skills); the study of vocabulary to develop guessing strategies; the identification of discourse markers and construction and an investigation into the speaker's or writer's opinion and attitude. Type 2 skills, then, are generally concerned with a more detailed analysis of text and for this reason are generally practised after type 1 skills have been worked on.

**9.3
A basic methodological model for the teaching of receptive skills**

We can now look at a model for teaching the receptive skills which is based on the discussion of methodological principles in the first part of this chapter. Just as in our model for introducing new langue (see Figure 4 on page 57) this model is not designed to be followed slavishly but is intended to provide general methodological guidelines.

The model has five basic stages which are:

Lead-in: Here the students and the teacher prepare themselves for the task and familiarise themselves with the topic of the reading or listening exercise. One of the major reasons for this is to create expectations and arouse the students' interest in the subject matter of the spoken or written text (see 9.2.3).

T directs comprehension task: Here the teacher makes sure that the students know what they are going to do. Are they going to answer questions, fill in a chart, complete a message pad or try and re-tell what they heard/saw? This is where the teacher explains and directs the students' purpose for reading or listening (see 9.2.3).

SS listen/
read for task: The students then read or listen to a text to perform the task the teacher has set.

T directs
feedback: When the students have performed the task the teacher will help students to see if they have completed the task successfully and will find out how well they have done. This may follow a stage in which students check their answers with each other first. (See 8.1.1(c) and examples in 9.4 and 9.5.)

T directs
text-related
task: The teacher may then organise some kind of follow-up task related to the text. Thus if the students have answered questions about a letter the text-related task might be to answer that letter. The reasons for text-related tasks have been argued in 5.5 and 9.2.4.

The five stages are concerned with type 1 skills. In other words the students perform one skill operation on the text and then move on to a text-related task. This procedure may vary, however, in two particular circumstances.

When the students have performed tasks for type 1 skills the teacher may then ask them to re-examine the text for type 2 skill work. Thus if the first task involved getting the general picture (see 9.4.4) the teacher might return to the text (after directing feedback) for a type 2 skill task such as deducing meaning. This takes place before the students move to a text-related task.

If the students perform very unsuccessfully in their first comprehension task (type 1) the teacher may redirect them to the same task to try again. This will take place before the text-related task.

These procedures are represented diagrammatically in Figure 8. The solid lines (——) represent a course of action that will generally be taken. The four stages of type 1 skill work and the three stages of type 2 skill work (if the

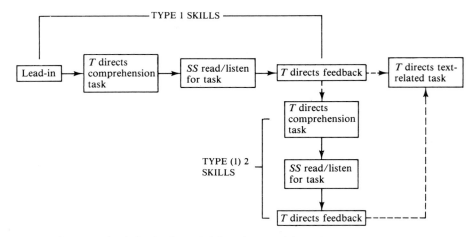

Figure 8 A methodological model for the teaching of receptive skills

type 2 option is taken up) are examples of this. The broken lines (----) represent optional courses of action. Thus the text-related task is optional (although we have stressed that it is a good idea) and so is the re-reading of/listening to the text for type 2 skills or for repair work on type 1 skills. The latter case explains the (1) in brackets.

In general, then, this is the model we will follow when looking at materials for reading and listening in 9.4 and 9.5.

9.4
Reading material

Before looking at examples of reading material we will make some general comments about reading in the classroom.

Reading is an exercise dominated by the eyes and the brain. The eyes receive messages and the brain then has to work out the significance of these messages. Unlike, for example, a listening text, a reading text moves at the speed of the reader (except where the reader is trying to read, for example, an advertisement that flashes past a train window). In other words it is up to the reader to decide how fast he wants to (or can) read a text, whereas a listener often has to do his best with a text whose speed is chosen by the speaker. The fact that reading texts are stationary is clearly a huge advantage.

It is often difficult to convince students of English as a foreign language that texts in English can be understood even though there are vocabulary items and structures the student has never seen before. But this is the case, not only for non-native speakers, but also for some speakers of English as a first language. Skills such as extracting specific information (see 9.1.3(b)) can be satisfactorily performed even though students do not understand the whole text; the same is true for students who want to 'get the general idea' of a text. It is considered vitally important to train students in these skills (e.g. the ability to understand what is important even though the reader cannot understand everything) since they may well have to comprehend reading in just such a situation in real life.

The same is of course true for listening, but because the reading text is static students are often tempted to read slowly, worrying about the meaning of each particular word. And yet if they do this they will never achieve the ability to read texts in English in anything but a slow and ponderous way. Certainly they will continue to have difficulty in quickly scanning (see 9.1.3(b)) or skimming (see 9.1.3(c)) a text for information unless the teacher insists on these skills being performed rapidly. In other words the teacher should insist on the comprehension task being performed in a limited amount of time: if this is regularly done the teacher will find the amount of limited time necessary becoming less and less.

We will now look at a number of examples of reading materials both published and unpublished using a variety of types of question.[7] We will look at *reading to confirm expectations, reading to extract specific information, performing tasks, reading for general comprehension, reading for detailed comprehension, recognising function, discourse patterns and markers* and *deducing meaning.*

9.4.1
Reading to confirm
expectations[8]

In the following example of a reading exercise the students are involved in reading in order to confirm their expectations about the information they think the text will contain. This technique places great emphasis on the lead-in stage (where students are encouraged to become interested in the subject matter of the text), encourages students to predict the content of the text (see 9.1.3(a)), and gives them an interesting and motivating purpose for reading.

(a) Eskimos[9]

The students are going to read a text about Eskimos. The subject is not necessarily in itself very interesting. The teacher puts up the following chart on the blackboard:

THINGS YOU KNOW	THINGS YOU ARE NOT SURE OF	THINGS YOU WOULD LIKE TO KNOW

He then asks the students to tell him things that they know about Eskimos, and writes up a few of these in note form.

He does the same with the other two columns. It is arguable that he might do this in the students' own language with a low level monolingual class. This is the lead-in stage.

At the end of this procedure he will have a number of 'facts' that the students either 'know', are not sure of, or want to know.

He now asks the students to read the following text as quickly as possible: their only task is to confirm (or not) the information written up on the blackboard. This is the *T directs comprehension task* stage.

Eskimos live in the Polar areas between latitude 66° N and the North Pole. There are Eskimos in Northern Canada, Greenland and Siberia.

This means that they are the only people who have their origins both in the Old World (Europe and Asia) and in the New World (America).

It is difficult to make an accurate estimate but there are probably about 50,000 Eskimos. Eskimos are not usually tall but they have powerful legs and shoulders. They have a yellowish skin and straight, black hair. Eskimos have a common language and can understand members of another group although they may come from many thousands of miles away. The most important unit in Eskimo society is the family. Marriage is by mutual consent: the Eskimos do not have a special marriage ceremony.

In the Eskimo community, the most important people are the older men. They control the affairs of the group. The economic system of the Eskimo communities works like a commune: they share almost everything. Eskimos live by hunting, fishing and trapping. When they go to hunt seals, they sail in *kayaks* (light boats made from skins) and when they hunt animals, they travel across the ice in sleds pulled by teams of dogs. The Eskimo snow house (called an *igloo*) is very well known, but, in fact, Eskimos usually live in houses made of wood and turf. When they are not hunting and working, Eskimos like to carve: they use ivory and wood and they often make very beautiful objects.

When the students have done this the teacher leads them through the points on the blackboard again and asks the students whether the text confirmed what they knew, told them things they were not sure of and wanted to know – or indeed disagreed with things they knew. This is the *T directs feedback* stage.

For the text-related task students can work in pairs where one member of the pair is a British television reporter, and the other an Eskimo. The reporter is making a programme about the life of the Eskimos and is therefore asking questions about how they live, etc. The students playing the role of the Eskimo will get their information from the text they have just read.

The 'reading to confirm expectations' technique is highly motivating and successful since it interests students, creates expectations and gives them a purpose for reading. The text-related task we have suggested is potentially productive of a great deal of oral language.

9.4.2
Reading to extract specific information

We will look at four examples in which students are asked to read a text to extract specific information, a skill we said was important (see 9.1.3(b)). An important feature of this type 1 skill is that students should see the questions, etc. they are going to answer before reading the text. If they do this it will be possible for them to read in the required way; they should scan the text only to extract the information the questions demand (see 9.4). We can now look at our examples.

(a) The QE2: yes/no questions[10]

The teacher and the students discuss different types of holiday for the lead-in stage, eventually coming round to the subject of luxury cruises. The teacher then tells the students they are going to read a text about a luxury liner, the QE2.

The teacher asks the students to read just the eight questions, and then asks if they have understood them. When this has been done the teacher tells the students to answer the questions by reading the text. They do not have to understand every word. The objective is only to find the answers to the questions, and they should do this as quickly as possible.

A   Read these questions. Then read the passage to find out whether your answer is 'Yes' or 'No'.

1 Is the ship in the picture small?   . . . . .
2 Are there many ships like the QE2?   . . . . .
3 Do most people prefer to travel by sea?   . . . . .
4 Is the QE2 expensive?   . . . . .
5 Can the ship carry 2,950 people?   . . . . .
6 Can the passengers swim on the ship?   . . . . .
7 Do they sell drinks on the QE2?   . . . . .
8 Can boys and girls watch films on the ship?   . . . . .

The ship in the picture is the Queen Elizabeth II, usually called the QE2. It is a large, modern passenger ship. There are not many ships like the QE2 now. Most people prefer to travel by air and not by sea. The QE2 is very slow and expensive compared with a modern jet plane. But some people do not like to travel by plane, and the QE2 is. . .well, different.

The ship is really an enormous floating hotel, almost a small floating town. The five-day voyage from Southampton, England to New York is a real holiday.

The QE2 can carry 2,000 passengers, and it has a staff of 950 running the ship and looking after the passengers. The ship has three restaurants, eight bars, a ladies' hairdresser's[1] and a men's barber's[2] shop. In addition, there are four swimming pools, two cinemas (they show many films for adults but there are some films for children, too), a casino, two libraries, a hospital, a bank, and a gymnasium. There are also some shops[3]. Yes, it is like a small city. But there are no cars, buses or trucks, and there is no smog; the air is clean and there is peace and quiet.

When the students have finished answering the questions they can check their answers with each other. The teacher then conducts feedback, finding out how well they did and explaining any misunderstandings. He may want to find out how many students got how many correct and which ones these were.

As a text-related task students are told that they are themselves taking a cruise on the QE2 and they should write a postcard to an English friend of theirs. The students and the teacher might discuss the kind of things they could say in such a postcard (particularly the use of the present simple and the present continuous – often found in postcards). After students have written their cards, the more interesting ones can be read out to the class or circulated among the students.

(b) Finding a book: open-ended questions[11]

In this example students are going to read a text explaining how a library catalogue system works. This text is extremely useful (rather than being intrinsically interesting) for students who will need to use British libraries.

The lead-in stage might involve the students and the teacher talking about libraries, how often they visit them, what they read, etc. The teacher then tells the students they are going to read about how a library works.

The teacher asks the students to read the following questions:

Level 1
Read these questions before looking at the text:

1   If you are not sure how to use the catalogues, who should you ask?
2   If you know the name of the writer of a book, which catalogue should you look in?
3   What is perhaps the most important information that catalogue cards give?
4   Look at the specimen catalogue card:
   (a) What is the title of the book?
   (b) What is the author's surname and initials?
   (c) What is the name of the publisher?
   (d) When was the book published?
   (e) How many pages are there in the book?

Now read the text and answer the questions above

The students are then instructed to read the following text in order to find the answers. They should do this as quickly as possible:

HOW TO FIND A BOOK

Catalogues: There are two kinds of catalogue, differing greatly in function. Readers should make use of both for they can then take full advantage of the important subject-information services, and should not hesitate to seek advice from the Enquiry Counter and the Cataloguing staff on the detailed use of these catalogues.

(I)   *The Name or Author Catalogue:* Here works can be sought under the name of the author, institution, editor or body responsible for the work, and also, where the work is best known by its name, for example, in periodical literature, under the title.

(II) *The Subject Catalogue:* Here books relating to one topic are brought together. There is an index to subjects arranged in alphabetical order.

Catalogue Cards: The cards in the catalogue, which are individual guides to specific items, indicate both location by subject and, within subject, location by size, i.e. octavos/quartos or folios. A specimen author card will demonstrate clearly what is meant here. It illustrates, bearing in mind that differences in detail do occur, the significance of information usually contained on a card.

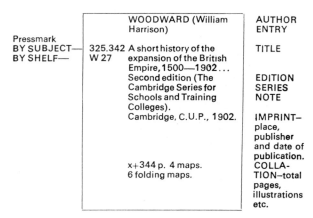

The teacher then conducts feedback on the text asking students to justify reasons for their choices.

The text also lends itself to type 2 skill activity – in this case more detailed comprehension work – and we will look at what this involves in 9.4.5(b).

If the teacher has done work on type 2 skills he can then move to the text-related task, which in this case involves the students in 'going to a library' and performing one of the following three tasks:

1 You are in the library. Ask one of the librarians at the enquiry counter how you can find two books that you want: give the title of one and the author of the other.
2 In the library you have tried to find the book that is on the specimen card (by W H Woodward). However, it is not on the shelf. Report the matter to the librarian and ask how you can obtain it. (It has probably been borrowed by another reader.)
3 Draw author catalogue cards for two books that you are familiar with and fill in as many of the details as you can, similar to those on the specimen author card.

This material was especially designed for students in England who are about to enter British educational institutions, and it is therefore especially specific to their needs.

(c) The departure board: open-ended questions[12]

Another example of the use of open-ended questions for information extraction is the following airline departure board:

AIRLINE	FLIGHT NUMBER	DESTINATION	DEPARTURE TIME
BA	384	São Paolo	10:01
SAB	486	Paris	10:07
BA	902	Zurich	10:18
LH	612	Stuttgart	10:26
PAN AM	786	Los Angeles	10:30
KLM	332	Madrid	10:35
SAB	604	Paris	10:41
KLM	622	Amman	10:55
KLM	801	Stockholm	10:58
LH	205	Delhi	11:00

(2) Get information from this Airport Departures notice-board, by reading quickly up and down columns, across rows, and by reading letters, numbers and times.

1 How many British Airways flights are there?

2 Where is flight 604 going to?

3 Which airline is flying to Amman?

4 Which flight takes off at 10.58?

5 How many different destinations are there?

6 How many planes take off between 10.25 and 10.45?

7 Where is the Pan Am flight going to?

8 When does flight 902 take off?

9 How many different airlines are there?

10 When does the flight for Stuttgart take off?

Once again the material the students work with is of the 'usefulness' rather than the 'interest' type (see 9.1.1). But this is the kind of reading skill that travellers need!

The teacher may conduct an oral lead-in about airports and travelling. He then asks the students to answer the questions about the departure information as quickly as possible. He then conducts feedback.

For the text-related task students could make dialogues in which one speaker is asking an information clerk for flight information. The latter gives answers based on the departure board, for example:

A: Could you tell me what time the flight to Sao Paolo leaves?
B: Certainly sir. It leaves at one minute past ten.
A: Thank you very much.
B: Not at all.   *etc.*

(d) Take your pick: transferring information[13]

In this example students read a page of advertisements about different language schools in England. The difference between this and other examples is that instead of answering questions students have to transfer the information they are looking for onto a chart.

Students and teacher may discuss language schools as part of the lead-in and the teacher then tells the students they are going to look at some advertisements for various schools. First, however, the students are given the following chart:

A   Use the information in the advertisements to complete this chart. Put a tick
     ($\sqrt{}$) in the appropriate box where the answer is "yes" and put a question mark
     if the answer is not clear from the advertisement.

	CROWN	CRAFT	PARADE
1 Location			
a) in London			
b) in country			
c) near sea			
d) easy to get to London			
e) in centre of town/city			
2 Accommodation			
a) in institution			
b) in hostel			
c) with families			
d) where student likes			
3 Shortest course available beginning in July			
a) 3 months			
b) 2 months			
c) 4 weeks			
d) 3 weeks			
4 Hours per week (normal course)			
a) over 20			
b) over 25			
5 Special courses offered			
a) summer			
b) intensive			
c) technical			
d) secretarial			
e) English literature			
f) speech and drama			
6 Minimum age			
a) 15			
b) 16			
c) 17			

They then fill in the chart based on this page of advertisements:

16 TAKE YOUR PICK!

CROWN SCHOOL OF ENGLISH

In the heart of London, close to Oxford Circus underground station.

Open throughout the year except for 2 weeks at Christmas and 1 week at Easter.

Minimum enrolment
4 weeks.

Age
16 and over.

Courses At All Levels

General English
courses 21 hours per week.

Special Courses in speech training and drama.
Also secretarial courses.
There is a bureau which provides assistance with accomodation.

PARADE SCHOOL OF LANGUAGES

On the south coast of England in popular seaside resort. Open throughout the year except for the month of December and 2 weeks at Easter.

Minimum enrolment

3 weeks (4 in July and August).

Age 17 and over.

Courses in General English
at all levels.

18 hours per week

Special Intensive courses

from April to October of 6 weeks' duration. Also courses in

Technical English

Limited accommodation

in adjacent hostels or with private families.
Trips to London and other places of interest arranged.

* * * * * * * * * * *

Craft House School

Country house in beautiful Thames countryside. Easy access to London
(train and bus services)

Three terms

5 January–22 March,
10 April–15 June,
20 September–18 December.

Minimum enrolment

One term

Residential only

Preference given to advanced students between ages 17-21.

SPECIAL SUMMER COURSES

1 July–28 August.
25 hours per week

+ guest lecturers on English Literature and way of life.

When they have finished students compare each others' charts to see if they have the same information. The teacher gives feedback where necessary. This text might lend itself also to a type 2 skill activity for detailed comprehension (see 9.4.5(a)).

For a text-related task students could pick the school they think looks most appropriate for them and write an application letter similar to the example on page 148.

When students read to extract specific information they are involved in a type 1 skill if this information extraction is the first operation they perform on the text. It is often chosen as the first reading activity because it is such an important skill in real life. Where students perform another type 1 activity on a text, however, they might work on the extraction of detailed information as a type 2 skill. Here, though, the extraction of specific information will be focused on detail subsequent to an original understanding of the text. As a type 2 activity extracting specific information does not have the same function as it does when it is the first operation performed on the text.

We have looked at a small number of examples of exercises designed to train students to extract specific information. There are obviously many more possibilities.

9.4.3 Performing tasks

In this section we will look at examples of texts for which students perform realistic tasks without going through any kind of comprehension stage since the task itself implies a general understanding of the text. We will look at two examples.

(a) Rosa Morello: filling in forms[14]

In this example students read a text and then have to fill in a form on the basis of what they read. Students are transferring information in a thoroughly realistic way.

This is the text the students see:

Read this DESCRIPTION.▼

Rosa Morello is from Colombia in South America. She is a student. She has come to London to study English.

Rosa is eighteen years old and single. She has dark hair, dark brown eyes and is 1.65m tall. She likes pop music, dancing, reading and good food. She is also interested in travel and languages.

In London, Rosa lives in a small flat with her friend Linda Morris. The flat is in north London.

And this is the form they have to fill in:

```
┌─────────────────────────────────────────────────────────────────────┐
│                   INTERNATIONAL STUDENT TRAVEL                       │
├─────────────────────────────────────────────────────────────────────┤
│  SURNAME ...MORELLO..................  FIRST NAMES ................  │
│  SEX ...............................  NATIONALITY ................  │
│  ADDRESS 144A CANFIELD GARDENS, TELEPHONE 01.-794.-6009 ........... │
│          LONDON NW6                                                 │
│  AGE ...............................  Attach passport photograph here: │
│  HEIGHT ............................                                 │
│  COLOUR OF HAIR ....................                                 │
│  COLOUR OF EYES ....................                                 │
│  OCCUPATION ........................                                 │
│  INTERESTS .........................                                 │
│          .......................                                     │
└─────────────────────────────────────────────────────────────────────┘
```

For feedback students can compare their forms before the teacher becomes involved.

As a text-related task the teacher asks the students to copy the form (without any of Rosa's details) onto a piece of paper. In pairs students interview each other in order to fill in the form with details of the student being questioned.

(b) Jobs vacant: replying[15]

In this example students read advertisements in order to reply to them, and their replies will be based on their understanding of the texts. This is the material to be used:

```
          BOUTIQUE ASSISTANT
Do you like PEOPLE?
Do you like CLOTHES?
Do you speak ENGLISH,FRENCH
& GERMAN?
Are you between 20 and 30?
If your answer is 'YES' to
these questions ...........
Write to Ms Marianne Weston
at the EUROBOUTIQUE,
Manchester International
Airport, Manchester.
```

Mother's Help or Au-pair girl wanted for:
Mark, 5, and Wendy, 2½

Are you over 18?
Do you like CHILDREN?
Do you like COOKING?
Do you want to learn ENGLISH?
Can you DRIVE?

If so, please write and give
full particulars to:
Mrs. Trafford,
8, Talbot Square,
London, W.8.

DRIVER WANTED
TO TEST-DRIVE
OUR NEW MODELS

IF YOU LIKE CARS
IF YOU CAN DRIVE
AND IF YOU'RE OVER 21

WRITE TO THE MANAGER:-

DALTON MOTORS·KINGSTON·SURREY

Choose one of the three jobs advertised and write a letter applying for the job. Start like this:

Dear ....
    My name is.................. and I'm ( ) years old.

Then write sentences starting like this:

I like ....
I speak ....
I can ....
I want to ....

Finish your letter like this:

If you would like to telephone me, my number is ....
           Yours faithfully,

                (SIGNATURE)

This reading activity can quickly develop into the kind of written communication activity we looked at in 8.2.2(d). The letters can be given to small groups of students who have to select the winning candidate for the various jobs.

    There are many tasks that students can perform with reading material: we have only shown two. It is important, nevertheless, to include this kind of reading exercise as well as those which train students in comprehension skills through the use of questions. Students will thus see reading as more than just question answering!

9.4.4
Reading for general comprehension

We will look at two examples of material designed to train students in reading for general information. They will be trying, in other words, to 'get the general picture' (see 9.1.3(c)).

    Getting the general picture – which we have called skimming – is a type of reading commonly performed. The aim of the reader is to read something quickly to get the general points.

(a) Ghosts: open-ended questions[16]
The teacher and the students talk about their belief (or lack of it) in ghosts. They recount any experiences they have had or heard about.

    The teacher then tells the students they are going to read a short passage about ghosts. They should do this as quickly as possible in order to get the main points from the text. They should then answer the questions which follow.

This is what the students read:

 What sort of people see ghosts?

Every year, about 300 people in Britain report seeing or hearing something supernatural. And they are only the ones who admit it. According to the experts, women are more likely to see ghosts than men. (Six out of ten reported cases come from women.) There are two possible reasons why this is so: either women are more sensitive than men or one of the requirements for seeing a ghost is to have an empty mind: to be thinking of nothing in particular.

At Battle Abbey in Sussex, where William the Conqueror defeated King Harold in 1066, the ghost of a Norman soldier was seen in 1974 by a seven-year-old boy. The boy was walking with his father and said, 'Who's that man with whiskers and a leather apron and shiny stuff all over him?' He was pointing at nothing, according to the father. Seven is the most psychic age of all, according to Andrew Green, member of the Society of Psychic Research.

Now answer these questions.

1   How many people probably see ghosts each year? 300 or more than that?

2   Why do you think women are more likely than men to see ghosts?

3   What do you think the 'shiny stuff' was in the seven-year-old boy's report of the ghost?

4   What do you think the seven-year-old boy saw the ghost doing? Walking slowly? Pointing? Looking over his shoulder? Describe what he was doing, using the construction, *'He saw him .... ing.'*

. . . .

. . . .

. . . .

Now use the same pattern to describe what you saw your friends doing yesterday.
E.g. *I saw Maria swimming in the swimming-pool.*

. . . .

. . . .

. . . .

The teacher then conducts feedback.

We might make a distinction here between questions 1–3 and question 4. The former are type 1 skill questions in that they are concerned with a general understanding of the text. The latter is a type 2 skill question. It focuses in on certain language details and operations which are not essential for the general understanding of the text. The teacher may, therefore, only ask students to answer questions 1–3 when he directs the task for the first time.

The teacher may not organise a follow-up task of the usual type here if he wants to concentrate on the grammatical pattern from question 4.

(b) Tomiko in New York: multiple choice[17]

We have not considered multiple choice questions before: briefly the idea is that the student is given a number of choices, only one of which is correct. Almost all reading comprehension used to be done with multiple choice questions, but teachers have become less enthusiastic about them recently since it has been suggested that in real life people do not have to make the same kind of choice, and that the choice actually causes more confusion than it helps students to understand. Multiple choice questions are still widely used, however, in testing.

In the following example, multiple choice questions will be used to get students to choose between different summaries of paragraphs in a letter.

The teacher reminds the students that Tomiko, a character in their textbook, is living in New York. She is writing to her sister Akiko in Tokyo.

The teacher then instructs the students to read this letter as quickly as possible:

September 30, 1979

Dear Akiko,

I love New York. It's a fabulous city and you can find everything you want here. There are movie theaters, museums, excellent restaurants and fantastic department stores and boutiques. Of course, New York is a very expensive city too – especially for a student with a part-time job.

Living in New York is exciting but my life is a little boring sometimes. Every day I get up at 8:30, have breakfast with Toshi and Lynn and go to work. At work I just type, answer the phone and type some more. Also, I don't have many friends at work, so I usually have lunch alone at a coffee shop. In the afternoon I go home and study or read. That's my day.

I have my English class in the evening. At least that's not boring. In fact, I really like it. I have an excellent teacher, and the other students are very nice – especially a guy from Brazil. His name's Tony and he plays tennis. I finally have someone to play tennis with.

I have to go now. I have to do my homework. Say hello to everybody for me and write soon.

Love
Tomiko

When the students have done this the teacher asks them to choose the best answers to the following three questions:

Circle the correct answers:
1 Paragraph 1 says   *a* Tomiko likes New York.
                          b Tomiko doesn't like New York.
                          c Tomiko wants a part-time job.
2 Paragraph 2 says   *a* Tomiko's life is exciting every day.
                          b Tomiko's life is a little boring.
                          c Tomiko's life is different every day.
3 Paragraph 3 says   *a* Tomiko likes her class.
                          b Tomiko doesn't like her class.
                          c Tony likes his class.

The letter is then used as a model for parallel writing (see 7.2.2).

Reading for general comprehension is a skill that involves absorbing only the main points of a text. The reader does not look for any specific information, but attempts to get a good general overall understanding of the text. Most informational texts can be used in this way provided that the language is within the reach of the students, and teachers can design their own questions to check general understanding if there are none with the text.

9.4.5
Reading for detailed comprehension

So far the reading skills that the students have been asked to practise have been of the type 1 kind. We can now look at type 2 skills which concern work that students do after they have read in one of the ways so far mentioned.

Very often after the students have read the text for the first time they then return to it to perform more detailed comprehension exercises which focus on details of the text. We will look at two examples.

(a) Take your pick: true/false questions

We have already seen the language school advertisements which were used to extract specific information by transferring this information to charts (see 9.4.2(d)). When this task has been performed the teacher asks the students to be involved in more detailed comprehension of the text. He puts them in pairs and asks them to decide (in their pairs) whether the following statements about the text are true or false:

COMPREHENSION PRACTICE
Are these statements true or false? If they are false, give the correct statement.
a The only way of getting to the Crown School is by bus.
b The Crown School closes for longer at Easter than it does at Christmas.
c You can also learn shorthand and typing at the Crown School.
d It is difficult to get to London from Craft House.
e Only advanced students can go to Craft House.
f Students do more than 25 hours a week on summer courses at Craft House.
g An intensive course at the Parade School lasts from April to October.
h There is plenty of accommodation in hostels opposite the Parade School.

i If you go to the Crown School in July, you have to enrol for a longer period than you do at the Parade School.

j Students who go to the Parade School have to be older than those who go to the Crown School.

The teacher then conducts feedback in the normal way, and may continue with the text-related task we detailed in 9.4.2(d).

(b) Finding a book: open-ended questions

In 9.4.2(b) we looked at a text concerning library cataloguing systems and saw the application of type 1 skills for extracting specific information.

After dealing with the text to extract specific information the teacher then asks the students to go back to the text in order to answer the following questions:

LEVEL 2
Answer these questions after you have finished LEVEL 1:

1 If you are looking for a particular book on *agriculture* but cannot remember the author's name, what should you do?
2 Where in the index to the subjects would you find a book on *accountancy*?
3 If you know the title of a well-known journal, but cannot remember any other details, is it possible to find it in the author catalogue?
4 What kind of information is usually found in the collation section of a catalogue card?

Having conducted feedback in the normal way the teacher can move to the text-related task (see 9.4.2(b)).

Most texts lend themselves to type 2 skills of the detailed comprehension kind. Detailed comprehension work gives students a good opportunity to study the finer points of the text and so learn more about how the language is used. The same is true of the next category of reading skills, *recognising function, discourse patterns and markers*.

9.4.6
Recognising function, discourse patterns and markers

In the following three examples of type 2 skills work students will concentrate on features of the text that have to do with its organisation. These features include the discourse construction and the functional ordering of the material. In other words we will be asking students to recognise the organisational skills that go into the writing of a text: readers have to be aware of such organisation in order to be able to make sense of what they are reading and in order to be able to interact with the piece of writing (see 2.4 and 9.1.3(f)).

(a) Pets: context questions[18]

In this example students are asked to recognise the function of cohesive devices in a text very much as we saw in 7.2.3. The idea is to train them to recognise the way in which such devices refer to information elsewhere in the text (in this case the reference is always anaphoric – that is the words '*it*', '*this*', '*they*', etc. refer to previous content in the text).

The students read the following text for the performance of type 1 skills:

JULIA ELLIOTT discusses the English love of pets and makes some suggestions.

A nation of pet-lovers

A RECENT survey in the United States showed that the average family there spent more money on its pets than on its children. Although this is a rather shocking statistic, it should not surprise anyone who has seen the doggy beauty parlours or the quiet shady groves where loved pets of all varieties are laid to rest for ever. It· is possible that the Americans are unique in treating their little friends in this way, but what information we do have would suggest that the English, too, are slavish in their attentions to the whims of their pets.

This can clearly be seen when we look at pet foods, which often contain more vitamins than human food or, at least, are seldom less nutritious. They certainly cost as much. Last year the British public spent two hundred million pounds on pet food alone, to say nothing of veterinary bills and animal furniture. It is difficult not to feel resentful about this when one considers what the same amount could do for victims of starvation and poverty, and so it is not unusual for me to get hot under the collar when I read about another old person who has left all his/her money to a dog or cat home.

There are a variety of reasons why I, personally, find the popularity of British pets alarming. Among other things they cause physical problems. An example of this is New York where they have great difficulty getting rid of the mess that dogs leave on the streets. Many people find this funny, but in a number of large cities it is a major problem. Animals can cause disease, too. It is the threat of rabies—a disease with no known cure—that has made the English government impose strict restrictions on animals coming into the United Kingdom. When the Spanish government recently destroyed a number of stray dogs as protection against the same threat, English tourists immediately wrote letters to the newspapers complaining about 'mass murder'.

Another problem is the carelessness of some pet owners. Most little children want a dog or a cat, and they continually pester their mothers and fathers until they get one. It is only when the 'sweet little thing' has been brought home that the parents realise how much time and money must be spent on 'Rover' or 'Bonzo'. At this point many of them abandon it. This brings me to my last point. Pets which are allowed to run free are often not sweet at all. English farmers lose hundreds of sheep a year, killed by someone's pet poodle or dachshund, and you must have read of children being mauled by pet alsations or even tigers.

You may think that I dislike all pets, but this is not true at all. I would only suggest that we have got our priorities wrong and that something should be done about it. For example, the authorities clearly have a responsibility to introduce stricter penalties for pet-owners whose animals savage livestock or harm little children. This might deter them from being so careless. Surely it would be a good idea, too, if we made dog licences more expensive. The increased revenue from them could be used for many needy causes.

As far as I'm concerned, it's time we stopped being sentimental about pets. I can see no reason, for example, why we should get upset when animals are cut up for medical experiments. If this will lead us to discovering cures for serious human diseases, then I say, 'keep cutting!'

We are a nation of pet-lovers. Wouldn't it be better to be lovers of human-beings?

169

After this first stage the teacher then gives the students the following questions:

CONTEXT QUESTIONS

a What does 'this' refer to in line 5?
b What are 'they' in line 22 and what does 'as much' in line 23 refer to?
c What is 'this' in line 29?
d Who or what is 'it' in line 75?
e What is it that something should be done about in lines 88/89?

After conducting feedback the teacher could include the following text-related task:

SUMMARY WORK

a Make a list of the four reasons the writer gives for being alarmed at the popularity of British pets.
b Make a list of the changes the writer suggests.
c Imagine that you are writing a report on the dangers of pets, and that in your short introduction you must briefly mention these dangers. Taking your information *only* from the text, write the introduction in not more than 80 words.

Summary writing is an important skill in real life, and it involves the concise description of written and spoken text, etc.

(b) Polenta: identifying function[19]

In the following exercise students are asked to recognise the function of the writing and to see how the same function can be achieved with two distinct language types.

Students work with type 1 skills on the following recipe:

POLENTA

Polenta is finely ground Indian corn meal; it makes a filling but excellent dish and this is the recipe as it is cooked by northern Italians with large families to feed.

1 lb of polenta will feed 6 hungry people. First prepare a very large heavy pan full of boiling salted water; when the water boils pour in the polenta, little by little, stirring all the time to eliminate lumps and adding more salt and pepper. It will take about 30 minutes to cook, and when ready is the consistency of a thick purée (rather like a purée of dried peas) and is poured out on to a very large wooden board, where it should form a layer about a quarter of an inch thick. Over it is poured a hot and rich tomato or meat sauce (see sauce bolognese for spaghetti), which is topped with grated Parmesan cheese. The board is placed in the centre of the table and everybody helps himself. Whatever is left over is trimmed into squares about the size of a piece of toast, and grilled over a very slow charcoal fire; the top crust of sauce and cheese remains undisturbed and the under side, being nearest the heat, is deliciously browned.

They are then asked to do the following exercise:

Re-write the recipe for Polenta by filling in the blanks:
Prepare _____. Pour _____.
Stir _____. Add _____. Cook for _____.
Pour on to _____. Pour _____. Top with
_____. Trim what is left _____.
Grill _____.

This is, of course a re-write exercise. Interestingly, though, the writer of the recipe uses imperative forms for instructions (e.g. 'Prepare a very large heavy pan . . .') as well as passive forms to describe the process (e.g. '(it) is poured out onto a very large wooden board'). The object of the exercise is to suggest that the descriptive use of the passive is another way of giving recipe instructions: the recipe could equally well be written completely in the passive.

This exercise, then, is revealing about both the use of the passive constructions and the use of the imperative form, which are performing an essentially similar function.

Two text-related tasks suggest themselves here. The first is for the students to write in English a recipe of one of their favourite dishes, and the other is to make Polenta.

(c) Behaviour patterns: identifying functional organisation[20]

The materials in the following example were prepared especially for Mexican students in higher education and the aim is to show the students how texts are organised functionally through the use of generalisation, reasons, exceptions and inference, etc.

Students are first asked to read a text, some of which is shown here:

The Evolution of Behavior

Here one of the key questions has to do with altruism: How is it that natural selection can favor patterns of behavior that apparently do not favor the survival of the individual?

by John Maynard Smith

Most species of gulls signal appeasement in fighting by turning their head sharply away from their opponent. This clearly identifiable display is called head flagging. Young gulls do not signal in this way; if they are threatened, they run to cover. One gull species, however, has proved to be an exception to the rule. Chicks of the ledge-nesting kittiwake species do employ the head-flagging display when they are frightened. Their anomalous behavior is the result of the interplay between innate behavior patterns and environmental forces. Unlike other gull species, which live on beaches, the kittiwake perches on tiny ledges of steep cliffs where there is no cover to which the chicks can run if they are threatened. The kittiwake species has responded to environmental pressures by accelerating the development of a standard motor pattern of adult gulls.

This explanation reflects a major change in the understanding of animal behavior. Formerly animal behavior was thought to consist of simple responses, some of them innate and some of them learned, to incoming stimuli. Complex behavior, if it was considered at all, was assumed to be the result of complex stimuli. Over the past 60 years, however, a group of ethologists, notably Konrad Z. Lorenz, Nikolaas Tinbergen and Karl von Frisch, have established a new view of animal behavior. They have shown that the animal brain possesses certain specific competences, that animals have an innate capacity for performing complex acts in response to simple stimuli.

171

Then they study the first paragraph in detail, analysing its organisation, using functional categories they have already been made aware of: the materials show them how the paragraph is organised.

Look at how John Maynard Smith constructs his argument in the first paragraph.

sentence 1   A generalization (G)
"Most gulls concede victory by moving their heads."

sentence 2   A definition (D)
"We'll call this head movement 'head flagging'."

sentence 3   An exception (E_1)
"Young gulls do not do head flagging."

sentence 4   An exception (E_2) to exception E_1
"But one species of young gulls does do head flagging."

sentence 5   Naming (N)
"This species is the ledge-nesting kittiwake."

sentence 6   Reason (R_1) for E_2
"Because of genetic inheritance and their environment."

sentence 7   Reason (R_2) about environment
"They have nowhere to run."

sentence 8   Inference (I_1)
"Young kittiwakes have adult behavior because of R_2."

Students are now asked to analyse a text (dealing with the same subject) in a similar way. This is the text:

DIFFERENTIATION in innate behavior patterns is the result of selection pressures arising from the environment. For example, adult gulls signal appeasement in fighting with a standard head-flagging display, turning their head sharply away from an opponent (*top*). Most young gulls do not employ the display; if they are threatened, they run to cover. Chicks of the ledge-nesting kittiwake species, however, do employ the head-flagging display when they are threatened (*bottom*). Unlike other gull species, which live on beaches, the kittiwake lives on tiny ledges of steep cliffs where there is no cover to which the chicks can run. Early development of the head-flagging behavior pattern contributes to the survival of the gulls. Hence natural selection favors the evolution of the kittiwake's anomalous behavior.

and this is how the students have to analyse it:

Look at the text above. *Scientific American* gives an almost identical argument to Maynard Smith's, in a different order, and with one extra inference.

Try to discover the sequence of argument in the seven sentences. Here are the ideas out of order:

Idea				
Exception E_2	☐		Inference I_2	☐
Inference I_1	☐		Exception E_1	☐
Reason R_2	☐		Generalization G	☐
			Reason R_1	☐

This material is particularly appropriate for students with a need to read technical and scientific English. The recognition of functional organisation is an important skill in the understanding of text, for if the reader does not perceive how an argument develops – and when information is designed to provide reasons for, or exceptions to, a generalisation, etc. – he may well not reach an understanding of the text in its entirety.

Our three examples, then, have attempted to train students in an understanding of how writing is organised and what devices are used for this organisation.

9.4.7
Deducing meaning

The following two examples are designed to train students in the ability to deduce meaning from context – a skill we said was important for native and non-native speakers alike (see 9.1.3(e)). In both cases the students are asked to make reasoned guesses of the meaning of words or phrases by choosing between possible alternatives. The guessing of meaning is one area, perhaps, where multiple choice questions are especially useful precisely because readers have to make choices between various potential meanings.

NOTES

IN THE SPRING OF 1976, Eleanor Coppola, her husband, Francis Coppola, and their children left California for the Philippines, where Francis Coppola would film *Apocalypse Now*. Mrs Coppola was asked to supervise a documentary film about the making of *Apocalypse*, and for this she scribbled notes to record the time, place, and action. As the months stretched into years, Mrs Coppola's notes became an extraordinary record not only of the making of a movie but of the emotional and physical price exacted from all who participated.

The production of *Apocalypse Now* has become a legend on its own—three years and millions of dollars spent filming in the Phillipines: the destruction of the sets by a typhoon; leading man Martin Sheen's heart attack mid-film; Marlon Brando's awesome arrival, enormously overweight, to play the part of a Green Beret. The filming itself became a drama of tension, passion, and catharsis.

With frame-by-frame precision, Eleanor Coppola brings us into the film-making drama to witness bizarre and spectacular sights: villages created and destroyed in an orgy of explosives; cadavers burning in piles; a giant stone temple built by 700 laborers and then demolished; cameras on dolly tracks floating away in a morass of mud; helicopters called off the set to fight in a civil war 150 miles away; a primitive native tribe whose members are

brought onto the set and whose ritual ceremonies become part of the film itself.

Behind the scenes, other dramas unfold: Francis Coppola taking great artistic and personal risks and suffering grave self-doubt; Vittorio Storato working for a perfection in his cinematography that is extraordinary—and fantastically expensive; Martin Sheen reaching a point in his portrayal at which he and his character merge in a moment of intense emotion and concentration; Brando, the master of dramatic realism, attempting for the first time in his career a different style of acting; and Eleanor Coppola herself: observing; commenting; filming a documentary; acting as wife, mother, and artist all at once; and struggling to maintain her control in the oppressive heat of the jungle and despite the inexorable demands placed upon her and everyone else involved—demands that will ultimately change lives.

As the focus of this remarkable journal turns to the author, Eleanor Coppola emerges as a woman of strength and complexity with human values that are rare in the film world of illusion. Her *Notes* take us behind the scenes of a motion picture as no other book has done, and at the same time brings us into a private world of exhilaration, pain, and dramatic conflict.

(a) Apocalypse Now[21]
Students have read this text to extract specific information.

They are then asked to answer the following questions:

Choose the alternative that best explains the following vocabulary from the text:

1 'a green beret' means
  a a hat
  b a type of American soldier
  c an inexperienced person

2 'dolly tracks' means
  a the 'railway' on which a camera platform moves
  b a boat on which cameras are carried
  c the places where cameras are stored

The important thing in these two questions is not the meaning of 'green beret' or 'dolly tracks' (neither are necessarily common items of vocabulary) but the students' reasoning processes when making their choice between the possible meanings.

(b) The tent people[22]

The same type of choice is offered in the following example of reading material for advanced students, but there is a marked difference in the case of two of the vocabulary items, 'dwellers' and 'tepee'. For both of these words students are asked to make an initial guess as to their meaning and then confirm or reject their original choice (and further deduce specific meaning) when the words reappear in slightly different contexts. The choices are offered not at the end of the complete text, but after the words have appeared in context. The process of deducing meaning is therefore made all the more real since it is immediate and involves the type of interaction with context that we discussed in 2.4.

This is the material:

THE TENT PEOPLE

"WE ARE NOT," said Chris, the first comer in the tepee village, "playing Indians." The dwellers in the valley in West Wales have not chosen their way of life as an easy option.

a) *dwellers* is likely to mean:
   i) people
   ii) animals
   iii) ideas
   iv) trees

To get there at all you have a long drive over mountain roads, and after you leave your car at the "no vehicle traffic" sign you have a fairly long rough walk to find the hidden valley where the tepees cluster on each side of a stream.

The tribe, as they call themselves, are gradually buying up the land on which their tepees sit but the farmer – who bought his land at £10 an acre has upped his price recently to nearly £700 which makes it very difficult.

b) *tepee* is likely to mean:
   i) a kind of animal
   ii) a tree
   iii) a type of accommodation
   iv) a person

Each person coming in passes a kind of entrance test, building tepee. Carol, mother of four children, ranging from eight to fourteen, said: "I met a couple of people from the tepee village and they asked me to come. I said I would be there in a fortnight – but I uprooted and went straight away. My great grandparents were American Indians so I suppose I just felt at home. It took me a fortnight to make the tent. The village has a big old heavy duty treadle sewing machine you can use."

c) *tepee* is likely to mean:
   i) a camping tent
   ii) an American Indian tent
   iii) a commercially produced tent
   iv) a circus tent

Outside her tepee looks like a traditional Indian home. Inside it is immaculate and extremely comfortable. Its walls are lined with pockets, the bedding rolls into durry mats which double as seating, the floor is thick with woven blue and green mats. A fire burns on a bed of rushes and she cooks in old fashioned iron pots and griddles.

The women boil water over their fires for their washing, although sometimes they will go down to the launderette in Carmarthen.

45 They bake a kind of unleavened bread, rather like Indian chuppatis, in their griddle pans;

d) *chuppatis* are likely to be:
   i) made of meat
   ii) made of paper
   iii) made of metal
   iv) made of flour

50 one man produced a beautiful rich fruit cake he'd baked in a tin over his fire. None of the women I saw wore trousers, preferring long, thick skirts. They live together but independently. There is a tepee which is used for the occasional communal meal or meeting and there is a sauna, constructed by the stream, which 55 all the village uses.
The women say they have discovered the need to get rid of possessions. There is room only for what is necessary, although there is no reason why that should not be 60 decorative as well as functional. But anything irrelevant has to be shed.
The tepee dwellers took the recent arctic weather extremely well.

e) *dwellers* is likely to refer to people who:
   i) do a certain job
   ii) have a certain character
   iii) live in a certain place
   iv) have certain ideas

65 "We couldn't get out but then as we don't manage to get out often anyway, that hardly mattered. We had local milk and eggs and when you buy your flour, beans, lentils and so on in 70lb sacks as we do, then you're better off than most people in towns."

f) *lentils* is likely to mean:
   i) a kind of vegetable
   ii) spices
   iii) building materials
   iv) fuel for fires

Deducing meaning, then, is a skill based to a large extent on the reader's judgment of possible meanings in context. It is something that readers do unconsciously, but which non-native speakers of English can be helped to develop as a skill when reading English.

9.5
Listening material

The teaching of listening skills will follow the methodological model in 9.3 in the same way as for the teaching of reading skills. Training students in listening skills, however, presents problems for both students and teacher not found with reading material.

Listening as a skill may be extremely similar to reading, but the text the listener has to deal with is considerably different from the written one. Most obviously, a listener cannot look at what he is trying to hear; he can only listen to it. Whereas the written word stays on the page and can be looked at more than once, the spoken word, unless recorded on tape or record cannot be repeated. Of course in a conversation it is possible to ask someone to say something again, but the fact remains that while a reader can look back at something as many times as he wants, the listener cannot.

Speech is very different from writing. Most people when they write do so grammatically; their language is grammatically correct. A good piece of writing develops an argument or a point of view (or a story, etc.) logically because the writer is aware of the need for clarity (see 5.6). Even the letter writer usually tries to make his thoughts especially clear. Introductory sentences introduce paragraphs and one idea is finished before the other is begun.

Speech, however, is very different. Of course a formal lecture may be planned in the same way as a good piece of writing, but spontaneous conversation is generally not very organised.

When people speak they do a number of things. In the first place they usually say too much! They say the same thing in a number of different ways so that a lot of what they say is *redundant*, or not necessary for the meaning of what is being said. Thus, for example, a nervous person might ask someone to dinner by saying:

I wonder . . . I mean I was wondering . . . if you might possibly . . . if you would like to come to dinner.

The message is an invitation to dinner; much of what was said did not help to communicate that message (although it communicated nervousness) and was therefore unnecessary. The listener has to work out what is necessary and what is unnecessary in a case like this. In other words he has to discard the redundant parts of what is said and only listen to the main message. This is a particular listening skill.

It's not just redundancy, however, that interferes with the clarity of what someone is saying. People invariably hesitate, repeat themselves, say things that are ungrammatical, and change their minds halfway through a sentence so that the listener has to switch quickly to the new topic. The following extract[23] illustrates these points. Jeremy is telling Roger a story. This is a transcript of a genuine recording of two English people speaking. The subject of the conversation is 'busking' which is when people perform in the open air (e.g. cafés, streets, etc.) and then ask the public for money:

ROGER: Somebody told me you once did some busking. Is that right?
JEREMY: Oh, yeah. Um, yes, I mean, it it I did I went busking what? just after university, or was it while I was at university? But anyway in the summer once in the (ROGER: Yeah.) south of France.

Even in this short exchange Jeremy uses language because he is hesitating ('Um, yes, I mean'). Then he tries to work out what he is going to say ('it it I did I went') and further complicates what he is saying by concentrating on whether or not he went busking during or after his university career ('I went busking what? just after university, or was it while I was at university?'). His final 'sentence' is ungrammatical in the sense that it has no verb ('But anyway in the summer once in the south of France').

It seems impossible that such a mess should be understood, and yet any English person listening to the conversation would be clear about the fact that the speaker once went busking in the south of France either during or after university.

One of our tasks when teaching listening will be to train students to understand what is being said in such conversations: to get them to disregard redundancy, hesitation, ungrammaticality and speakers changing their minds. After all, they do it in their own languages, so it seems reasonable to suppose that we can train them to do it in English, although clearly in acceptable stages: we would probably not give the beginner the sort of conversation we have just looked at on his first day of class!

The major problem that teachers and students encounter when tackling listening material, however, is not these speech 'phenomena' but the actual way listening material is presented to the student. He may be asked to listen to his teacher for listening training, and this may be very beneficial: but there is a limit to the activities the teacher can perform. Not only that, but it would seem sensible to let students hear voices apart from that of their teacher. The most common method of presenting listening material is through the use of a tape recorder. This is clearly sensible since there is no limit to the different types of listening material that can be put on tape. But the tape recorder brings many disadvantages into the classroom. In the first place it is not always a very good machine and the tapes are sometimes less than totally clear. People speaking on tape cannot be seen, and yet much of what we hear in real life takes place with the speaker being present. A speaker on a tape cannot be interrupted (although he can be stopped) to ask for clarification, and the tape continues to run at a steady speed not chosen by individual students. In other words, understanding taped material is very difficult! But tapes are still the best means of letting the student hear the spoken language (especially in a non-English-speaking country).

The difficulties inherent in the use of listening materials lead us to a number of conclusions about how such material should be handled. Firstly we should be sure in almost all cases to give a clear lead-in to what the students are going to hear: more than ever, expectations are important here. Secondly wherever possible there should be some kind of visual backup to the listening material that will help students to come to grips with the text. The questions and tasks that we give the students should be especially designed to be of genuine help in their learning of listening skills and, as far as possible, not be confusing. Lastly, and perhaps most importantly, we should be sure that the quality of our tape and our machine is sufficient for the circumstances in which the listening exercises are to take place.

We will now look at a number of examples of listening material from published sources using a variety of types of question. We will look at *listening to confirm expectations, listening to extract specific information, listening for communicative tasks, listening for general understanding, recognising function, deducing meaning* and *inferring opinion and attitude*.

9.5.1
Listening to confirm expectations

Just as we can ask students to read to confirm expectations (see 9.4.1) so we can ask students to listen for the same reason. The technique has the same advantages with listening as with reading: the students' expectations and interest are aroused, and they have a definite purpose for listening. We will look at two examples.

(a) Eskimos

In 9.4.1 we saw how a text about Eskimos could be used for reading to confirm expectations: the teacher elicited information from students about what they knew/didn't know/weren't sure of concerning Eskimos (see pages 154 and 155).

In this example the teacher would start in exactly the same way, using the same procedure to elicit information from students. The text used in 9.4.1(a) can serve as the model for a talk the teacher would then use for listening comprehension, but the teacher will modify the written version so that it sounds more like a real talk. He might do this in the following way:

I'd like to talk about Eskimos ... um ... Eskimos are the people who live in the Polar regions and here we are talking about the areas between latitude 66° North and the North Pole ... very cold areas of course! In fact there are Eskimos in Northern Canada ... er ... in Greenland, and ... er ... and in Siberia. This means that they are the only people ... the only people who have their origins ... who come from the Old World ...

The teacher feedback and the text-related task could then be the same as in 9.4.1(a).

(b) Lyn's crash[24]

In this example for elementary students a visual is used to build up expectations about what the students are going to listen to. The students are shown the following photograph and are asked to speculate about what has happened. They discuss

A Open class discussion

1 Funny things are always happening to people. One day, a very funny thing happened to Lyn Donovan, the girl in the photograph. The photograph was taken immediately after the incident. Look at it and try to imagine what happened.

A strange incident

2 On the tape is an account of the whole story. Listen to it and note down:

what Lyn was doing_____
what she saw _____
how she felt _____
what the old lady was doing ____

3 Now say exactly what happened.

B Role playing—in groups of 4

Roles: Lyn Donovan
Driver of the car behind
Policeman
Witness

Imagine and act out the conversation which took place after the accident. Begin like this:

Policeman — Hello. What happened here?
Lyn — Well, I was driving along the road when I saw................

C Group discussion

Has anything funny (ie amusing or strange) ever happened to you, your friends, or your family? Tell your group about it.

witness	run over
crash into	look for
false teeth	I don't believe it
on your hands and knees	It's true
shocked	Well, I never
surprised	How strange
frightened	Good heavens

their speculations among themselves and with the teacher. They then look at the four questions in **A2** to guide them in their listening. This is what they hear on the tape:

Son Hi, mum!
Mother Ah, there you are. I was getting worried about you. It's late.
Son Yes, I bumped into Lyn and went to the pub for a drink. She was telling me about a funny thing that happened to her yesterday.
Mother Oh, what was that?
Son Well, she was driving home from work when suddenly she saw an old lady on her hands and knees in the middle of the road.
Mother On her hands and knees in the middle of the road?
Son Yes, in front of her car. She was so shocked that she stopped without warning, and the car behind crashed into her.
Mother Oh! Was she hurt?
Son No, she wasn't, fortunately.
Mother Where did this happen?
Son Near the church on York Street, where they're repairing the road.
Mother And what was the old lady doing on her hands and knees?
Son I'm just coming to that . . . so Lyn got out of her car and the other driver got out of his. Then the old lady picked something up, and walked away without saying a word.
Mother Well, I never! She was lucky Lyn didn't run her over.
Son Well, yes. Then a policeman came; but he didn't believe their story.
Mother Oh?
Son Luckily there was a witness, a man waiting for a bus. He saw it all. Guess what the old lady was doing.
Mother I haven't the faintest idea.
Son She was looking for a false tooth!
Mother A false tooth?
Son Yes. It fell out as she was crossing the road. The witness heard her mumbling, 'Oh, my gold tooth'.
Mother I don't believe it.
Son It's true. Ask Lyn.

They then have a feedback session with the teacher in which they discuss how the dialogue matched up to their original expectations. **A3** in which they are asked to retell the story helps them to do this.

In this material the text-related task is provided in **B Role playing**.

The use of visuals to create expectations with listening material cannot be overstated (see page 177).

Listening to confirm expectations, then, involves the student in the lead-in stage in a way that is interesting and highly purposeful.

9.5.2
Listening to extract
specific information

The ability or skill of listening to extract specific information is as important for listening as it is for reading: indeed to some extent it is more difficult when listening to spoken English because of the speech phenomena we mentioned in 9.5, and therefore needs more work.

The two examples we are going to look at both involve filling in charts but there is, of course, no reason why other question types should not be used.

(a) The road accident[25]

Once again the subject of the material (for early intermediate students) is a road accident.

The students are shown the following small map and the tables/charts to be filled in.

Listen to these three accounts of a road accident and complete the table below:

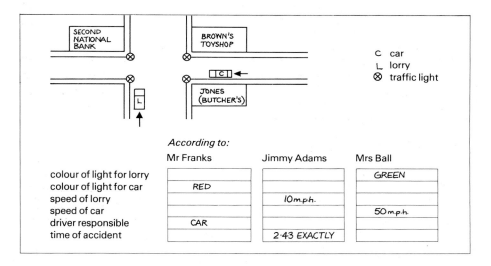

According to:

	Mr Franks	Jimmy Adams	Mrs Ball
colour of light for lorry			GREEN
colour of light for car	RED		
speed of lorry		10 m.p.h.	
speed of car			50 m.p.h.
driver responsible	CAR		
time of accident		2·43 EXACTLY	

The teacher explains that there has been an accident, and makes sure that the students understand the information that they have to listen for (e.g. driver responsible/time of accident, etc.). Notice that some of the entries have already been made; this will help the students since they have less detail to concentrate on.

The students hear three short conversations. Here are the first two:

Conversation 1

POLICEMAN: Now, Mr Franks. I'd just like to read your statement back to you and then you can sign it.

MR FRANKS: Fine.

POLICEMAN: 'I was standing in front of the Second National Bank building at about 2.40 p.m. I saw a small red car approaching the junction of Churchill Avenue and York Road. It was coming towards me along Churchill Avenue at about 40 miles per hour. The traffic lights on York Road changed to green and a delivery lorry began to move forward at about 5 m.p.h. The driver of the car didn't see that his traffic light had changed from amber to red and ran into the side of the lorry.'

MR FRANKS: That's correct. I'll sign it.

Conversation 2

POLICEMAN: Now, Jimmy, did you get a good view of the accident?

JIMMY: Oh, yes. I was standing outside Brown's toyshop and I saw it all quite clearly.

POLICEMAN: Do you know what time it was?

JIMMY: Yes, I checked my watch. It's a quartz watch, you know. It was 2.43 exactly.

POLICEMAN: Good. Now, how fast was the delivery lorry moving?

JIMMY: Well, quite slowly – about 10 miles an hour. It was coming up York Road and I suppose the driver realised the lights were going to change. But they were still red when he went over them.

POLICEMAN: I see. What about the car?

JIMMY: It was a red Volkswagen. It was coming along Churchill Avenue at about 30 miles per hour. The driver braked when he saw the lorry crossing the Avenue.

POLICEMAN: Did you see what colour his traffic light was?

JIMMY: Yes, it changed to amber just before he crossed it.

During the feedback session the teacher can check with the students that the charts have been filled in correctly. As a follow-up task he can ask students to work in groups. In these groups they have to write the policeman's report to his superior about what he thinks really happened. This will involve the students in a discussion of the three different accounts after which they will have to reach a consensus (see 8.1.1) before writing the report.

(b) Athletes[26]

In this example students listen to a lengthy conversation but are only asked to extract a relatively small amount of information from what they hear.

The teacher might start the lead-in by getting the students to discuss some well-known athletes. He might ask the students to speculate about the kind of training such athletes do.

The teacher then asks the students to study the following chart:

3. Listening
A reporter is talking to some athletes about their training programmes. Listen and complete the chart.

	Bo Lundquist Swedish cyclist	Anne Cole British swimmer	Bob Maley American long-distance runner
Gets up at			
Starts training at			
Finishes training at			
Spare time activities			

When the students are clear about what they have to do they hear the following conversation on tape:

EXTENSION 3 Listening

ANNOUNCER: And in today's 'Sportsworld' we have a special report from Karen Finch who is with the athletes in the Olympic Village in Los Angeles.
The line's clear. Can you hear me Karen?
(FX crackly line – BBC news report from US)

KAREN: Fine, Barry, just fine.

ANNOUNCER: Great. So here is Karen Finch with her report from the Olympic village.

KAREN: Well, I have three athletes with me in the studio. First Bo Lundquist.

BO: Hej!

KAREN: Bo is a cyclist and he's here with the Swedish team. This is your first Olympics, isn't it, Bo?

BO: Yes, it is.

KAREN: And how do you feel about it?

BO: Happy, very happy.

KAREN: Let's talk about your training schedule, Bo. I imagine it's pretty hard.

BO: Yes, it is. *I get up at five* ...

KAREN: *Five*! And do you start training then?

BO: Well, I have a cup of coffee first. *I start training at about five-thirty.* You know, it's quite cold then.

KAREN: Right! I'm sure it is. When do you finish training, Bo?

BO: Well, I practise cycling on the track for about two hours. Then I have a short break for breakfast. After that, I do exercises for another few hours. I suppose *I finish at about midday.*

KAREN: So you're free after *twelve.* What do you do then?

BO: You mean, what do I do in my spare time?

KAREN: Right.

BO: Well, *we usually go swimming down at the beach in Malibu for the afternoon.* That's all. I go to bed early. I want to win a gold for Sweden.

KAREN: Well, I hope you do. Thank you, Bo Lundquist. Next with me in the studio is a British girl. She's a member of the swimming team. European champion in free style – Anne Cole. Hello, Anne.

ANNE: Hello.

KAREN: Anne, you heard Bo Lundquist talking about his training programme. Tell me about yours. For example, do you get up so early?

ANNE: Well, not quite so early. *I get up about six-forty-five.*

KAREN: Do you start your training straightaway, Anne?

ANNE: No, not exactly. I have a very light breakfast at seven and *I try to get to the pool by half past.*

KAREN: I see. How long do you train for?

ANNE: All day.

KAREN: You mean you swim all day?

ANNE: (laughs) Oh, no! I swim for about four hours – have lunch and then do track work and body strengthening exercises in the afternoon. *I suppose I train until four o'clock in the afternoon.*

KAREN: That's a long day.

ANNE: It's all right.

KAREN: What about your free time? What do you do?

ANNE: Well, I like to relax when I'm training, so *I read a lot and watch a lot of television –* I like American TV. *I sometimes go dancing at the Olympic Club.*

KAREN: Dancing?

ANNE: Yes, but I go to bed early on most nights.

KAREN: Thank you, Anne, and good luck to you. Finally, here's Bob Maley. Bob's a long distance runner – the American 3000 metres champion.

BOB: Hi!

KAREN: Hello, Bob. How is your training going?

BOB: Fine, just fine. I have a really good programme and I think I'm in first class condition.

KAREN: Tell me about it, Bob.

BOB: Well, I don't like training early in the morning. I don't know why. I just don't like it. So *I start around about ten.*

KAREN: Mmm. And what about lunch?

BOB: I don't have lunch. Lunch makes me tired. *I train all through the day until about five o'clock.*

KAREN: Really? *Until five?*

BOB: Yes! then I shower and I go home.

KAREN: So you live right here in Los Angeles, do you, Bob?

BOB: Yes. I'm married. We live on campus at the University.

KAREN: What do you do in your spare time, Bob?

BOB: I don't have much spare time. I'm studying to be a doctor.

KAREN: Don't you have any free time?

BOB: Not much. But when I relax *I like listening to music.* Music is really special to me.

KAREN: Well, thank you, Bob, Anne and Bo. Good luck! This is Karen Finch at the Olympic Village in Los Angeles.

ANNOUNCER: Thank you, Karen. And now for our other sports news. Tennis ...

The students and the teacher then check that the chart has been filled in correctly. For a follow-up task related to the text students work in pairs in which one member plays the role of either an athlete or a famous politician, actress, writer, etc. The other member of the pair interviews this personality rather as Karen interviewed the athletes on the tape. After the interview the pair can write a short report for a magazine on the life of the personality who was interviewed.

Extracting specific information when listening is a vital skill especially since so much is said in conversation that is redundant and unnecessary. Students should get a lot of practice in this type 1 skill.

9.5.3
Listening for communicative tasks

The four examples in this section ask students to listen in order to perform some kind of communicative task which is as much like real life as possible – although (d) below is to some extent different from the first three examples.

The performing of the communicative task is, however, somewhat unreal, particularly in examples (a) and (b), for here students are asked to do something as if they were themselves one of the people they hear talking. Despite this unreality, however, the performing of the task involves the students in lifelike reactions to what they hear.

(a) The telephone message[27]

In this example students have to take down a telephone message based on a telephone conversation they hear. In writing down the message they are behaving as if they were one of the speakers in the conversation.

Students are told that they must imagine that they are Lynne Thomas, Jack Cooper's secretary. They are then shown the following material:

7. A telephone message

Listen to a telephone conversation at Weston Aeronautics. Lynne Thomas, a secretary, answers the phone and takes a message. Listen and write down the message.

```
┌──────────────────────────────────┐
│        TELEPHONE MESSAGE         │
│  To:                             │
│                                  │
│  From:                           │
│                                  │
│  Message:                        │
│                                  │
└──────────────────────────────────┘
```

This is what the students hear:

Exercise 7 Listening
(Internal phone rings)
LYNNE: Hello. Lynne Thomas speaking.
MIKE: Oh. This is Mike Landon here. Is Jack Cooper there by any chance?
LYNNE: I'm afraid not. He's away for a day or two. Back on ... let's see ... Monday morning.
MIKE: Blast! Oh, well, perhaps I can leave a message for him.

LYNNE: Yes, of course. Just a minute. (rustle of paper)
        Now let's see ... *to Jack Cooper from Mike
        London.*
MIKE: No, Landon ... L A N D O N.
LYNNE: Sorry. Yes, got that. And what's the message?
MIKE: Well, it's just this: *Could he come to a meeting on
        Monday afternoon at 5 p.m.?*
LYNNE: That's this Monday coming, *October 12th?*
MIKE: Right. It's to discuss *the new factory in France.*
LYNNE: Fine. I've got that ... I'll see that he gets it as soon
        as he comes in on Monday.
MIKE: Good. Goodbye.

  To: *Jack Cooper* From: *Mike Landon* Message: *meeting
  Monday 5 p.m. – discuss new factory in France*

After the teacher and students have checked that the message pads have been
filled in appropriately (e.g. the grammar doesn't necessarily have to be right,
but the meaning of the message must be clear) the teacher can put the
students in pairs in which they have to take down similar messages based on
similar phone conversations. This will be more successful if the teacher gives
students role cards, etc. (e.g. *A*: You are Lynne Thomas, Jack Cooper's
secretary. Cooper is away for two days. *B*: You are Jane Goodchild and you
need to know whether your design for a new turbo shaft has been approved).

(b) The flat agency[28]

Again in this example, students are involved in taking down information from
a conversation in which they have to imagine they are taking part. In this case
they have to fill in a form with personal details – a realistic task.

  Students are told that they must imagine that they work in a flat agency (a
key concept that the students must obviously understand). They are the
agency employee in the conversation and should fill in the agency application
form based on the conversation. This is the form the students then study:

Fill in this form while you listen

TOWN AND COUNTRY FLAT AGENCY ⊕	Application Form
Name .... Mr/Mrs/Miss	Occupation ....
Address..	Size of flat wanted ....
Tel.No...	Offer ....

This is the conversation the students hear:

3 LISTENING (1)
Listen and fill in the form on page 25.

MAN: Good morning! Can I help you?
WALTER: Yes, I'm looking for a flat.
MAN: Mmm. What size?
WALTER: Two bedrooms, I think.
MAN: Two bedrooms...mmm...just a minute please...
        where's the application form...ah...here...now,
        your name, please.
WALTER: Moaney. Walter Moaney.

MAN:	Can you spell that?
WALTER:	MOANEY.
MAN:	N E Y...Married?
WALTER:	Yes, I am.
MAN:	Address?
WALTER:	5 Station Road.
MAN:	And your telephone number?
WALTER:	5423168.
MAN:	Once again, please.
WALTER:	5 4 2 3 1 6 8.
MAN:	Thank you. And what do you do, Mr Moaney? What's your occupation?
WALTER:	I'm an engineer.
MAN:	Right...well...let's see...two bedrooms...what about this...8 West Road...
WALTER:	Sorry...where...what address?
MAN:	8 West Road. That's near the station and the shops.
WALTER:	Mmm...Yes, I'll go and see it.

The students can then check with each other that they have the same information on their forms. The teacher can be called on in case of doubt.

For a text-related task the students work in pairs. One is the employee who was on the tape and the other is his boss. The former has to describe Walter Moaney and his needs to the latter.

(c) Directions[29]

We have already studied an example of someone giving directions (see 9.2.2) and this example is somewhat similar. Understanding directions is clearly vitally important and in this example students have to follow the directions they hear.

The students are asked to look at the following map and the teacher draws their attention to the box marked 'you are here'. The students are told to listen in order to mark the route of the directions they hear. This is the map they see:

4.12 **Active listening**

Task: Someone gives directions. Mark the route you hear on the map below.

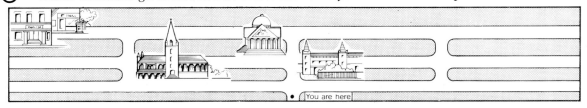

This is what the students hear:

LISTENING TEXT
S1: Excuse me. How can I get to the nearest bank please?
S2: The nearest bank. Mm. Go down this road on your left. Then turn right and go down the second street on your left. There's a bank on the left opposite the post office.

Once again the students can check each others' maps to see if they have the same information. The teacher can help if necessary.

This example is used in the specimen lesson plan (see 11.5.1) where it is quoted as 'recent work' done by the students. It is then picked up in the lesson plan for the teaching of asking for and giving directions.

(d) Jigsaw listening[30]

Jigsaw listening is the term invented by Marion Geddes and Gill Sturtridge[31] to describe an activity in which different students get different information from different listening passages which they then have to share in order to perform some kind of task. In other words three students may each listen to a taped conversation. The conversation they listen to is different in each case (each person listens to only one conversation) thus giving each student a different piece of the 'jigsaw'. The students then join together to use their 'pieces' to put the jigsaw together. In many ways the idea is similar to the story construction activities we looked at in 8.1.6 and 8.2.5 except that here the original input comes from listening material, not pictures or written sentences.

In this example, called 'The meeting' students are told that there is to be a business meeting in Birmingham next week that four men are going to attend. Some of them will be travelling by train.

The class is then divided into three groups. Each group is going to hear one telephone conversation in which two of the men discuss arrangements for the meeting. Using this information they should answer the following two questions and fill in the following chart using information from the railway timetable that is given to them:

1 When *exactly* is the meeting?
2 Where *exactly* will the meeting be?

NAME	Time of departure	Place	Time of arrival	Place
1 2 3 4				

WEEKDAY TIMETABLES			
LONDON (Euston)	09.10	MANCHESTER	08.10
Watford	09.26	Stoke-on-Trent	09.42
Coventry	10.17	Stafford	10.19
BIRMINGHAM (New St)	10.45	Wolverhampton	10.39
		BIRMINGHAM (New St)	10.59

These are the three conversations that the groups hear:

Conversation 1
BRADWELL: 340 1148. Jack Bradwell speaking.
WHITE: Oh hello Jack. It's Don. Don White here.
BRADWELL: Oh hello Don. How are things up in Birmingham?

WHITE: Oh not too bad. Listen . . . I'm just phoning about the meeting. It's next Thursday.

BRADWELL: Aha . . . yes, yes. I've got my diary here, let's have a look. Er . . . yes, next Thursday the 14th.

WHITE: That's right. Now it'll be here in Birmingham at 11.15 on Thursday in the Rose Hotel.

BRADWELL: Good. Let's see, there's a train leaving just after 9 o'clock. I'll get that. That'll give me thirty minutes to get from the station to the hotel. Where is the Rose Hotel by the way? Is it the one opposite the park?

WHITE: Oh no . . . that's the Red Rose restaurant. Don't go there. No, the Rose Hotel is just around the corner from my office here. It's opposite the library.

BRADWELL: Right. See you on Thursday. Bye Don.

WHITE: OK. Bye Jack.

Conversation 2

STEVENS: Hello. Tony Stevens speaking.

WHITE: Oh hello Tony. It's Don White here. How are you?

STEVENS: Oh hello Don . . . fine . . . fine. What's the weather like in Birmingham?

WHITE: Oh not too bad. Now look Tony, it's about the meeting next Thursday here.

STEVENS: Ah yes . . . yes . . . it's for 11.15 isn't it?

WHITE: That's right. Now it's at the Rose Hotel at a quarter past eleven. Now you know where it is don't you?

STEVENS: Oh yes . . . of course I know the Rose. Right. Thursday the 14th at 11.15 at the Rose. I'll catch the 10.17 from here and that gets in around 10.45.

WHITE: Right . . . OK. Now listen, look out for Jack Bradwell . . . He's coming up on the same train from London.

STEVENS: Right. I'll see him on the train then.

WHITE: Oh there's just one more thing Tony. Can you telephone Bob Gordon for me and make sure he knows where and when to come?

STEVENS: Of course I'll do that now. Oh, by the way, I'm just going off on a business trip so you won't be able to contact me again before next Thursday.

WHITE: All right. Well I think everything's all right.

STEVENS: Fine. I'll ring Bob Gordon now. See you in Birmingham on Thursday. Bye.

WHITE: OK, yeah, thanks. Cheers Tony.

Conversation 3

GORDON: Bob Gordon speaking.

STEVENS: Hello Bob. It's Tony Stevens here. How are things?

GORDON: Fine. How about you?

STEVENS: Oh not so bad. Listen, I wanted to talk to you Bob about next Thursday. I hope you haven't forgotten.

GORDON: No . . . no. I've got it in my diary . . . just looking it up. Thursday the 14th . . . meeting in Birmingham. Don't know when or where though.

STEVENS: Right, well Don White asked me to tell you. It's in Birmingham at a quarter past eleven in the Rose.

GORDON: D'you mean the Rose Hotel or the Red Rose restaurant opposite the park?

STEVENS: The one opposite the park. I've never heard of the Rose Hotel. Er . . . now you've got the time right? 11.15. OK?

GORDON: Yeah . . . fine. 11.15. I may be a few minutes late. There's a train from here at 8.10. I'll take that one. Which train are you getting?

STEVENS: I'm catching the 10.17. It gets in at about 10.45.

GORDON: OK. See you Thursday then. Cheers Tony.

STEVENS: Bye Bob.

In each group the students have now filled in their table as far as possible and they will have listened for the answers to the questions. The teacher will have stressed that they must find out when and where *exactly* the meeting is to be.

The teacher then rearranges the class. He takes a student from each group and now has a new group of three. He makes another group of three, and so on, until the whole class is divided up into groups of three where each student comes from one of the original groups. In each new group of three each student will have listened to a different conversation. They are then given the following 'discussion stage' questions:

DISCUSSION STAGE

1 Find out from the other groups the names of the other people attending the meeting. Complete the table.
2 Check with the other groups that everyone knows when the meeting is and *exactly* where it is.
3 Who told each person where the meeting is?
4 If there are any problems what do you think will happen?

Clearly there will be problems when the students come to question 2 if they are alert. In the third conversation Stevens told Gordon that the meeting was to be in the Red Rose restaurant whereas both White and Bradwell are going to meet at the Rose Hotel. Students can then discuss what they think will happen: will Bradwell meet Stevens on the train and correct Stevens's mistake? What will Gordon do if he arrives at the Red Rose restaurant and finds no-one there?

'The meeting', then, works as a listening exercise: students listen for the answer to two questions in order to fill in a table/chart (which we suggested was a useful and realistic skill). But the jigsaw activity is also communicative in the sense that students communicate information to each other as a result of what they have heard.

Getting three different groups using three different tape recorders may, of course, cause difficulty. We will look at the use of tape recorders in 9.5.8.

Exercises that involve the students in doing something with what they hear (such as the four examples above) are extremely beneficial because they

9.5.4
Listening for
general
understanding

reflect real listening (except, perhaps, for (d)) and are thus highly motivating.

In the following two examples students listen to conversations in order to get a general idea of what the main points are. Once again, the ability to 'get the general picture' from a piece of authentic spoken rather than written English is often more difficult and is a vital skill.

(a) The bus service[32]

In this example students are told that three people are going to give their opinions about the local bus service. The students' task is to get a general idea of what these people think and of whether they are users of the service. This is what the students hear:

Interviewer: First of all I asked Bob Giddens 'What do you think of the bus service?'

Bob Giddens: My personal view on that is I come to work in my car because the bus service is so lousy. If they improved the bus service where[1] I could get home erm in the times I think reasonable I would use then use[2] the bus service, but until then, no way.[3] . . . But um yes I definitely think it can be improved by adding other routes to the town because they all spread into the town centre using the t-town centre as the . . . centre point, which[4] I think they could do more by having some ring-buses going round the outskirts of the town, because um . . . if you want to get from one side of town to the other you've got to go to the town centre, change your bus and then go on[5] to another bus to wherever you want to go; so if they had some ring-buses you could get on and go right round the outskirts of the town.

Interviewer: Mrs Smith lives in the same town and she said:

Brenda Smith: I mean I think the bus service is appalling. Luckily for me I don't use it that often[6] unless I have to go shopping.

Interviewer: What . . . how could the bus service be improved?

Brenda Smith: Well they . . . they could turn up . . . for one thing. I mean you look at a timetable and you think oh well five minutes to wait and it turns out to be an hour, which is not very nice when you are in a hurry.

Interviewer: Then I asked Pam Campbell, 'How often do you use the bus service?'

Pam Campbell: Well, fortunately, I don't have to use the bus service too often because a girl who works in my office gives me a lift into work, but I must admit when I do . . . use it I-I curse it very often. I have waited at times up to fifty minutes at the station for a bus that goes in my direction and then I have to t-walk some fifteen minutes at the end of it and I think there should be some way of warning people when a bus is *not* going to arrive and certainly much more frequent bus services.

When they have listened to the tape they fill in this chart.

A Complete the form with a ✓ for 'Yes' and a ✗ for 'No'.

	Bob Giddens	Brenda Smith	Pam Campbell
Approves of the bus service			
Usually travels to work by bus			

A text-related task would be to get the students to interview each other about public transport in their town (or the town they are living in).

(b) The busker[33]

We have already seen a part of this piece of listening in 9.5. The material is designed for higher intermediate students and the conversation is completely authentic.

Students talk about busking – what it means and how it is done, etc. – before being prepared to listen to someone talking about their busking experience.

They are then shown the following set of pictures and told that their task is simply to order the pictures correctly in the box at the bottom right depending on the busker's story:

1	2	3	4	5

THE PRACTICE OF ENGLISH LANGUAGE TEACHING

This is the conversation the students hear:

Listen to the first part of Jeremy's story. Put the letters A to E in the right order in the table in the Workbook. Are you ready?

Roger: Somebody told me that you once did some busking. Is that right?

Jeremy: Oh, yeah. Um, yes, I mean, it it I did I went busking what? just after university, or was it while I was at university? But anyway in the summer once in the (*Roger:* Yeah.) south of France.

Roger: Why was this? Were you **hard up***￼ or something?

Jeremy: No. It's part of er – if you think you're a folk singer –

Roger: Yeah.

Jeremy: – if you've i i if you imagine you're a folk singer, then you've got to go busking some time. It's part of the experience (*Roger:* How-) of being a folk singer.

Roger: How er wha- How did you get on? I mean, wha wha what happened?

Jeremy: Well, it wasn't bad. You see, I di- I was a very lucky type of busker. It I wasn't er doing it to stay alive.

Roger: No.

Jeremy: I bought a return ticket from Dover to to Nice, so that if anything went wrong,

$\left\{ \begin{array}{l}\text{I could get straight back again.}\end{array}\right.$ Um –
Roger: $\left\{ \begin{array}{l}\text{You were all right. Yes. Yes.}\end{array}\right.$

Jeremy: Thi ii it really went very well. I started by going round the cafés every

$\left\{ \begin{array}{l}\text{evening – and – passing a hat round.}\end{array}\right.$
Roger: $\left\{ \begin{array}{l}\text{Yeah. And the(n)} \ldots \text{Good Lord! Wha What}\end{array}\right.$ did you play? Guitar or something?

Jeremy: Yes. (*Roger:* Yeah.) Guitar, and sang sort of fairly ordinary folk songs. In those days it was er all

$\left\{ \begin{array}{l}\text{Dylan and Joan Baez}\end{array}\right.$ type stuff.
Roger: $\left\{ \begin{array}{l}\text{Yeah. Yes.}\end{array}\right.$

And you were a raving success, were you?

Jeremy: (*laughs*) Tha- That might be exaggerating a little. (No?) we I think I was **moderately***￼ successful and I was joined by a a a young French um guy I met (*Roger:* Yeah.) who didn't sing and didn't play the guitar, but was a superb hat-carrier.

Roger: $\left\{ \begin{array}{l}\text{Oh, I see. Yes. Yes. –}\end{array}\right.$
Jeremy: $\left\{ \begin{array}{l}\text{Er – So I would sing the songs and he'd}\end{array}\right.$ carry around the hat.

Roger: Yeah. Yeah. Di-

Jeremy: It It It went pretty well. Of course there was one – er – Quite a lot of people gave us quite a lot of money (*Roger:* Uhm.) except for the English. They wouldn't give us a penny.

The students' task is fairly simple and involves only a general understanding of what is being said in order to be able to put the letter **A** in the first box (for example).

Listening for general understanding, then, is an important skill to encourage in our students. The two examples we have looked at were specifically designed to allow the students to concentrate only on getting the general picture rather than on extracting specific information or working on more detailed type 2 skills.

9.5.5 Recognising function

We will look at an example of type 2 skill work in which students are trained to recognise the different functional meaning conveyed by different intonation patterns (see 2.1.2).

(a) Tag questions[34]

In this example students are being trained in the ability to discriminate between two common intonation patterns used with tag questions. Tag questions are those that occur at the end of a statement using the auxiliary operator to make the question, e.g. 'It's hot, isn't it?', 'You didn't come yesterday, did you?', etc. We have already discussed the different intonation patterns that can be used for this in 2.1.2.

The students are working on a conversation between a character called Peter and someone called Maggie. In this exercise Peter's questions are taken out of the original conversation to form the focus of the work.

First of all the students see the following examples:

| 1 *Peter:* You've been to Zanada, haven't you. ● . . . | *Am I right?* | 1 | 2 | | | | |
| | *Agree with me* | 1 ✔ | 2 | | | | |

| 2 *Peter:* Oh, yes, I remember. You went a couple of years ago, didn't you? ● . . . | *Am I right?* | 1 | 2 ✔ | | | | |
| | *Agree with me* | 1 | 2 | | | | |

This shows them how the falling intonation has the function of expressing certainty that the listener should agree ('Agree with me') whereas the rising intonation is performing a genuine request for confirmation ('Am I right?').

The students now do the following exercise: every time they hear a 'bleep' (●) they must say whether Peter is asking 'Am I right?' or is asking the listener to agree with him. Students have to tick the appropriate box for each question.

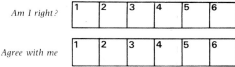

| *Am I right?* | 1 | 2 | 3 | 4 | 5 | 6 |
| *Agree with me* | 1 | 2 | 3 | 4 | 5 | 6 |

TAPESCRIPT OF EXERCISE

Examples. First, just listen to Peter. When is he asking if he is right or not? When is he asking Maggie to agree with him?

Peter: You've been to Zanada, haven't you. ● . . .
Peter: Oh yes, I remember. You went a couple of years ago, didn't you? ● . . .
Now do the exercise. After each BLEEP, tick the appropriate box in the Workbook.

Peter: Now, let's see . . . It's er, it's a mainly
agricultural country, isn't it. ● . . .
Peter: Well yes, I know, but there's not much
industry once you've left the coast, is there? ● . . .

Peter: I see . . . Mm, so the North would be the
best place to go to, wouldn't it. ● . . .
Peter: Yeah. Mind you, I should think the South is
very beautiful, isn't it. ● . . .
Peter: (*laughs*) Yeah. That's right. Oh and what about
transport? It'd be better to hire a car, wouldn't it? ● . . .
Peter: Really? That's cheap. It costs that much a day
here, doesn't it. ● . . .
Peter: Yeah, well that's fine, Maggie. Thanks a lot. Bye.

Students have been able, then, to hear a number of examples of a commonly used language device in speech: they have had training in discrimination between the two possible functions of such a device.

9.5.6
Deducing meaning

We will look at one example in which students are asked to deduce meaning. The same listening material will be used for 9.5.7.

(a) The union committee meeting[35]

In this example advanced students are listening to authentic material of a complex nature both for type 1 skill work – general comprehension – and type 2 skills (deducing meaning and inferring attitude).

    The students have already listened for general comprehension to the following taped conversation (the introduction is included):

SECTION 3 Extensive Listening 3

THE SITUATION: Terry Wilkins, a cameraman at Coastal Television, has been dismissed for smoking in the studio which is designated as a 'No Smoking' area. Sally Green, the Chairperson of the local branch of A.T.T. (The Association of Television Technicians) has called a Committee Meeting to discuss the Union's attitude to the dismissal.

At the meeting are the following people:

Paul Barnes, who sounds like this:

    I mean, as far as I'm concerned, the Management are just trying to make their point.

Jill Mortimer, who sounds like this:

    Don't you think that if we were to set up some sort of an enquiry and perhaps put the Management on the spot . . .

David Kennedy, who sounds like this:

    I'm sorry the day has come when the Union is really playing into the hands of the Management.

PART ONE The meeting is started by Sally Green.

SALLY: We're here now to discuss, er, what action we could take – um – as the Union Committee and then put these forward – these ideas forward to the Union. Um – have we got any comments first of all – general comments (PAUL: Well . . .) – on this situation?

PAUL: Yeah. I think the thing to do is to, er, to-to look at what possibilities we have, you know . . .

JILL: Because the Management is in the wrong aren't they – I mean, er – I think we'd all agree that – um – he shouldn't have been dismissed just for something like smoking (SALLY: Umm.) in the studio.

DAVID: Yes, I think I can tell you why he was dismissed. I think the reason he was dismissed is because he – um – is a nuisance to the Management.

JILL: Oh, David. (PAUL: No, well I . . .) Do you really think . . .?

PAUL: Yes, I think you're going a bit too far there, really, David.

DAVID: No, no. You know as well as I do that every time there's any complaint from us, it's Terry who goes and puts our case to the Management.

JILL: Oh, that's all very well, but then he's acting as our representative. Why should that land on him? (SALLY: That's very silly.)

DAVID: Look, (PAUL: Sorry, sorry David.) the Management don't like him. He's – he's very effective. I mean, he always represents our interests well, doesn't he? So, (JILL: Yeah, yeah.) what happens? They catch him smoking and they use it as a pretext to get rid of him.

PAUL: Look – sorry, sorry.

SALLY: Wouldn't that be provoking the Union into further action? (DAVID: Yeah, OK.) More militant action than . . .

DAVID: Yes, I suppose that's – that's . . . No. I'm not sure if it's that actually. I think the real reason that they want to do it is intimidate us in order to weaken the Union.

PAUL: Oh, but surely, surely you'd agree that – um – the Management has the right to sack somebody who's broken a rule that's been agreed upon by everybody. I mean . . . (SALLY: Umm . . .)

DAVID: Technically I would agree with you but –

PAUL: Didn't we accept this ruling David? About smoking in the studio?

DAVID: Yes, yes. We accepted the rule that we shouldn't smoke in the studio (JILL: OK.) but we didn't accept as an automatic consequence of breaking the rule that the person should be dismissed and that's what's happened. (JILL: Ah well, surely then . . .) I'll lay odds – I'll lay odds that if it had been say, I don't know, Sally or somebody like that who was smoking, they wouldn't have been sacked.

PAUL: Why? Well, I – sorry.

DAVID: Because they're not trouble-makers (ALL: Aah . . .) as far as the Management's concerned.

PAUL: I think – I don't know about you – um, Jill? I think – I think the Union – um – has to look after the interests of its members (ALL: Of course.) within limits and I accept that the Management were probably too hasty and too quick and it seems a bit –

DAVID: Too hasty! I'll say they were too hasty! (JILL: I think you're going a bit too far.)

PAUL: Well I think you're running away with yourself a little bit, David. Really. (DAVID: No, I . . .) I mean, if you're talking about, you know, fighting back and . . .

DAVID: Look. Look, you're living in cloud-cuckoo land because you've got to be realistic about this. I am – well, I don't think there's any doubt about it, that if it had been somebody else they wouldn't have been sacked. Now – OK so he broke a rule (JILL: But, but –)

PAUL: Let's be realistic. The Management has certain rights, David. I mean, they are the Management. I mean, this is a professional Association of people.

DAVID: I agree they've got certain rights, but so have we. We've got a right to be protected –

PAUL: But not a right to smoke in the studio. Not a right to smoke – not a right to break rules.

DAVID: I'm not suggesting that we should try and set the place on fire – I mean, who is? But what I'm saying is that if a chap's caught for smoking, then it doesn't follow that he should be dismissed straightaway. It only follows as far as the Management's concerned if he happens to be Terry, who, as we all know, is somebody – a bit of a thorn in the Management's side.

SALLY: Could I take it from this then that everybody's more or less agreed that, er, the Management did act rather hastily. (ALL: Mmm.)

PAUL: I think they have to be informed of our disfavour – if you like. (DAVID: Yes.)

SALLY: How would we go about informing them and, er, not just informing them but, er, letting them know that, er, we do feel rather strongly about this.

JILL: Well, we must obviously make some sort of representation – you know – um – to negotiation perhaps with the Management –

PAUL: I think we should seek some kind of formula actually, for future reference (JILL: Yes, well exactly.) for working out (DAVID: I couldn't agree more.) what happens when someone breaks a rule. (DAVID: Yes, certainly.) I think we should have (JILL: Yes) been consulted, really.

DAVID: Yes. We should have been consulted and I've got a good formula and I'll tell you what it is.

JILL: Go on then.

DAVID: Go on strike.

The students are then asked to listen to the conversation again to answer the following questions:

2 LANGUAGE IN CONTEXT

a. Listen to Part One and decide what the following words or phrases mean.
- *a)* '. . . they use it as a pretext to get rid of him.'
- *b)* 'I'll lay odds that . . .'
- *c)* '. . . you're running away with yourself a little bit . . .'
- *d)* 'You're living in cloud-cuckoo land.'
- *e)* '. . . a bit of a thorn in the management's side.'

Unlike the examples in 9.4.7 students are not being offered an explicit choice of meanings here. They will have to make their choices from their own alternative meanings of the words or phrases.

9.5.7
Inferring opinion and attitude

The ability to recognise a speaker's attitude and opinion is often a high-level skill and involves the listener's understanding of the speaker's register (does he use formal or informal language, is he tentative or blunt?, etc.) as well as of the functions he is performing. This will be shown clearly in our example.

(a) The union committee meeting

The listening material is the same as for the example in 9.5.6 above. One of the purposes of the taped discussion is to give students an ability to recognise the speakers' use of different language forms to convey different functions more or less strongly or formally, etc. Students have previously worked on this type of language.

Once again, then, the students listen to the extract but this time they must answer the following questions:

3 READING BETWEEN THE LINES

a. Listen to Part One again and say which of the following statements are true and which are false. You should justify your answers by referring to what the speakers actually say.
- *a)* Paul Barnes bluntly disagrees with the reason David Kennedy gives for Terry Wilkins' dismissal.
- *b)* When David Kennedy says that Wilkins was dismissed because he always put the Union members' complaints to the management, Jill Mortimer reacts quite strongly.
- *c)* Sally Green tentatively disagrees with David Kennedy's argument that the management were looking for an excuse to dismiss Terry Wilkins.
- *d)* Paul Barnes argues strongly that the management has the right to dismiss someone who has broken an agreed rule.
- *e)* David Kennedy tentatively agrees that the management were too hasty.
- *f)* Both Jill Mortimer and Paul Barnes bluntly disagree with David Kennedy's analysis of the reasons for Terry Wilkins' dismissal.
- *g)* Jill Mortimer tentatively argues that the Union should make representations to the management and start negotiations.

Their basis for inferring the speakers' attitudes is the speakers' choice of language forms, intonation and stress. In order to say that the statements of the questions are true or false students will have to refer to exactly what was said.

This highly detailed listening exercise is nevertheless useful simply because it is in the choice of specific language items, etc. that speakers make their attitude to what they are saying clear.

9.5.8
Using the tape recorder

Almost all the examples of listening material we have looked at have involved the use of a tape recorder; in the jigsaw listening example in 9.5.3(d) we suggested the use of three machines at the same time!

It is clear that listening to a tape recorder is not incredibly easy, particularly for the student at the back of a class of forty. For this reason we may expect to have to play the listening passage more than once – although it will clearly be satisfactory if this is not necessary. Students should be persuaded, though, that it is possible to complete the comprehension task and that they should try not to panic (a common reaction of students when unaccustomed to listening to tape-recorded passages).

When the teacher conducts a feedback stage to find out how well students have performed the comprehension task(s) he may find that certain parts of the listening text have been misunderstood. It will then be a question of going to that part of the tape which was difficult. Finding your place on a tape is not always easy and teachers should practise with the machines they are going to use before taking them into class.

There is no reason why the teacher should not allow the students to operate a tape recorder when he is confident that they will treat it properly. The jigsaw listening exercise obviously involves the students in this way. Here the teacher should make sure that the students are familiar with the controls and should explain to them that they should try to complete the comprehension task by listening to the tape straight through, at least for the first time. They may then of course play it – or parts of it – as many times as they want.

Of course ideally most listening exercises would be done by students working on their own with their own machines: that way they could work at their own speed. Most schools and institutes, however, are not equipped luxuriously enough to make this possible and a single tape recorder will be used for the whole class.

The teacher, then, should be prepared to play a tape more than once, repeating the same segment of a tape where necessary. But in almost all cases, the first time the students listen they should listen to the whole passage.

9.6
Conclusions

We have discussed in some detail the teaching of receptive skills and we have stressed the importance of the teacher's role in creating expectations and enthusiasm for the text that is to be heard or read. We have pointed out the need for authentic or authentic-looking texts and we have provided a methodological model for the teaching of listening and reading skills.

In showing a considerable variety of listening and reading exercises we have tried to explore some of the many ways of helping students to acquire receptive skills. Many of the comprehension question-types can easily be used by a teacher with a text that he chooses for his own class. Where commercially produced tapes are not available, for example, he may well record material himself with a colleague or colleagues and then use some of the techniques we have shown here.

Discussion

1 Do you think beginner students can be expected to work with genuinely authentic texts? If so, what kind of reading and listening would be appropriate?
2 Which do you think are the most important criteria for the selection of reading and listening material: interest or usefulness? Give reasons for your answer.
3 Are there any situations in which you would not use a lead-in stage? Give examples.
4 Do you think that a teacher might start the treatment of reading/listening material with type 2 skill work? Give reasons for your answer and examples, where appropriate.
5 What are the advantages of getting students to read quickly?
6 What do you understand by 'speech phenomena'?

Exercises

1 Look at the textbook you are using (or are familiar with). Find out if the textbook has material specifically designed for the teaching of listening and reading skills.
2 Find a reading text in your textbook (or a book you are familiar with) and say whether the text is authentic, simulated-authentic or non-authentic. Say whether the content reflects interest or usefulness.
3 Find a reading text that would be appropriate for the confirming type of exercise we saw in 9.4.1.
4 Take a reading text that could be used for either reading to extract specific information or reading for general understanding. Write questions, etc. for each type of reading using as many question-types as you can.
5 Write a conversation which could be used for the communicative task-type of listening.
6 Take a written text from any source and re-write it so that it could form the basis for a talk to be used for listening comprehension (see the examples in 9.5.1).

References

1 Many of the points about expectations, interest, etc. are raised in N Coe (1978).
2 For more on skills involved in listening and reading see J Willis (1981) pages 134 and 142.
3 Taken from E Brinton et al. (1971).
4 Taken from E Davies and N Whitney (1979).
5 Taken from G Broughton (1968).
6 Taken from L G Alexander (1978).
7 For an excellent summary of different question-types and their uses see J Suárez (1979).
8 I first saw this technique demonstrated by Mick Wadham.
9 The text is from R Rossner et al. (1979a).
10 The questions and the text are from R Rossner et al. (1979b).

11 The material is from R Jordan (1980).

12 The material is from E Davies and N Whitney (1979).

13 The material is from D Byrne (1977).

14 This material comes from E Davies and N Whitney (1979) (adapted).

15 The material comes from B Abbs and I Freebairn (1977).

16 Taken from P Mugglestone (1979).

17 Taken from O Castro and V Kimbrough (1979).

18 The material is from J W Arnold and J Harmer (1978).

19 The text is from *Mediterranean Food* by Elizabeth David (Penguin 1965).

20 The material is taken from M Scott (1981).

21 The text is taken from the book jacket of *Notes* by Eleanor Coppola (Simon and Schuster 1979).

22 The material is taken from P Barr et al. (1981).

23 The extract is from R Kingsbury and R Scott (1980).

24 Taken from M. Webster and L. Castañon (1980).

25 The material is from R Rossner et al. (1980).

26 Taken from B Abbs and I Freebairn (1979).

27 Taken from B Abbs and I Freebairn (1979).

28 Taken from B Abbs and I Freebairn (1977).

29 The material is from L G Alexander (1978).

30 The material shown in this example is from M Geddes and G Sturtridge (1979).

31 See M Geddes and G Sturtridge (1978).

32 Taken from L Gore (1979).

33 The material is from R Kingsbury and R Scott (1980).

34 Taken from L Gore (1979).

35 The material is from J Harmer and J W Arnold (1978).

10 Class management

In this chapter we will consider various aspects of class management including *the role of the teacher, student groupings*, and *discipline*. In general we can say that class management is important in so far as it involves the efficiency of the teacher and the learning activities. The most effective activities can be made almost useless if the teacher does not organise them efficiently; if the teacher, with a group of adolescents, allows a discipline problem to arise, learning will be adversely affected. A teacher who always teaches to the whole class (e.g. who does not use any pair or group work) is wasting valuable opportunities for the students to get maximum practice and for the learning to be therefore more efficient.

**10.1
The role of the teacher**

In Part B of this book we saw a variety of activities that ranged from presentation of finely-tuned input to the communication output of the various communicative activities in Chapter 8. We have seen a number of different reading and listening activities.

It will be obvious that the teacher's behaviour for these various types of activity will be different. Indeed in 4.2 we discussed the components of a balanced activities approach and saw how in presentation, for example, the teacher was 'in firm control' (see page 36) whereas for communication output (see 4.2.6) we said that the 'role of the teacher should change' (page 38).

The role of the teacher, then, will depend to a large extent on the function he performs in different activities. We will examine the roles of *controller, assessor, organiser, prompter, participant* and *resource*.

10.1.1
The teacher as controller[1]

The teacher plays the role of controller when he is totally in charge of the class. He controls not only what the students do, but when they speak and what language they use. Clearly the introduction of new language often involves the teacher in a controlling role, particularly at the accurate reproduction stage. We have suggested that there is a good reason for conducting a short drilling session where the teacher indicates exactly what is to be said (or written) and who is going to say (or write) it. Thus the *instruct-cue-nominate* cycle is the perfect example of the teacher as controller. (See 4.2.3 and the many examples in Chapter 6).

It is important to realise, however, that this control is not necessarily the most effective role for the teacher to adopt. Indeed if he wishes the students to use language in any way, then control will have to be relaxed since if all the language used is determined by the teacher the student will never have the opportunity to learn properly (see, for example, 4.2.1 and 4.2.6).

The teacher as controller, then, is useful during an accurate reproduction stage, and in general during lockstep activities (see 10.2.1). But even during immediate creativity, for example, it is vital that this control should be relaxed to some degree, and during communicative activities or the practice of receptive skills, the teacher as controller is wholly inappropriate.

10.1.2
The teacher as assessor

Clearly a major part of a teacher's job is to assess the students' work, to see how well they are performing or how well they performed. A difference has to be made, however, between *correcting* and *organising feedback*.

During an accurate reproduction stage, where the teacher is totally in control, he will be correcting student error and mistake (see 6.3.3). His function, we have suggested, is to show where incorrectness occurs and help the student to realise what has gone wrong and to put it right.

Where students are involved in immediate creativity, or where they are doing a drill-type activity in pairs (e.g. asking and answering set questions) the teacher may still correct, but we suggested that such correction might be 'gentle' (see 5.4.2 and 6.3.3). *Gentle correction* involves showing that incorrectness has occurred, but not making a big fuss about it. In the accurate reproduction stage the teacher asked students who had made mistakes to say the sentences correctly: he spent some time making sure that they could do so. Gentle correction, on the other hand, involves the teacher in saying things like 'Well that's not quite right . . . we don't say 'he goed . . .' we say 'went'' but not insisting that the student then repeats the sentence in the same controlled way. Where students are working in pairs or groups in a fairly controlled situation the teacher may inject this type of correction without completely destroying the atmosphere since he is not stopping the activity in the same way as he would if he asked for repetition and then insisted on a short drill.

Organising feedback is a major part of assessing students' performance (for their benefit) so that they can see the extent of their success or failure. The teacher waits until an activity or task has been completed and then tells the students how well they did.

We must make a distinction between two kinds of feedback. *Content feedback* concerns an assessment of how well the students performed the activity as an activity rather than as a language exercise. When the job application role play has finished, for example, (see 8.1.7(c)) the teacher first discusses with the students the reasons for their choice of the successful applicant. He does the same in the travel agent activity (see 8.1.7(a)) when he discusses why the Hyatt Regency is the hotel that students should have chosen for their holiday. In both cases he is reacting not to the students' accurate use of language, but to the result of their communication. The same would be true of a teacher's reaction to the news broadcast (see 8.2.6(a)): the teacher would first discuss the effectiveness of the presentation of the news. Content feedback, in other words, centres on the content or subject matter of an activity: it aims to give students feedback on their degree of communicative efficiency.

Form feedback, on the other hand, tells students how well they performed in terms of the accurate use of language. Most correction during the presentation stage is a type of form feedback (see 6.3.3). Where communicative activities are taking place the teacher will record particularly common errors and mistakes (either by writing them down or by recording them in some way). After giving content feedback he can then ask students what was wrong in the examples he collected. This may then form the basis for a mini-presentation of language which the majority of students are getting wrong (see 5.4.4).

The teacher should take great care not to make form feedback dominant after communication activities: content feedback should usually come first and the teacher must decide when form feedback is appropriate and when it is not.

It is vital for the teacher to be sensitive to his students in his role as assessor and to realise when correcting is inappropriate.

10.1.3 The teacher as organiser

Perhaps the most important and difficult role the teacher has to play is that of organiser. The success of many activities depends on good organisation and on the students knowing exactly what they are to do. A lot of time can be wasted if the teacher omits to give students vital information or issues conflicting and confusing instructions.

The main aim of the teacher when organising an activity is to tell the students what they are going to talk about (or write or read about), give clear instructions about what exactly their task is, get the activity going, and then organise feedback when it is over. This sounds remarkably easy, but can be disastrous if the teacher has not thought out exactly what he is going to say beforehand.

Certain things should definitely not be done when organising an activity: teachers should never, for example, assume that the students have understood the instructions. It is wise to check that the students have grasped what they have to do, and where possible, the students' native language can be used for this. Teachers should never issue unclear instructions; it is wise to plan out what you are going to say beforehand and then say it clearly and concisely. In lower level classes with monolingual groups, the students' language can be used for this. It is essential for the teacher to plan exactly what information the students will need. For example, if an information gap exercise is being used (such as those in 7.1.2) students must be told not to look at each other's material. If they do the exercise will be ruined. If students are reading for specific information (see 9.4.2) they must clearly understand that they are not to try to understand everything, but only read to get the answer to certain questions. If they do not understand this a lot of the point of the exercise will be lost. Lastly the teacher must be careful about when he gets students to look at the material they will be using for the activity. If he hands out material and then tries to give instructions he will find that the students are looking at the material and not listening to the instructions!

In Part B of this book we have seen many activities and described how the teacher will organise them. Especially in Chapter 8 we have listed the stages the teacher should go through when organising communication activities.

The organisation of an activity and the instructions the teacher gives are of vital importance (see 5.8) since if the students have not understood clearly what they are to do they will not be able to perform their task satisfactorily.

The organisation of an activity can be divided into three main parts. In the first the teacher gives a *lead-in*. Like the lead-in for presentation or for the treatment of receptive skills this will probably take the form of an introduction to the subject. The teacher and students may briefly discuss the topic in order to start thinking about it. This procedure is detailed, for example, in 8.1.7(c). In 8.1.3(a) (the 'describe and draw' game) the teacher's lead-in might be very simple, e.g. 'You're going to test your artistic powers by drawing a picture. The idea of this exercise is to see how well you can talk about a picture and give instructions'. In the case of many of the reading and listening exercises we looked at in Chapter 9 the lead-in concerned a familiarisation with the topic (see, for example 9.4.1(a) and 9.4.2(a)).

When the lead-in stage has been accomplished the teacher *instructs*. This is where he explains exactly what the students should do. He may (as in many of our examples in Chapter 8) tell the students they are going to work in pairs and then designate one member of each pair as *A* and the other as *B*. In the 'describe and draw' example the teacher then gives each student *A* a picture and says, 'Do not show this picture to *B* until the end of the game'. When all the *A* students have their pictures the teacher says, 'I want all the *B* students to draw the same picture as the one *A* has. *A* will give you instructions and you may ask him questions. You must not look at *A*'s picture until the game is complete'. At this stage, particularly in a monolingual class, it may be a good idea to get a translation of these instructions to make sure the students have understood. In certain cases the teacher may well organise a demonstration of the activity before giving instructions (see the information gap practice activities in 7.1.2).

Finally the teacher *initiates* the activity. He gives a final check that students have understood, e.g. 'Has anyone got any questions . . . no? . . . good. Then off you go!'. The teacher may ask the students to see if they can be the first to finish, thus adding a competitive element which is often highly motivating.

The *lead-in* → *instruct* (*demonstrate*) → *initiate* → *organise feedback* sequence can almost always be followed when the teacher is setting up activities – when the teacher is acting as organiser. For the sequence to have the right effect the teacher must remember to work out carefully what instructions to give and what the key concepts for the activity are (much as he works out what key concepts are necessary at the lead-in stage when introducing new language). His job is then to organise the activity as efficiently as possible, frequently checking that the students have understood. Once the activity has started the teacher will not intervene (where pair/group work is being used) unless it is to use gentle correction (see 10.1.2) or to prompt (see 10.1.4).

10.1.4
The teacher as prompter

Often the teacher needs to encourage students to participate or needs to make suggestions about how students may proceed in an activity when there is a silence or when they are confused about what to do next. This is one of the teacher's important roles, the role of prompter.

In 7.1.4(2) we looked at follow-up questions and real answers and we saw the teacher prompting the student to use these devices. He encouraged the student to ask another question and was ready with a suggestion about what that question might be in case the student could not think of one himself. We also said that in simulations the teacher might need to prompt the students with information they have forgotten.

The role of prompter has to be performed with discretion for if the teacher is too aggressive he starts to take over from the students, whereas the idea is that he should be helping them *only* when it is necessary.

10.1.5
The teacher as participant

There is no reason why the teacher should not participate as an equal in an activity especially where activities like simulations are taking place. Clearly on a lot of occasions it will be difficult for him to do so as an equal (since he often knows all the material and all the details, etc. such as with information gap exercises, jigsaw listening, etc.). In 8.1.7 we said that a teacher might join simulations as a participant, sometimes himself playing a role.

The danger is that the teacher will tend to dominate, and the students will both allow and expect this to happen. It will be up to the teacher to make sure it does not.

Teachers should not be afraid to participate since not only will it probably improve the atmosphere in the class, but it will also give the students a chance to practise English with someone who speaks it better than they do.

10.1.6
The teacher as a resource

We have stressed the importance of teacher non-intervention where a genuinely communicative activity is taking place in the classroom and this means that the teacher is left, to some extent, with nothing to do. He still has two very important roles, however. One is to be aware of what is going on in his role as assessor – although discreetly – and the other is to be a kind of walking resource centre. In other words the teacher should always be ready to offer help if it is needed. After all he has the language that the students may be missing, and this is especially true if the students are involved in some kind of writing task, for example.

We must qualify this role, however, by saying that the teacher should not be available as a resource for certain activities such as the communication games we looked at in Chapter 8 (see page 115). In other words there are certain activities where we want to force the students to perform in English entirely on their own with no outside help: in this case the teacher will not be available to help. But there are many other activities – writing individually or in pairs or groups, discussing, planning an advertisement, etc. where the teacher should make it clear that he is available as a resource, as a source of information, if the students need such information.

10.2 Student groupings[2]

In previous chapters we have often talked about activities where students work in pairs or in groups.

We will now consider briefly the relative merits and uses of various student groupings. We will consider *lockstep, pair work, group work* and *individual study.*

10.2.1 Lockstep[3]

Lockstep is the class grouping where all the students are working with the teacher, where all the students are 'locked into' the same rhythm and pace, the same activity (the term is borrowed from the language laboratory). Lockstep is the traditional teaching situation, in other words, where a teacher-controlled session is taking place. The accurate reproduction stage usually takes place in lockstep (although this is not necessarily the only way it can be done) with all the students working as one group and the teacher acting as controller and assessor.

Lockstep has certain advantages. It usually means that all the class are concentrating (although this may not always be so), and the teacher can usually be sure that everyone can hear what is being said. The students are usually getting a good language model from the teacher, and lockstep can often be very dynamic. Many students find the lockstep stage (where choral repetition, etc. takes place) very comforting. There are, in other words, a number of reasons why lockstep is a good idea.

There are also reasons, though, why the use of lockstep alone is less than satisfactory. In the first place, students working in lockstep get little chance to practise or to talk at all. Simple mathematics will show that if a ten-minute accurate reproduction stage takes place in a class of forty, and if each student response takes thirty seconds (including instructing and correcting) only half the class will be able to say anything at all. If this is true of controlled sentences, then the situation with language use is far more serious. In a class of forty only a very small percentage of the class will get a chance to speak.

Lockstep always goes at the wrong speed! Either the teacher is too slow for the good students (and therefore there is a danger that they will get bored) or he is too fast for the weak students (in which case they may panic and not learn what is being taught). Shy and nervous students also find lockstep work extremely bad for the nerves since they are likely to be exposed in front of the whole class.

Most seriously, though, lockstep, where the teacher acts as a controller, cannot be the ideal grouping for communicative work. If students are going to use the language they are learning they will not be able to do so locked into a teacher-controlled drill. And if they are to gain student autonomy they must be able to do so by using the language on their own. Lockstep, in other words, involves too much teaching and too little learning!

This rather bleak view of lockstep activities does not mean we should abandon the whole-class grouping completely. As we have said, it has its uses. Where feedback is taking place after a reading or listening task clearly it will be advantageous to have the whole class involved at the same time both so that they can check their answers and so that the teacher can assess their performance as a group. Where pair and group work are to be set up clearly the whole class has to listen to instructions, etc.

10.2.2
Pair work

We have mentioned pair work before (e.g. for question and answer practice, information gap exercises, simulations, etc.) and students can be put in pairs for a great variety of work including writing and reading.

Pair work seems to be a good idea because it immediately increases the amount of student practice. If we refer back to our imaginary class of forty students we can immediately see that at any one time (in an oral pair work exercise) twenty students are talking at once instead of one. Pair work allows the students to use language (depending of course on the task set by the teacher) and also encourages student co-operation which is itself important for the atmosphere of the class and for the motivation it gives to learning with others. Since the teacher as controller is no longer oppressively present students can help each other to use and learn language. The teacher will still, of course be able to act as an assessor, prompter or resource. With pair work, then, students can practise language use and joint learning.

Certain problems occur with pair work, however. Teachers are often worried about the use of the students' native language in monolingual groups. Usually, however, students will use English if they are motivated to do so and the teacher explains what the reason for the activity is. Incorrectness is another worry, but as we have repeatedly said accuracy is not the only standard to judge learning by: communicative efficiency is also vitally important and pair work encourages such efficiency.

Teachers sometimes worry about noise and indiscipline when pair work is used particularly with children and adolescents. A lot depends here on the task the teacher has set and on his attitude during the activity. If a teacher goes and concentrates on one pair in the corner of the room to the exclusion of the others, then indeed the rest of the class may forget their task and start playing about! If there is a danger of this happening the teacher should probably remain at the front of the class (where without interfering in any way he can get a general idea of what is going on) and then organise feedback when the pair work task is over to see how successful it was. He should try and make sure that the pair work task is not carried out for too long. Students who are left in pairs for a long time often become bored and are then not only not learning, but also become restless and perhaps badly behaved. If the noise rises to excessive levels then the teacher can simply stop the activity, explain the problem and ask the students to continue more quietly. If this does not work the activity may have to be discontinued.

It is important, though, to remember that the type of pair work the teacher will organise depends on the type of activity the class is working with. In Chapter 6 we saw many examples where students worked in pairs doing drills, or asking and answering questions using language that had just been presented. Sometimes they will merely be practising a learnt dialogue (see, for example, 6.5.3(b) where students have a brief pair work session in which they repeat the dialogue before using it – later – as a model for their own conversations).

The point being made here is that it may be a good idea to familiarise students with pair work at the beginning of a course by giving them this kind of very short, simple, task to perform. As students get used to the idea of working in pairs the teacher can extend the range of activities being offered.

A decision has to be taken about how students are put in pairs. Teachers will have to decide whether they will put strong students with weak students or whether they will vary the combination of the pairs from class to class. Many teachers adopt a random approach to putting students in pairs while others deliberately mix students who do not necessarily sit together.

There seems to be no research to give an answer to the ideal combinations for either pairs or groups (see 10.2.3).

The teacher should probably make his decision based on the particular class and on whether he wishes to put special students together, whether he wants to do it at random (e.g. by the letter of the alphabet which begins the student's name) or whether he simply puts students sitting next to each other in pairs.

Pair work, then, is a way of increasing student participation and language use. It can be used for an enormous number of activities whether speaking, writing or reading.

10.2.3
Group work[4]

Many of the activities in Chapter 8 were designed for students in groups (see for example 8.1.1(a), 8.1.6(a), 8.2.5(b), etc.) and teachers have been realising for some time now the advantages of organising the students into groups of five, for example, to complete certain tasks.

Group work seems to be an extremely attractive idea for a number of reasons. Just as in pair work, we can mention the increase in the amount of student talking time and we can place emphasis on the opportunities it gives students really to use language to communicate with each other. When all the students in a group are working together to produce, for example, an advertisement, they will be communicating with each other and more importantly co-operating among themselves. Students will be teaching and learning in the group exhibiting a degree of self-reliance that simply is not possible when the teacher is acting as a controller.

In some ways group work is more dynamic than pair work: there are more people to react with and against in a group and therefore a greater possibility of discussion. There is a greater chance that at least one member of the group will be able to solve a problem when it arises, and working in groups is potentially more relaxing than working in pairs, for the latter puts a greater demand on the student's ability to co-operate closely with only one other person. It is also true to say that group work tasks can often be more exciting and dynamic than some pair work tasks.

Of course the worries that apply to pair work (like the use of the students' native language, noise and indiscipline) apply equally to group work: the problems do not seem insuperable, though, and the solutions will be the same as those for pair work.

Once again the biggest problem is one of selection of group members. Some teachers use what is called a sociogram where, for example, students are asked to write down the name of the student in the class they would most like to have with them if they were stranded on a desert island. This technique certainly tells the teacher who the popular and unpopular students are, but will not help to form groups of equal sizes since popularity is not shared round a class in such a neat way.[5] At the beginning of a course a sociogram will anyway not be appropriate since students will often not know each other.

A lot of teachers form groups where weak and strong students are mixed together. This is often a good thing for the weak students (although there is a danger that they will be overpowered by their stronger brethren and will thus not participate) and probably does not hinder the stronger students from getting the maximum benefit from the activity. Sometimes, however, it is probably a good idea to make groups of strong students and groups of weaker students.

The teacher can then give the groups different tasks to perform. It is worth pointing out here that one of the major possibilities offered by group work is just this fact: that where there are students of different levels and interests in a class, different groups can be formed so that not all the students are necessarily working on the same material at the same time.

Group size is also slightly problematical: in general it is probably safe to say that groups of more than seven students tend to be less than totally appropriate since the amount of student participation obviously falls and the organisation of the group itself may start to disintegrate. But this is not always the case and a lot depends on the activity being performed. Where decisions have to be taken as a result of the activity it is probably a good idea to have an odd number in each group since in that way a split decision is impossible (see for example the activity in 8.1.1(b)). In more general tasks (e.g. designing material together or doing the first stage of jigsaw listening, etc.) the necessity for odd numbers in the groups is obviously not so great.

A major possibility for group work is the idea of *flexible groups*. Here students start in set groups, and as an activity progresses the groups split up and re-form; or they join together until the class is fully re-formed. An example of this type of flexible grouping is 8.1.6(a) where students start in groups of six and then re-form with each member of the original groups now being a member of another group. The activities in 8.1.1, however, in which students work to reach a consensus, start by having small groups of students. Gradually these groups are joined together. Thus if the class starts in groups of three, two groups will then be joined to make groups of six, then of twelve, etc. (see pages 113 and 114).

One other issue confronts us with group work, and that is the possibility of having group leaders. We have already said that different groups may be doing different tasks. There is nothing intrinsically wrong with the idea that while one group is doing a fluency activity, another group should be doing something like an accurate reproduction stage or a listening or reading activity. It may be advantageous in such cases to have one student acting as a group leader. He could have two functions: one would be to act as the *group organiser*, making sure that a task was properly done, that the information was properly recorded or collected, etc., and the other could be as a *mini-teacher* where a student could conduct a drill or a dialogue, etc. In the latter case the teacher would have to make sure that the student was properly primed for his task. Certainly in mixed-ability groups (where students do not all have the same level of English) the idea of a student acting as a mini-teacher is attractive. In practice, though, even where groups are leaderless, students tend to take on definite roles. While one student is permanently commenting on what is happening (e.g. 'We seem to be agreeing on this point') another is permanently disagreeing with everybody. Some students seem to need to push the group towards a quick decision while others keep quiet unless they are forced to speak. This seems to be a matter of individual personality and few teachers are equipped to make reasoned judgments about exactly how to handle such situations. Ideally all teachers would take a training in psychology including a lot of work on group dynamics: if teachers have not done this, common sense and a degree of sensitivity seem essential.

Group work offers enormous potential. It can be used for oral work, tasks where decisions have to be taken, joint reading tasks, listening tasks, co-operative writing and many other things: it also has the great advantage of allowing different groups of students to be doing different things in the same classroom.

10.2.4
Individual study

Somehow we must try and let students work on their own and at their own speed at some stage during the class. They can do this, of course, even where they are all doing the same task.

Individual study is a good idea precisely because students can relax from outside pressure (provided that there is no time limit or competitive element) and because they can rely on themselves rather than on other people. Both reading and writing work can be the focus for individual study (although see 8.1.1(c) and various ideas in 8.2 about the use of pair and group work with reading and writing material). Ideally, where materials exist and where conditions permit, there would be stages at which individual students could have a choice of different activities.

We have advocated the use of pair and group work for a variety of reasons, both practical and psychological. But students also need some time on their own, and various reading and writing exercises can be particularly appropriate for this. When planning activities for a class (see 11.4) the teacher should not forget to take this factor into consideration.

10.3
Discipline[6]

Many teachers find the subject of discipline distasteful since it conjures up visions of repressive teachers and – for the English at any rate – the horrors of the Victorian classroom so grippingly described by Charles Dickens. Nevertheless, the majority of teachers who have difficulty with language teaching when their students are children or adolescents do so because their students are inattentive, badly-behaved or quite simply out of control.

Discipline here does not mean a series of punishments meted out to badly-behaved students (although see 10.3.3): discipline here refers to a *code of conduct* which binds a teacher and a group of students together so that learning can be more effective. In other words, the object of 'discipline' is not to take action when things get out of hand, but to ensure that things never reach that stage. It is important, too, to realise that the code of conduct that determines the behaviour of a class is as necessary for the teacher as it is for the student. Both the former and the latter are bound to follow the code.

A code of conduct involves the teacher and students in forms of behaviour in the classroom. Certain things do not comply with these forms of behaviour such as arriving late for class, coming to class without textbook and materials, 'forgetting' to do homework, bringing sweets/chewing gum into the classroom, making a lot of noise, not paying attention, etc. Probably all of these acts would be considered 'bad' behaviour by a majority of teachers; the students, too, will feel the same if such acts fall outside a recognised code of behaviour.

The point being made here is that both students and teacher need to know what the code is. When they do they will then know what forms of behaviour are unacceptable, not just for the teacher, but for the rest of the group as well. If this code is established properly then the likelihood of problems is far less then if it is not. Prevention, in other words is better than a cure.

We will examine the area of discipline further, and we will look at the *causes of discipline problems, prevention rather than cure* and *action in case of indiscipline*.

10.3.1 Causes of discipline problems

There seem to be three possible reasons for discipline problems: the teacher, the students and the institution. We will examine each of these in turn.

(a) The teacher

The behaviour and the attitude of the teacher is perhaps the single most important factor in a classroom, and thus can have a major effect on discipline. We can make a list of things that teachers should probably not do if they want to avoid problems:

Don't go to class unprepared: Students automatically identify teachers who are not sure what to do in the classroom. Particularly for those classes that might cause trouble, the teacher has to appear to be well prepared and knowledgeable in his subject.

Don't be inconsistent: If the teacher allows students to come to class late without taking action one week he cannot then chastise them for doing the same thing again the week after. Teachers have to be consistent, in other words, about what the code of conduct is otherwise the students will lose respect for it.

Don't issue threats: Teachers who threaten students with terrible punishments and then do not carry them out are doing both the class and themselves a disservice. Hopefully threats are not necessary, but it is absolutely fatal to say that some action is going to be taken if it is not.

Don't raise your voice: One of the great mistakes of many teachers is to try and establish control by raising their voices and shouting. This almost always has disastrous consequences for it contributes to a general raising of the level of noise in the classroom. Very often a quiet voice is far more effective.

Don't give boring classes: We saw in Chapter 1 how important students found it that classes should be interesting (see page 6). It seems true that perhaps the greatest single cause of indiscipline is boredom. Interested students do not misbehave in the same way.

Don't be unfair: A teacher cannot allow himself to be unfair, either to the class as a whole or to individuals. Teachers should always try to avoid having favourites or picking on particular individuals. Most teachers, of course, have students that they like or dislike more than others, but a major part of their job is not to show these preferences and prejudices in the classroom.

Don't have a negative attitude to learning: A teacher who does not really care and who is insensitive to the students' reactions to what is happening in the classroom will lose the respect of his students – the first step to discipline problems.

Don't break the code: If part of the code is that the students should arrive on time, then the teacher must too. If there is a ban on chewing gum then the teacher should not chew gum. If homework must be handed in on time then it must also be corrected promptly. A teacher who behaves in a way that is considered anti-social and which is disapproved of if imitated by the students will destroy the code of conduct, for it either exists for the group as a whole (including the teacher) or it does not exist at all.

(b) The student

A teacher who does everything to avoid trouble may still have discipline problems because of the students: and all practising teachers know that while one group may cause no trouble, another may be difficult to handle.

There are, of course, many reasons why students behave badly and we can mention a few of these:

Time of day: The attitude of the students is often affected by when the class takes place. If the students are all tired after a long day of study they may find exacting classes too challenging. If the class takes place just before lunch students may tend not to pay too much attention as the lunch hour approaches. Early morning classes may cause students to be sleepy; classes after lunch are often full of drowsy students. The teacher must take these factors into account when planning the class (see Chapter 11).

The student's attitude: A lot depends on how the student views the class, the teacher, and the subject being learnt. Clearly therefore it is important for these to be seen in a positive – or at least neutral – light. For many reasons, though, students are often hostile to English classes and their teachers. We will discuss ways of avoiding this in 10.3.2. Where a student starts with a negative attitude, however, much can be done: if the class is interesting – if the student can become interested even against his better judgment – a lot of the problem will disappear.

A desire to be noticed: It is generally accepted that adolescence is a difficult time and that young adolescents often need to be noticed or have a desire to be recognised in some way. This is not just special to adolescents, however, and most teachers are familiar with students in their classes who demand attention. What is special about adolescents, perhaps, is that they are quite prepared to be disruptive in order to gain the recognition they need. It seems somewhat short-sighted, then, to label such bad behaviour as in some way wicked and punish it harshly. Much more important is the possibility of channelling this behaviour and involving the student; if recognition is what he needs then the teacher should try to make sure that it can be given within the context of the language class.

Two's company: Two students being disruptive together are far more effective than one! They may encourage each other in their anti-social behaviour and gradually influence the whole group. Action in such cases has to be taken fairly rapidly, and much can be achieved if students are reseated, if the troublemakers are separated, and if particularly disruptive students are made to sit at the front.

Students, then, have a number of reasons for behaving badly: they cannot always be easily controlled and much will depend on the particular group and the particular teacher. In general, though, a bored student is a discipline problem, whereas an interested student who knows and understands the code is not.

(c) The institution

A lot depends on the attitude of the institution to discipline and student behaviour. Ideally there will be a recognised system for dealing with problem classes and students. It is to be hoped that the teacher can consult co-ordinators or department heads when in trouble, and that cases of extremely bad behaviour can be acted upon by such people.

If the institution does not have a recognised policy for dealing with discipline problems then it is up to the teachers to press for such a system. Ultimately a student who causes a severe problem has to be handled by the school authority rather than by the teacher on his own and it is therefore in the teachers' interest to see that there is a coherent policy.

Teachers should be careful about showing that they disagree with the policy of the institution (where they do) since this can have a bad effect generally on other classes in the same area. Teachers who disagree, for example, about things like the choice of textbook, should not show this disagreement too openly to the students, but work to have the decision changed with the administration.

There are many causes of discipline problems, some of which we have looked at in this section. Generally we have been dealing with classes of children and adolescents, but many of the comments we have made apply equally well to adult classes for here too the teacher must have some kind of code of conduct and must take account, for example, of the time of day when the class takes place.

Having discussed some of the reasons for problems we will now look at how discipline problems can be prevented.

10.3.2
Prevention rather than cure

It is much more difficult to deal with discipline problems than it is to teach a well-behaved class. This will be obvious to all teachers and our task, therefore, would seem to be that of ensuring that the class is well-behaved. Based on the previous discussion (see 10.3.1) we can make some proposals for preventing discipline problems from arising.

(a) Establishing a code of conduct
The first thing a teacher should do with a new class is to establish the code of conduct that we have continually mentioned. What exactly is considered, for example, anti-social behaviour? What is the best type of behaviour for effective learning?

Clearly the establishing of a code of conduct is most effectively done in the students' own language, and ideally it will take the form of a discussion on the first day with a new class (the teacher will, however, want to stress that the students' native language is to be used sparingly, and he will talk about the importance of using English only, in practice and communicative activities). If the teacher asks the students what they think the code should be he will probably elicit most of the things he already has on his list.

The code should take account of a number of things such as lateness, bringing the right materials to class, homework, sweets in the class, inattention, the unnecessary use of the students' native language, etc. The teacher should have established on his own what the 'minimum' code is and then, as a result of the discussion, come to an agreement about exactly what constitutes anti-social behaviour.

The teacher should use the first few classes partly to establish a style of learning and teaching: at the same time the code can be reinforced by taking action immediately the code is broken. Students can be asked why another student's behaviour is wrong; what part of the code is being broken? By involving the group in this process a group responsibility can be developed which will enhance the learning process.

It is important to show the students that the main reason for the code is to have effective learning, and that to have badly-behaved classes is to ensure that the students will not learn well.

(b) Being fair and consistent
Once the code has been established its administration is crucial. The two qualities that are necessary are fairness and consistency. The teacher must be sure to react to code-breaking in the same way every time and he must be sure to treat all students equally. No student should be allowed to 'break the code' without action being taken for such a student will immediately be seen as the teacher's favourite. This is bad for the class and for the student. Teachers should not, either, lean heavily on one student exclusively.

(c) Being well-prepared
There are a number of reasons why it is vital to be well-prepared when teaching children and adolescents – although of course it is vital to be

well-prepared whoever you are teaching. A well-prepared teacher will know what is likely to interest and stimulate his class. If he follows the procedure we will outline in Chapter 11 he will have planned his class not just on the basis of language to be taught, but also on the basis of what activities are suitable (on that day at that time), what skills have to be taught, and what the content of the lesson should be. He will have thought, in other words, about what the most effective thing for that class will be.

A well-prepared teacher will also have a number of ideas for the class that he may never use – a sort of 'emergency package' for unexpected events.[7] His ideas might include quick games, writing activities, listening activities and other tasks. He will have these so that if he has time over or if he quickly has to change his plan (see (d) below) he can produce an activity that will be suitable. All teachers should collect a store of activities that can be used 'on the spur of the moment' when the situation merits it.

(d) Being adaptable and interesting

In Chapter 1 we discussed the need for interesting classes and we discussed the need for adaptability.

The well-prepared teacher may know exactly what he is going to do but may still not provide classes that are interesting enough. And yet, as we have said, an interested student rarely causes problems.

The well-prepared teacher may have planned a class that he is sure will interest his students only to find that they show no enthusiasm whatsoever. He will have to make a quick decision about whether to continue with the activity or whether to change quickly to something else. In the same way the teacher may find that students suddenly become very bored with an activity they were previously enjoying. Unless there is a good reason why not he may decide to switch quickly to another activity.

The teacher may find that the noise level in the class is getting too high and that the class generally is getting out of control (see 10.2.2, for example). In such a situation a quick writing task may solve the problem. A quick listening test of some kind may also bring the class to order. This type of 'change of activity' is infinitely preferable to taking some kind of disciplinary action.

A teacher has to be sensitive to the behaviour of his class. If he persists with an obviously boring and unsuccessful activity it will not be surprising if discipline problems occur. If, on the other hand, he is able to change the activity when it becomes unsatisfactory he may avoid this situation. We now see why the emergency package is necessary.

Of course teachers don't change what they are doing only for such negative reasons. Students who have been working hard often need a break, and the teacher might well organise a quick game to relax them. Often the teacher will introduce an enjoyable activity simply because the students have not really enjoyed the class so far. Sometimes the teacher might introduce an activity that is interesting (but not completely relevant to what is being studied) for the same reason.

The well-prepared teacher, then, is prepared to be adaptable as a prevention against boredom and indiscipline and he never forgets that interested students learn.

If the teacher establishes a code of conduct and is fair and consistent, and if that teacher is well-prepared and adaptable there is no reason why significant discipline problems should arise. Nevertheless teachers do have discipline problems and action sometimes has to be taken. We will now consider such action.

10.3.3
Action in case of indiscipline

There are a number of things a teacher can do when students behave badly, but in general two points can be made. Any 'punishment' that hurts a student physically or emotionally is probably dangerous and harmful in many ways. Its effect cannot be measured and it probably encourages in the student behaviour and psychology that we would want to avoid as educators. With this in mind we should also be sure that any punishment is in line with the policy of the school or institute where the class is given.

The ability to control a group of students when things get out of hand depends to a large extent on the personality of the teacher, and some teachers certainly appear to find it easier than others. There are, however, a number of measures that can be taken.

(a) Act immediately

We have continually stressed the need for a code. When it is broken the teacher should act immediately. If the indiscipline involves anti-social behaviour in the classroom the teacher should take steps at once. Where it involves things like not bringing books to class the teacher should speak to the student either during or immediately after the class.

The longer a discipline problem is left unchecked, the more difficult it is to take action.

(b) Stop the class

Where the indiscipline involves disruptive behaviour the teacher should immediately stop the class. This is a clear indication to all the students that something is wrong. The teacher may then tell the students who are behaving badly what is wrong. Many teachers refuse to re-start the class until the student has settled down; they simply stop the class, make it clear that the student's behaviour is unsatisfactory, and wait until things improve.

(c) Reseating

An effective way of controlling a student who is behaving badly is immediately to make the student sit in a different place. Certainly where troublesome students are sitting together they should be separated. Often if students are moved to the front of the class they will behave better.

(d) Change the activity

Particularly where a majority of the class seem to be gradually getting out of control, a change of activity will often restore order. Thus a quick fast-writing task will often quieten students down and at the same time provide good writing practice. The same effect can often be achieved by a reading task or a listening exercise.

In general, anti-social behaviour can usually be cured if the student is given something to do which will involve him.

(e) After the class

Where one student is continually giving trouble the teacher should probably take that student to one side after the class is over. It will be necessary to explain to the student why his behaviour is anti-social. At the same time the student should be given a chance to say why he behaves in this way. The teacher can also clearly spell out the consequences if he continues to behave badly.

(f) Using the institution

When problems become extreme it will be necessary to use the institution – the school or institute – to solve them. Many institutes will then seek the help of the child's parents (where children are concerned). This seems a reasonable thing to do since it is important for parents to be involved in their children's education. They can be contacted in cases of continual lateness, truancy, forgetting to bring materials and bad behaviour.

The institution, of course, has the final power of expulsion; it is to be hoped that it is almost never used. The institution does also have the power to warn students of the consequences of their action, to change students from one class to another and to explain to students its attitude towards bad behaviour.

Teachers should not have to suffer serious problems on their own. They should consult their co-ordinators, department heads and principals when they need help.

There are, of course, other possible courses of action where indiscipline takes place; the options we have looked at avoid the possibility of either physical assault or humiliation: both are seriously wrong particularly for children and adolescents.

**10.4
Conclusions**

In this chapter we have discussed the subject of class management. We have seen that a teacher has a number of different roles and that the adoption of only one of these (e.g. teacher as controller) will be detrimental to a varied and interesting class. Teachers must be aware of the different roles they can adopt and know when and how to use them.

We have discussed student groupings and shown how lockstep on its own is not sufficient. We have shown the advantages and disadvantages of pair work, group work and individual study and discussed their importance during the learning process, showing that it is during group and pair work that a lot of real learning (rather than teaching) takes place since the students can use language really to communicate with one another.

We have discussed the difficult problem of discipline and said that it involves a code of conduct designed so that learning can be efficient and effective. We have shown some reasons for indiscipline and then tried to suggest a number of ways to ensure that discipline problems never arise. We have also suggested some action that can be taken when the code of conduct is not adhered to.

Discussion

1 When do you think the teacher should act as a controller? Why?
2 Can you think of any other roles the teacher might adopt in the classroom?
3 How much time do you think should be devoted to lockstep, pair work, group work and individual study?
4 Why do you think group work is important?
5 Can you think of any other reasons why discipline problems might occur other than those quoted in 10.3.1?
6 Do you agree with the various courses of action in 10.3.3? What other action would you be prepared to take in cases of indiscipline?

Exercises

1 Take any two activities from Chapters 6, 7, 8 and 9 of this book and say what roles the teacher will be adopting for each activity and why.
2 Look at the textbook you are using (or one you are familiar with) and identify those activities which are intended for pair and/or group work.
3 Take any activity from your textbook (or one you are familiar with) which is concerned with practice output or communicative output and say how you would organise the activity.
4 Take a reading and/or listening exercise from your textbook (or one you are familiar with) and say what you will do for the lead-in stage. What instructions will you give?
5 What items would you include in a 'code of conduct' for a class of thirteen-year-olds? Make a list and then decide how you would present the code to the class.

References

1 For a provocative view of the traditional role of the teacher see A McLean (1980). Others showing concern about the over-emphasis on the teacher as controller are S Salimbene (1981) and A Gerwitz (1979) who argue for more student-based learning.
2 L McLean (1978) helpfully shows the relationship between some different student groupings and different teacher roles.
3 The teacher's role in lockstep can change. W Plumb (1978) shows examples of this.
4 On group work see M Long (1977), D Byrne (1976) pages 80–82, and S Statman (1980).
5 M Long (1977) suggests that it is not necessarily important to have groups of equal size if the sociogram (or similar device) suggests unequal groups.
6 A number of ideas here result from collaboration with Jean Pender and other colleagues at the Instituto Anglo-Mexicano in Guadalajara.
7 P Mugglestone (1975) gives some examples of active listening in this way. Jean Pender has given talks stressing the need for 'Spare activities' at the 1980 Mextesol and 1981 TESOL conventions.

11 Planning

In previous chapters we
have come to
conclusions about a
general methodological
approach (see Chapter 4)
and we have looked at a
number of ideas for
various learning and
teaching stages (see
Chapters 5 to 9). We

have discussed the need for the teacher to adopt different roles and for
different student groupings (see Chapter 10). We are now in a position
to consider how we can include such ideas in our own classes in less
than a purely random way.

The best techniques and activities will not have much point if they
are not, in some way, integrated into a programme of studies and few
teachers would take an activity or piece of material into class without
first having a reason for doing so. The best teachers are those who think
carefully about what they are going to do in their classes and who plan
how they are going to organise the teaching and learning.

In this chapter we will consider such issues and come to some
conclusions about the guiding principles behind lesson planning. We
are concerned about how to plan a class (whether it is of forty-five, fifty,
sixty or seventy-five minutes' duration) taking into consideration what
the students have recently been doing and what we hope they will do in
the future. We will not consider an overall plan of study (for a term
or a year), since decisions about the syllabus and general course
content are often taken not by the individual teacher but by a school
authority: we will confine ourselves to the teacher's role in planning
(although in 11.1 we will make some comments about how such
courses are generally described).

We will look at *planning, textbooks and the syllabus, planning
principles, what the teacher should know, the pre-plan* and *the plan.*

11.1 Planning, textbooks and the syllabus

All too often overall decisions about course content are not taken by
teachers, but by some higher authority. Of course it will be necessary for a
large institution to know that the same kind of teaching is taking place in all
of its classes at the same level, but previous decisions about the exact syllabus
and the textbook to be used can often tie the teacher to a style of teaching
and to the content of the classes if he is not careful.

Many institutions present the syllabus in terms of the main textbook to be used: by a certain date teachers are expected to have covered a certain number of units in the book. At the same time teachers are often provided with a list of supplementary material and activities that are available. Whether or not the course is tied to a particular textbook, its syllabus will generally have a list of language items at its core (see 3.1): the assumption being made is that these language items will be new for the students and should therefore be introduced to them in the order of the syllabus.

Where a textbook is involved there are obvious advantages for both teacher and students. Good textbooks often contain lively and interesting material; they provide a sensible progression of language items, clearly showing what has to be learnt and in some cases[1] summarising what has been studied so that students can revise grammatical and functional points that they have been concentrating on. Textbooks can be systematic about the amount of vocabulary presented to the student and allow the student to study on his own outside the class. Good textbooks also relieve the teacher from the pressure of having to think of original material for every class. Indeed there is a greater variety of published material for teaching and learning English than ever before.

But textbooks can also have an adverse effect on teaching for a number of reasons. As we have already said they tend to concentrate on the introduction of new language and controlled work: a teacher relying too heavily on the textbook will often not be encouraged to provide enough roughly-tuned input or output practice (see Chapter 4). Textbooks also tend to follow the same format from one unit to the next. There are good reasons, perhaps, why this should be the case: they are thus easier to 'get to know' and to handle, both for teacher and student, and they are also easier to design and write. But this similarity of format generally involves a rigid sequence. Almost all textbooks at the elementary level start by introducing new language, for example, and they then follow a sequence of practice combining the new language with language the students already know. Reading and listening generally have a set place in the sequence and each unit looks more or less like those that come before and after it.

The discerning teacher with time to spare can move around the material selecting what he wants to use and discarding parts of the units that seem to him to be inappropriate. Most teachers, though, are under considerable pressure both because they are obliged to complete the syllabus and because they teach a number of classes. They are also influenced by the attitude of the institution, their colleagues and the students who sometimes see the textbook not just as the provider of a syllabus but also as a programme of study and activities that has to be closely followed.

There are two major reasons why such an attitude may not be in the best interests of either students or teachers. In the first place a teacher who over-uses a textbook and thus repeatedly follows the sequence in each unit may become boring over a period of time for he will find himself teaching the same type of activities in the same order again and again. In such a situation, even with good textbooks, students may find the study of English becoming routine and thus less and less motivating. Classes will start appearing increasingly similar and the routine will become increasingly monotonous. One of the cornerstones of good planning is the use of variety in teaching precisely to offset this tendency (see 11.2).

The other major reason for worrying about textbooks is that they are not written for your class. Each class is potentially different from any other (see 11.3.3) and while most published books are written with a 'general' student audience in mind your class is unique. It may not comply to the general pattern and the students need to be treated individually.

The balanced activities approach (see 4.3) is especially concerned with the lack of variety in textbooks for two reasons. In the first place textbooks rarely provide a balanced selection of activities, and as we have seen, concentrate on language presentation and controlled practice. The lack of roughly-tuned input and communication output means that the teacher will have to look outside the book if he is to provide the balance that is so necessary. The need for balance is a methodological consideration (see 4.3) since it is through this balance that students are exposed to a variety of learning experiences that will help them to acquire and learn English.

The need for balance is also a motivational consideration since, as we have said, a teacher who follows a programme of similar activities day after day will bore the students. In 11.2 we will study the need for variety in lesson planning in some detail. The balanced activities approach realises the need for balance, in terms of the different activities with which the students are faced, in order to provide them with an interesting and varied programme of study. And the best person to achieve the correct balance is the teacher who knows his students and can gauge the need for variety and what the balance should be. This is particularly true in the planning of activities during the pre-plan stage (see 11.4(a)).

It is not being suggested that textbooks are somehow destructive: the better ones are written by teachers and writers with considerable knowledge and skill and have much to recommend them. But the textbook rarely has the balance that a teacher would want for his class. The textbook, in other words, is an aid (probably the most important one there is) and not a bible. The teacher will have to work out the best way to use the textbook: he should never let the textbook use him, or dictate the decisions he takes about the activities in which the students are going to be involved. The contents of the pre-plan (see 11.4) will show how other considerations (apart from just textbook and syllabus) are incorporated into the planning process.

11.2 Planning principles

The two overriding principles behind good lesson planning are variety and flexibility. Variety means involving students in a number of different types of activity and where possible introducing them to a wide selection of materials. Variety means planning so that learning is, for the students, always interesting and never monotonous. Flexibility means the ability to use any number of different techniques and not be a slave to one methodology. Flexibility is also important when dealing with the plan in the classroom; for any number of reasons what the teacher has planned may not be appropriate for that class on that particular day. The flexible teacher will be able to change the plan in such a situation. Flexibility is the characteristic we would expect from the genuinely adaptable teacher (see 4.3).

We have already commented on the danger of routine and monotony and how students may become de-motivated if they are always faced with the same type of class. This danger can only be avoided if the teacher believes that the learning experience should be permanently stimulating and interesting. This of course is difficult to achieve, but at least if the activities the students are faced with are varied there will be the interest of doing different things. If new language is always introduced in the same way (e.g. if it is always introduced in a dialogue) then the introduction stages of the class will become gradually less and less challenging. If all reading activities always concentrate on extracting specific information and never ask the students to do anything else, reading will become less interesting. The same is true of any activity that is constantly repeated. Our aim must be to provide a variety of different learning activities which will help individual students to get to grips with the language. And this means giving the students a purpose and telling them what the purpose is. Students need to know why they are doing something and what it is supposed they will achieve. We have stressed the need for a purpose particularly with communicative activities (see 5.3) and receptive skills (see 9.1.2): but the teacher must have a purpose for all the activities he organises in a class and he should communicate that purpose to his students.

In any one class there will be a number of different personalities with different ways of looking at the world. The activity that is particularly appropriate for one student may not be ideal for another. But the teacher who varies his teaching approach may be able to satisfy most of his students at different times.

Variety is a principle that applies especially to a series of classes. Over a two-week period, for example, we will try and do different things in the classes. Variety also applies to a lesser extent to a single class period (see 11.4). Although there are some activities that can last for fifty minutes it seems generally true that changes of activity during that time are advisable. An introduction of new language that lasted for fifty minutes would probably be counter-productive, and it is noticeable how an over-long accurate reproduction stage tires students and fails to be very effective. We would not expect, either, to ask the students to engage in reading comprehension for a whole class. We might, however, be able to base a whole class on one reading passage, but only if we varied the activities that we could use with it. Thus we might get students to read to extract specific information; this could be followed by some discussion, some intensive work and some kind of written or oral follow-up. Children, especially, need to do different things in fairly quick succession since they will generally not be able to concentrate on one activity for a long stretch of time.

The teacher who believes in variety will have to be flexible since the only way to provide variety is to use a number of different techniques: not all of these will fit into one methodology. Teachers should be immediately suspicious of anyone who says they have the answer to language teaching for this will imply a lack of flexibility.

Good lesson planning is the art of mixing techniques, activities and materials in such a way that an ideal balance is created for the class. In a general language course there will be work on the four skills (although a teacher will probably come to a decision about the relative merits of each skill): there will be presentation and controlled practice, roughly-tuned input (receptive skill work) and communicative activities. Different student groupings will be used.

If the teacher has a large variety of techniques and activities that he can use with his students he can then apply himself to the central question of lesson planning: '*What is it my students will feel, know or be able to do at the end of the class (or classes) that they did not feel or know or were not able to do at the beginning of the class (or classes)?*'. We can say, for example, that they will feel more positive about learning English at the end of the class than they did at the beginning as a result of activities that were enjoyable; we can say that they will know some new language that they did not know before; we can say that they will be able to write, for example, a type of letter that they were not able to write before.

In answering the central question the teacher will create the objectives for the class. He may involve the students in a game-like activity because his objective is to relax the students and make them feel more positive about their English classes. He may give them a reading passage to work on because his objective is to improve their ability to extract specific information from written texts. He may introduce new language because his objective is that the students should know how to refer to the past, for example.

We will return to these issues in 11.4 and 11.5 but first we will look at what the teacher should know before he starts planning.

11.3
What the teacher should know

Before the teacher can start to consider planning his classes he needs to know a considerable amount about three main areas: they are *the profession, the institution*, and *the students*.

11.3.1
The profession

Clearly a well-prepared teacher needs to know a lot about his job before he can start to make successful plans. There are six major areas of necessary knowledge.

(a) The language for the level

Clearly the teacher must know the language that he is to teach his students. By 'know' we mean that the teacher must be able to use the language himself and also have an insight into the rules that govern its form and its use. This is obviously the result not only of the teacher's own knowledge of English but also of preparation and study where facts about language can be absorbed.

(b) The skills for the level

The teacher himself needs to 'know' the skills he is going to ask his students to perform. It is no good asking them to write a report if the teacher cannot do it himself.

(c) The aids available for the level

The teacher has to know what aids are available and appropriate for the level he is teaching. These may include wall pictures, flashcards, tapes and tape recorders, overhead projectors, sets of books and material and, of course, the blackboard.

(d) Stages and techniques in teaching

The teacher needs to know and recognise different teaching techniques and stages. He needs to know the difference between accurate reproduction and communicative activities so that he does not, for example, act as a controller in both cases. He also needs to be able to recognise stages in the textbook he is using so that he realises when an activity is controlled rather then free and vice versa. In particular, then, he must have a working knowledge of the issues we discussed in Chapter 5 and the principles behind the teaching of receptive skills.

(e) A repertoire of activities

The well-prepared teacher has a large repertoire of activities for his classes. He can organise presentation and controlled output practice; he can direct students in the acquiring of receptive skills and organise genuinely communicative activities. This repertoire of activities enables him to have varied plans and achieve an activities balance.

(f) Classroom management skills

The well-prepared teacher will have good classroom management skills (see Chapter 10). He will be able to adopt a number of different roles, will be able to use different student groupings, and will be able to maintain discipline.

These areas are all vitally important for a teacher and they all imply a lot of work particularly where a level is being taught for the first time. Without these areas of knowledge a teacher is in a poor position to make decisions about lesson planning.

11.3.2
The institution

The teacher needs to know a lot about the institution in so far as it is involved with his teaching. The following five areas of knowledge are crucial.

(a) Time, length, frequency

It sounds silly to emphasise that the teacher should know at what time, for how long and how often classes take place. Nevertheless this is clearly important since it will affect all planning.

(b) Physical conditions

The teacher needs to know what physical conditions exist in the place(s) that he is going to teach. It is no good taking in an electrically powered tape recorder if there is no socket for a plug in the classroom! When planning it will be important to bear that kind of detail in mind as well as more major considerations like the condition of the chairs and blackboard, the brightness of the lighting, the size of the room, etc.

(c) Syllabus

It is clearly important to be familiar with the syllabus the institution has for the levels that are being taught. The teacher will have to be sure in general terms that he can cover the majority of the syllabus where possible. It is impossible to plan within an institution without such knowledge.

(d) Exams

It is also extremely important to know what type of exams (if any) the students will have to take and when, since clearly a major responsibility of the teacher will be to try and ensure that the students are successful in tests and exams.

(e) Restrictions

The teacher should be aware of any restrictions imposed by the institution upon his teaching: apart from the obvious restrictions of physical size and shape of the classroom, there are also the limitations of class size, availability of aids and physical conditions (see (b) above).

Clearly a knowledge of all these things is vital if the teacher is to make plans that are realistic in the circumstances.

11.3.3
The students

The teacher needs to know a considerable amount about his students. We have already made the point that each class is unique (see 11.1.) and as a result, each class will need to be treated differently. Nowhere is this more true than in planning, where the teacher selects the activities that will be suitable for the students. In order to do so he obviously needs to know a lot about them.

The teacher needs to know *who the students are, what the students bring to the class* and *what the students need*.

(a) Who the students are

It is obviously necessary for the teacher to know about the following things:

Age: How old are the students? Are they children? Adolescents? In each case they will need to be treated differently (see 1.3) from each other and from an adult class. Are they all more or less the same age?

Sex: Are they all girls/women? Is there a mixture of the sexes? Are they all men? In an ideal world the sex of the students should make no difference to the activities and content of the lesson. In practice, however, there are still countries where a teacher may well feel that what is suitable for one sex is not suitable for the other.

Social background: It is important to know if your students are rich or poor; whether or not they are used to luxury or are oppressed by it. What kind of behaviour is usual in the social class to which they belong? In a classless society where wealth were adequately shared this might not be so important. Such societies do not exist, however! Especially where a small minority of the students come from a different social background to the rest of the class it will be vital to take this fact into account when planning the content of your class.

Occupation: Clearly the occupation of your students will help you to make decisions about your planning. Where a teacher is fortunate enough to have thirty students who all have the same occupation (see 1.1(b)) his task will be considerably easier since he can make assumptions about what things the students know and what activities they are used to. Certainly this is the case with secondary school classes, etc., but with adults there is usually a variety of different occupations represented by the students.

Of these four items the most difficult to ascertain will be the students' social background. The teacher might well prepare a confidential questionnaire at the beginning of the term/semester to help him get an idea of such information.

(b) What the students bring to the class

The teacher needs to know how the students feel about learning English and what they 'know'. Again there are four major areas for him to investigate:

Motivation and attitude: How do the students feel about learning English? Are they generally positive about coming to class? Do they feel friendly or hostile towards the culture that English represents for them? What is their attitude to teachers and to their English teacher in particular? Clearly special efforts will have to be made with hostile students having negative attitudes and the teacher might well place a greater emphasis on motivating the students than on anything else, at least for a time.

Educational background: Closely tied to motivation and attitude is the educational background of the students. Clearly the content of the class will be different if the students are postgraduates than if they have never got beyond primary education. At the same time the educational experiences of the students are important. Some students who have been previously unsuccessful may need more encouragement than usual. Again the teacher may think it a good idea to issue a questionnaire – or at least talk to the students informally – at the beginning of the term/semester.

Knowledge: The teacher will want to know about various aspects of the students' knowledge. For example he will obviously want to know how much English the student knows. At the same time, though, he will want to know how well the student performs in his own language: can he write academic papers, does he write informal letters fluently?, etc.

Another important major area of knowledge concerns the world in general. How much do students know about current affairs? Are there parts of the world about which they appear to be largely ignorant? Are there large areas of knowledge they do not have? It is vital to know this since much planning will be unsuccessful if the teacher assumes knowledge of current events, etc. which the students do not have. It might be worth adding here that teachers are often scathing about their students' apparent ignorance; if this is the case they should try and work out what world knowledge *they* are unfamiliar with. It is a salutory experience.

Interests: The teacher will want to know what the students' interests are (and he will be lucky if he can find a majority interest in various subjects). Often he will take planning decisions on the basis of student interest rather than anything else (see 11.4): it should not be forgotten that interest is a primary ingredient of motivation.

c) What the students need

We have said that different types of student will need to be treated differently (see 1.3): we also saw that people learn languages for a variety of different reasons (see 1.1). Particularly in the light of why our students are studying language we must analyse what their needs are.

If we are teaching a group of medical students who are unlikely to have to use oral English in their professional lives, but who need to be able to read medical textbooks in English, we might at once identify the ability to read scientific texts (medical, in this case) as the students' need and therefore design a course consisting exclusively of exercises and texts designed only to give students this ability. If our students, on the other hand, are training to be travel guides we might identify their biggest need as being the ability to give quick oral descriptions and answer factual questions in English (as well as the ability to 'organise' people and give directions, etc. in English). The point being made is that where possible teachers or co-ordinators should find out exactly what it is their students really need English for[2] and use this knowledge to make decisions about course design. What skills should have greater emphasis? Is there a need for communicative oral activities or should the emphasis be on writing? The analysis of student needs helps to answer these questions and provide a sound basis for course decisions.

The fact that a student need has been identified, however, does not necessarily mean that all decisions about course design and planning can be taken immediately. Two more considerations are important; student wants and methodological principles.

The fact that the medical students' need is to be able to read medical texts in English does not necessarily mean, however, that all they want to do for all and every English class is read medical texts. They might want to learn some oral English, be able to write informal letters, etc. The travel guide's needs may be largely oral but the students might also want to be able to read English novels, etc. In other words, needs and wants are not necessarily the same and the job of the course designer and lesson planner is to try and reach a compromise between the two. Thus the main theme running through our course for medical students might be the reading and understanding of medical texts. But this might be integrated with oral work about the texts, or might even run side by side with work on oral social English. What is being suggested is that we will have to pay attention to what the students want even where it seems to conflict with student needs.

Even where wants and needs are compatible and well-established, however, there may be good reasons for using material which is not especially directed towards those needs. We have already stressed the concepts of variety and flexibility in lesson planning and they are no less important with specialist classes than for the 'general' class. Even where students are studying English for a specific purpose (ESP, see 1.1(b)) the teacher will want to include a variety of motivating activities. The initial enthusiasm of students who are studying ESP can easily be destroyed unless the teacher remembers general planning principles.

The majority of students, however, will be studying English for a reason that makes their needs difficult to identify (see 3.1.1). In such cases we will teach the four skills, making our decisions about how much weight to give each skill (and the language to be used) as best we can.

A detailed knowledge of the students, then, is essential when planning what activities to use and what subject matter to teach. It is important for the students to be interested in the subject, but it is also important that they should be able to cope with its level of difficulty (not just of the language, but also the content): where there are clearly definable student needs it is important for the students to see that the teacher has taken account of these needs and is organising classes accordingly – although bearing in mind our comments about needs and wants and the importance of general planning principles.

A detailed knowledge of the students, who they are, what they bring to class and what their needs are will give the teacher a good idea of how to provide a programme of balanced activities that will be most motivating and most beneficial for those students.

11.4
The pre-plan

The teacher who is knowledgeable about the institution, his profession and the students, is ready to start making a plan. Before he actually writes down the detailed contents of such a plan he will need to think generally about what he is going to do. This is where the pre-plan is formed.

The idea of the pre-plan is for the teacher to get a general idea of what he is going to do in the next class or classes. Based on his knowledge of the students and the syllabus he will consider four major areas here: *activities, language skills, language type* and *subject and content*. When he has, as a result of considering these areas, got ideas of what he wants to do he will decide whether such ideas are feasible given the institution and its restrictions. When this has been done he possesses his pre-plan, and he can then move to the final stage, the plan. We can summarise this in Figure 9:

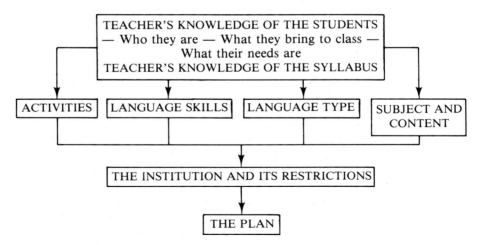

Figure 9 The pre-plan

We will now consider the four major elements of the pre-plan:

(a) Activities[3]
'Activities' is a loose term used to give a general description of what will happen in a class. It is important to realise that here we are not talking in any

way about items of language; we are talking about what, generally and physically, the students are going to do.

A game is an activity; so is a simulation. The introduction of new language is an activity; so is parallel writing or story reconstruction. Listening is an activity and so is an information gap task; social talk is an activity, so is an oral composition.

An activity is what the teacher thinks of when he is asked, 'What are you going to do in class today?'. Rather than give details the teacher will often say, 'Oh, I've got a nice group-writing task and then we're going to do a song.'

When teachers think of what to do in their classes it is vital to consider the students and what they have been doing recently. If, for example, they have been doing largely controlled work (e.g. presentation and controlled practice) then the teacher may well take a preliminary decision to plan a freer activity. Only subsequently will he decide what skill or skills this might involve. If the work has been very tiring, challenging, and over-serious the teacher may make an immediate decision to include an activity whose main purpose is to give the students an enjoyable time. If, on the other hand, the last two classes have largely consisted of communicative activities the teacher may decide to include language input or controlled work.

Teachers should make decisions about activities independently of what language or language skills they have to teach. Their first planning thought should centre round what kind of class would be appropriate for the particular group of students on a particular day. It is in this consideration of activities as a starting point for lesson planning that the teacher can ensure a motivating balance of the type we have discussed (see 4.3 and 11.1).

It will also be necessary to consider activities not only on the basis of what the students have been doing recently but also in terms of the class period itself. In other words we must consider what activities to include in a period of, say, sixty minutes, and how to balance the different activities within that period of time. We have already said (see 11.2) that a lengthy session of accurate reproduction would probably be de-motivating and unsuccessful. Where presentation is included in a class we will want to make sure that students are not only involved in a lockstep accurate reproduction stage, but are also involved in other motivating activities. In general our aim will be to provide a sequence that is varied and does not follow one activity with a completely similar activity and then follow that with one that is the same.

The decision about what activities are to be included in a plan is a vital first stage in the planning process. The teacher is forced to consider, above all, what would be most beneficial and motivating for the students.

(b) Language skills

The teacher will have to decide what language skills to include in the class. Sometimes, of course, this decision will already have been taken when the activity has been selected (e.g. listening). In the case of more general activities, though (e.g. communicative activity, roughly-tuned input, etc.) the teacher will then decide whether he wishes to concentrate on one skill or a combination of skills. Even where the choice of activity has determined the skill to be studied (e.g. listening) it will still be necessary to decide what sub-skills the class are going to practise. In Chapter 9 we looked at a number of different ways of listening: when planning the teacher will select which of these types of listening is most appropriate.

The choice of language skills to be practised and studied will be taken in accordance with the syllabus. The latter will often say what skills and sub-skills should be taught during the term or year and it will be the teacher's job to cover these over a period of time. The teacher will also make his choice on the basis of his students' needs. He will also bear in mind what the students have been doing recently, just as he does when thinking of activities.

(c) Language type

The teacher will have to decide what language is to be focused on during the class. There is, of course, a great range of possibilities here. The teacher may decide that he wants the language to be used to be 'general and unpredictable'. This would be the case if he were going to organise a 'reaching a consensus' activity or perhaps a simulation (see 8.1.1 and 8.1.7). He might decide, however, that he wanted to focus on *yes/no* questions using '*was*' and '*were*'. These are the two extremes (completely free language and completely controlled). The teacher may choose to concentrate on a language area: he might want his students to 'talk about the past' using a variety of past tenses or in general to concentrate on 'inviting'. Much will depend on the language in the syllabus.

The choice of language type is a necessary decision: all too often it is the first decision that teachers make and thus classes take on the monotonous controlled aspect that we discussed in 11.2. Here it is only one of four major areas the teacher has to think of when drawing up the pre-plan.

(d) Subject and content

We have considered what kind of activity would be suitable for our students and we have decided on language skills and type. The last and in some ways most important decision still has to be made. What kind of content will our class have? We may have decided that a simulation activity is appropriate but if the subject of that simulation does not interest the students in any way the choice of activity is wasted. Although we have said it is the teacher's job to interest students in, for example, a reading passage it will surely be more motivating to give the students a reading passage that they would find interesting with or without the teacher (but see 9.2.2).

The teacher who knows who his students are and what they bring to class will be in a much better position to choose subject and content than a teacher who does not. And this knowledge is vital since one of language's main functions is to communicate interest and ideas.

These four areas, then, form the basis of the pre-plan. It should be noticed that two of them are not in any way concerned with decisions about language, but are based on what will interest and motivate the students. This reflects everything we have said about language use since language is a tool for doing things, not just an abstract system.

A teacher who concentrates on activities and subject and content will benefit the students far more than the teacher who only concentrates on language skills and type.

When the teacher has a general idea of what he is going to do in his class as a result of considering the four areas in the pre-plan he will then consider the institution and the restrictions it imposes. If he has decided that he wants to take a song into class he must make sure that this is possible: is a tape of the song available and are the tape recorders in good working order? Is the activity he would like to take into class suitable for the number of students he has to teach? How should he organise the activity for that number of students? Will he be able to do all the things he wants to in the time available, and if he can how should he order the class? What should come first?

The experienced teacher considers all these details without, perhaps, consciously realising he is doing so. The new teacher, or the teacher starting a job in a new school or institute will have to bear all these points in mind.

The teacher now has a clear idea of what he is going to do in his class: he is ready to make a detailed plan.

11.5
The plan

The plan we are going to consider is extremely detailed and it should be understood that most experienced teachers do not write down what they are going to do in such a complicated way. The detail in our plan and in the specimen plan in 11.5.1 is felt to be necessary, however, for two reasons. Firstly, the inexperienced teacher needs a clear framework of reference for the task of planning, and secondly the form of the plan forces the teacher to consider aspects of planning that are considered desirable.

There is one particular situation in which a detailed plan is beneficial and that is when a teacher is to be observed: by providing a plan such a teacher clearly shows why he is doing things in the classroom, and where an activity is not totally successful, the observer can see how it would have gone if it had been performed or organised more efficiently.

The plan has five major components: *description of the class, recent work, objectives, contents* and *additional possibilities*. When we have discussed these we will look at a specimen plan.

(a) Description of the class

The teacher may well carry this part of the plan in his head: the more familiar he becomes with the group the more he will know about them.

The description of the class embraces a description of the students, a statement of time, frequency and duration of the class, and comments about physical conditions and/or restrictions. We will see how this works in the specimen plan on page 232.

(b) Recent work

The teacher needs to have in his head – or on paper – details of recent work the students have done. This includes the activities they have been involved in, the subject and content of their lessons and the language skills and type that they have studied. Only if all this is known (or remembered) can the teacher make reasonable planning decisions about future classes (see especially 11.4(a)).

(c) Objectives

The teacher will write down what his objectives are for the class. He will usually have more than one since there will be a number of stages in the class and each one will be there to achieve some kind of objective.

Objectives are the aims that the teacher has for the students and are written in terms of what the students will do or achieve. They are written in general terms (e.g. 'The objective is to relax the students'), in terms of skills (e.g. 'to give students practice in extracting specific information from a text') and in terms of language (e.g. 'to give students practice in the use of the past simple tense using regular and irregular verbs, questions and answers'). The written objectives will be more or less specific depending on how specific the teacher's aims are.

The objectives, then, are the aims the teacher has for the students. They may refer to activities, skills, language type or a combination of all of these.

(d) Contents

By far the most detailed part of the plan is the section in which the contents are written down. Here the teacher spells out exactly what he is going to do in the class. The 'Contents' section has five headings:

Context: Here the teacher writes down what context he will be using for the activity. Context means 'what the situation is: what the subject of the learning is'. The context for introducing new language might be a flight timetable; the context for an oral composition might be a story about a man going to the zoo. The context for a simulation might be 'The travel agency'.

Activity and class organisation: Here the teacher indicates what the activity will be (see 11.4(a)) and says whether the class will be working in lockstep, pairs, groups or teams, etc.

Aids: The teacher indicates whether he will be using the blackboard or a wall picture, the tape recorder or the textbook, etc.

Language: Here the teacher describes the language that will be used. If new language is to be introduced he will list some or all of the models. If the activity is an oral communicative activity he might only write 'unpredictable'. Otherwise he may write 'advice language', for example, and give some indication of what kind of language items he expects.

Possible problems: Many activities can be expected to be problematic in some way. The teacher can often anticipate, for example, that the new language for a presentation stage may cause problems because of its form. The introduction of the past simple may cause problems because of the different verb endings: question forms are often difficult because of word order, etc. The teacher should be aware of these possible problems and have considered ways of solving them. Certain activities have complicated organisation. Again the teacher should be aware of this and know how to overcome it.

(e) Additional possibilities

Here the teacher writes down other activities he could use if it becomes necessary (e.g. if he gets through the plan quicker than he thought or if one of his activities has to be stopped because it is not working well).

All these details, then, form the major part of the plan.

We can now look at an example of the kind of plan we have been discussing.

**11.5.1
A specimen lesson plan**

We will now look at a specimen lesson plan which closely follows the model we have described. It is designed for an adult class that has been studying for about forty-two hours – the students are at the beginning of their second term.

In order to show how the plan operates most of the activities will come from earlier chapters of this book. The reader will have to imagine, therefore, that such material is readily available.

The reading material (which also occurs in Chapter 9) comes from a textbook at this level[4] which it is assumed the students are using as the class text. The recent work is based on the syllabus of this textbook.

Where page numbers, etc. are given the reader should refer back to earlier chapters in this book.

Specimen plan

A – Description of class

Students between the ages of 16–25.
21 women, 9 men (6 secretaries, 5 housewives, 10 university students, 3 teachers, 1 doctor, 1 businessman, 4 secondary students).

The class takes place from 7.45–9.00 p.m. on Mondays and Wednesdays. The students are generally enthusiastic, but often tired: concentration sometimes suffers as a result. Students have completed approximately 42 hours of English.

B – Recent work

Introduction of 'there is/ there are' with maps, etc. Localisation used in pairs and lockstep (see 7.1.4). Students write short paragraphs describing places.
Invitation language ('would you like to ____') in dialogues and freer practice.
Invitation letters written (see 8.2.2(a)).
Introduction/practice of present simple + frequency adverbs.
Controlled practice of this + sentence writing.
Controlled practice sessions mixing present continuous/simple.
Noughts and crosses game using frequency adverbs as cues.
A listening exercise in which students follow directions (see 9.5.3(c)).

C – Objectives (*For details see* 'Contents' *below*).

1 To involve students in conversation. To practise using verbs of liking and to introduce ways of agreeing and disagreeing.
2 To give students practice in reading to extract specific information (scanning).
3 To give students realistic writing practice. To encourage the use of present simple/continuous tenses.
4 To introduce students to ways of giving directions.
5 To relax students and give them a chance for genuine oral communication using all and any language at their disposal.

D – Contents

Objective 1: (Estimated time: 15 minutes)

(a) *Context*: Topics for discussion. Students and teacher choose. Hopefully to do with holidays and/or cruises.

(b) *Activity and class organisation*: Students write down sentences expressing likes and dislikes about the topic. The teacher introduces a way of agreeing and a way of disagreeing. *S1* reads his original sentences and *S2* agrees/disagrees and follows this with his sentences.

The activity starts in lockstep: students then work in small groups. For a full description of this activity see 7.1.5(b)).

(c) *Aids*: None except blackboard for written explanation of language. Students need paper and a pen.

(d) *Language*: 'I like/don't like (the topic) because + sentence.'

'I agree, and + additional remark.'

'I'm afraid I don't agree. (I think) + opinion.'

+ unpredictable language.

(e) *Possible problems*: Students have difficulty with (especially) disagreement language. Students make a number of errors in the sentences they write. The teacher will not correct these mistakes (unless serious) and will then use gentle correction. Error/mistakes with the agreement/disagreement language will be corrected, however, at the beginning of the session.

Objective 2: (Estimated time: 10 minutes)

(a) *Context*: Text about the QE2.

(b) *Activity and class organisation*: Students read text individually to answer eight yes/no questions. Students check each others' answers in pairs. The teacher then conducts feedback. For a full description of this activity and Objective 3, including a copy of the text, see 9.4.2(a)).

(c) *Aids*: The reading passage in the textbook.

(d) *Language*: The language of the text.

(e) *Possible problems*: Students may not use the right reading skill (e.g. scanning). The teacher will make his instructions especially clear in this respect.

Objective 3: (Estimated time: 15 minutes)

(a) *Context*: Students are passengers on the QE2 writing postcards to their friends/families.

(b) *Activity and class organisation*: The teacher explains that students are going to write postcards as if they were passengers on the QE2. The teacher elicits language that students might use (e.g. what the passengers do every day/what they are doing now/what there is on the ship, etc.). The students write postcards in pairs. Two pairs then make a group of four to compare and correct postcards. Some postcards are then read to the class. The teacher collects postcards to look at them later.

(c) *Aids*: Students should have pencil and paper.

(d) *Language*: General and fairly unpredictable, although some emphasis on present simple/continuous and 'there is/are'.

(e) *Possible problems*: Students may not have vocabulary/language, etc. that they think they need. The teacher will act as a resource (see page 204) in this case.

Objective 4: (Estimated time: 25 minutes)

(a) *Context*: A stranger in a town who doesn't know his way.

(b) *Activity and class organisation*: The teacher introduces students to a dialogue in lockstep. Students then practise in pairs. They then make up their own dialogues using the wallchart of a town.

(c) *Aids*: Blackboard for initial drawing and wallchart of (e.g. Salisbury) (see page 79).

(d) *Language*: The original dialogue is:

A: Excuse me!
B: Yes?
A: How can I get to the bus station, please?
B: Go down this street. Take the second left and it's on your right.
A: Thank you very much.
B: Don't mention it!

(e) *Possible problems*: Length of dialogue (particularly directions). The students' ability to orientate themselves on the wallchart map. The teacher will conduct a certain amount of accurate reproduction work to solve the first problem and elicit a number of examples to solve the second.

Objective 5: (Estimated time: 10 minutes)

(a) *Context*: Photographs of surrealist paintings.

(b) *Activity and classroom organisation*: Students work in pairs. One student has a picture that the other student has to duplicate without looking at the original. (For a full description of the describe and draw game see 8.1.3(a)).

(c) *Aids*: Flashcards. Students need pencil and paper.

(d) *Language*: In general the language of description, but largely unpredictable.

(e) *Possible problems*: Noise and the use of the students' native language. The teacher will ask the students to communicate fairly quietly, and will stress the importance of English use in this activity.

E – Additional possibilities

1 Students give an oral or written description of their favourite work of art.
2 An 'ask the right question' game (see 7.1.3(a)).
3 Text about hovercraft to compare with the QE2.

A number of points can be made about this lesson plan. In the first place decisions were taken based on what students had been doing recently (recent work). It appears that students had not been doing much reading and that a lot of their oral work had been either in lockstep or was at best controlled practice output. There had not been many opportunities for students to express themselves, and the listening had been done as input to prepare the way for teaching students how to ask for and give directions.

The record of recent work immediately led to a number of decisions in the pre-plan. In the first place there was a need for some reading practice. Secondly it was clearly time to involve students in some kind of communicative oral activity, and it would not be a bad idea to give them an enjoyable way of communicating in this area. There was also a need for students to be involved in expressing themselves, and finally the listening input could be taken up to form the basis for some language presentation.

These, then, were the considerations that affected the pre-plan. The first activity in the plan aims to answer the need for self-expression while at the same time giving students a simple way of agreeing and disagreeing. It also serves as a general lead-in to the topic of the reading text.

The reading passage comes from the textbook the students are using and the follow-up task serves the dual purpose not only of giving the students a realistic task within their reach but also of recycling language that they have recently been studying.

The dialogue activity picks up language used in the listening activity of a previous class and teaches useful language that the students would obviously need if they ever went to an English-speaking country.

The 'describe and draw' activity has the dual advantage of giving students genuinely communicative language use while at the same time being enjoyable and motivating. Its position at the end of the class is intentional since by that stage students may well feel the need for a more enjoyable activity which will end the class on a high note.

11.6 Conclusions

In this chapter we have considered how to approach the planning of language classes. We have shown how an over-reliance on the textbook and the syllabus may well cause the teacher to de-motivate his students and anyway may not teach them in the most efficient way. We have stressed the need to think of the activities that would be suitable for our classes pointing out the need for variety, flexibility and balance.

We have discussed what the teacher should know before making a plan. This includes knowledge of the profession including ideas for different activities and a knowledge of useful techniques. Teachers should also know everything that is necessary about the institution. Most importantly though the teacher should know who and what his students are, and what needs they have.

We looked at a pre-plan in which teachers make general decisions about what they are going to teach: these decisions are made on the basis of activities, language skills, language type and subject and content. We emphasised the fact that language type (e.g. the traditional syllabus) was only one of the necessary components of the pre-plan and that equally important are activities and subject and content where the teacher makes decisions based on how the students feel and what they have been doing recently.

Finally we looked at how an actual plan could be put together, stressing that experienced teachers probably do not write plans in such great detail but that to do so forces the teacher to consider important aspects of planning (and will always be useful if the teacher is to be observed).

Discussion

1 Do you agree that variety is a cornerstone of good lesson planning? Do you think that it is possible to have too much variety?
2 Do you think that activities can last for a whole class period? Give reasons for your answer.
3 How important is it for teachers to know about their students? Are there any other things he should know apart from those mentioned in 11.3.3?

4 What do you think of the specimen plan in 11.5.1? Would it be appropriate for the kind of students you teach?

5 What difficulties can you foresee in trying to work out a balanced activities approach to planning and teaching?

Exercises

1 Look at a unit in the textbook you are using (or are familiar with). What activities are there in the unit? Do you think you would have to include extra material, etc. when teaching the unit? If so what?

2 Look at the unit in the textbook you are using (or are familiar with) and say what language skills and language type are included in the unit. Is the language for presentation or controlled practice, or is there some provision for communicative output?

3 List the recent work your class (or an imaginary class) have done and make decisions about what activities you would include in the next lesson.

4 Make a lesson plan for your class.

5 In general terms plan out the next six classes for your students.

References

1 See, for example, R Rossner et al. (1979a & b), B Abbs and I Freebairn (1977, 1979, 1980) and J Garton-Sprenger et al. (1979) although in the latter case the summarising occurs after a number of units.

2 An example of a questionnaire designed to discover student needs is R Mackay (1978). For a more detailed and controversial approach to needs analysis see J Munby (1978).

3 The importance of activities is stressed in P Mugglestone (1977).

4 The book the students are using is R Rossner et al. (1979 b).

Appendix: Evaluating materials[1]

At various stages of his professional life the teacher will be involved in the selection of material for his students. Sometimes these materials will be of a supplementary kind (e.g. to complement a coursebook) and sometimes they will be the coursebooks themselves.

There may be various reasons for looking closely at materials to see if they are appropriate for a group of students: the teacher may have seen exciting material at a teachers' meeting or convention. He may have seen enticing publicity about a new course, or he may have heard about some successful materials from a colleague. Often the desire to look for new materials stems from a dissatisfaction with what is being currently used, and the teacher or course planner may want to compare a number of different alternatives.

Whatever the reasons for considering whether or not materials are appropriate for a group of students, the decision that a teacher or course planner takes is vital. It is vital because the teacher will take at least some of his ideas from the textbook, and may even use it as the basic syllabus for a course (see 11.1). Where a number of teachers in an institution are using the same book it will have a powerful influence over what type of teaching takes place in that institution.

Before attempting to evaluate materials, however, the teacher must have come to some conclusions about his students and what their needs are. This knowledge is necessary for him to be able to judge the materials in the light of his knowledge of the students who may eventually use them. Once he has drawn up a profile of his students and their needs he can then go about evaluating materials that seem to be suitable for the students in two ways. One of these ways is to study the book and see how well it matches your students and their needs. The *materials evaluation form* (see pages 241–244) will be useful for doing this. Another is to *pilot* the course. This means that the book (or materials) is tried out on a small group of students and the results measured before a decision is taken about whether all the students will use the material. Once again, after such piloting, the materials evaluation form will be useful here.

There are two steps, then, in the evaluation of materials: the first is to have a profile of the students and their needs which leads you to conclusions about the type of material which would be appropriate for them, and the second, subsequent step, is to apply this knowledge to the completion of the materials evaluation form, which aims to measure how far the materials under consideration match up to student needs and the general methodological principles which the teacher holds.

The profile of student needs has three major components. In the first the teacher describes his students, saying who they are and what they bring to class (this is the same as the class planner, who also needs this information to take planning decisions – see 11.3.3); the second is to describe student needs in terms of when the students are likely to use English and what skills they should acquire in the language (see 11.3.3(c)). The third part of the student profile describes in general terms the type of material the teacher would like to see for his students. We can summarise the profile of students' needs in the following way:

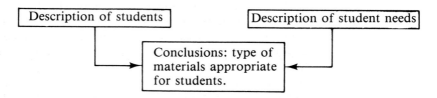

Figure 10 Profile of student needs for materials selection

The 'description of students' will answer questions in the following way:

DESCRIPTION OF STUDENTS

1 Age: _____
2 Sex: _____
3 Social/cultural background: _____
4 Occupation(s): _____
5 Motivation/attitude: _____
6 Educational background: _____
7 Knowledge (a) English level: _____
            (b) Of the world: _____
8 Interests and beliefs: _____

Based on the above, what conclusions can you draw about the kind of materials that would be suitable for your students?

_____

_____

We now have an idea of the kind of materials that would be appropriate for the students based on their personal characteristics. The second stage is to come to some kind of conclusion about what their needs are.

DESCRIPTION OF STUDENT NEEDS

1 What contexts and situations (if any) will your students probably use English in at some future date?

a _____

b _____

c _____

2 Give an order of priority for the different language skills (including sub-skills) that your students will need when using English.

a _____

b _____

c _____

d _____

e _____

3 Now say what percentage of class time should be spent on these various skills.

a _____ d _____

b _____ e _____

c _____

4 Based on the above say (a) what level the students need to reach and (b) what kind of language they need to be able to use or understand (e.g. formal/informal, spoken/written, scientific/business, etc.).

We now have a clearer idea about what our students' needs are and we can move to some conclusions about the type of material we wish to look at.

CONCLUSIONS: TYPE OF MATERIALS APPROPRIATE
FOR STUDENTS

Based on the description of students and their needs, say what type of materials you think would be most appropriate for these students.

_____

_____

_____

_____

These descriptions of students and their needs can be arrived at in a number of ways and may have more or less specific results depending on who the students are.

Finding out what the students' needs are may be done very formally (see for example R Mackay (1978)) especially where there is a clear demand for a high level ESP course. The needs analysis will take the form of questionnaires, interviews with students and their teachers and/or employers, and a study of the kind of English they will have to cope with. A more informal way of arriving at conclusions about student needs is teacher intuition together with conversations with the students concerned.

Where students have a very specific purpose for studying English the entries on the 'description of student needs' form will be precise. Where students are studying general English (particularly in a secondary school situation) the entries will clearly be less specific. Nevertheless, it will still be possible to come to informal (but informed) decisions about such things as priorities for certain skills. The fact that students are studying general English may mean that it is less easy to say that certain skills should predominate, but the mere fact of saying this will lead to decisions about the kind of materials the teacher wishes to use.

Armed with a knowledge about his students the teacher can now evaluate materials that seem to be more or less appropriate for his students' personalities and needs. The evaluation of materials, however, should be as formal and principled as possible, and that is why there is a need for the materials evaluation form.

In the materials evaluation form questions are asked which demand the answer 'yes' or 'no' and an additional comment. After completing the form the teacher is asked to say whether he recommends the course for his students: by the time he gets to this point he will have already come to a number of decisions about the materials as a result of completing the form, and should therefore be in a position to make this decision.

The materials evaluation form has seven major headings: *practical considerations, layout and design, activities, skills, language type, subject and content* and *guidance*. Under *practical considerations* the teacher is asked to say whether the price of the materials is right for the students (it should be remembered that some coursebooks are very expensive) and if the integral parts of the course (e.g. tapes, teacher's book, etc.) are available. If the answer to these first two questions is 'no' then there is no need to complete the form since the teacher will have to decide not to use the materials.

Under *layout and design* the teacher is simply asked to judge whether the materials look attractive to the students. This does not necessarily mean full-colour photographs: for science students the design should be suitably scientific-looking in a clear and interesting way.

The next four headings refer to the concerns of course and lesson planning that we mentioned in 11.4. It is under these headings that we look at the content and methodology of the materials under consideration. The first concern is, as in 11.4, the range and balance of *activities* in the material. The teacher wants to be sure that there is a reasonable balance of the sort we discussed in 4.3. Particularly important is that there should be a substantial amount of language input and that there should be a variety of communicative activities. The teacher wants to be sure that the practice activities are useful and motivating and that presentation of language takes place in realistic and motivating contexts. Under *skills* the teacher measures whether the course answers the students' needs from the description of those needs that he has previously prepared. Thus the teacher asks whether the right skills are included and whether the balance between the different skills is appropriate for the group. He also answers a question about skill integration which we said was an important principle in methodology (see 5.5). In Chapters 6–9 we have seen many examples of how practice in using different skills can be integrated with the practice of other skills.

Under *language type* the materials evaluation form asks the teacher to consider whether the language in the materials is realistic (see, for example, our comments about questions and answers in 7.1.4(2), whether the language is at the right level for the students, whether it is of the right type (e.g. students studying English for medicine will probably not want materials with purely social English) and whether the progression of 'new' language is logical and appropriate for the students. This last point concerns how, and in what order, students are asked to produce new language. In general we would expect students to be able to build on what they already know so that there will be some connection between what they have just learnt and what they are learning now. The connection does not necessarily have to be grammatical only, however, and may concern situations in which language is used, or further extensions of an interaction. Perhaps what we are looking for here is a sequence that will be intelligible to the learner rather than unconnected items thrown into a course at random.

Under *subject and content* we analyse what topics, etc. are included in the course and whether they match up to our students' personalities, backgrounds and needs. We ask, therefore, if the subject and content is relevant to our students' needs, whether it is – at least sometimes – realistic, whether it is interesting for the students, and whether there is sufficient variety to sustain motivation.

Lastly the materials evaluation form asks whether there is sufficient *guidance* not only for the teacher, but for the students. In the former case we would expect clear explanations of how the material can be used to its maximum advantage. In the latter case we would expect the materials to be clear, easy to follow (in terms of instructions, etc.), and to have clearly stated objectives that both students and the teacher can understand.

When the teacher has finally completed the materials evaluation form he is asked to recommend whether the materials should (continue to) be used. We can now look at the complete materials evaluation form. After many of the questions, references will be given in brackets to various parts of this book so that readers can take up these references if in doubt about what exactly the questions mean or imply.

Materials evaluation form

NAME OF MATERIALS UNDER CONSIDERATION

AUTHOR(S) _____

PUBLISHER _____
LEVEL _____

A – Practical considerations

1 Is the price of the materials appropriate for your students?

Yes ☐ *No* ☐ *Comment* _____

2 Are the integral parts of the materials (coursebook, tapes, teacher's book, etc.) available now?

Yes ☐ *No* ☐ ⌐*Comment* ――――――――――――――――――――――――――

B – Layout and design

1 Is the layout and design of the materials appropriate for your students? (Refer to description of students/student needs.)

Yes ☐ *No* ☐ ⌐*Comment* ――――――――――――――――――――――――――

C – Activities

1 Do the materials provide a balance of activities that is appropriate for your students? (See 4.3, 11.1 and 11.4(a).)

Yes ☐ *No* ☐ ⌐*Comment* ――――――――――――――――――――――――――

(You may also want to refer to Exercise 3 on page 40 and Exercise 1 on page 236)

2 Is there a sufficient amount of communication output in the materials under consideration? (See 4.2.6 and 5.3 for a description of what this means, and Chapter 8 for a large number of examples of this type of activity, both speaking and writing.)

Yes ☐ *No* ☐ ⌐*Comment* ――――――――――――――――――――――――――

3 Do the materials provide enough roughly-tuned input for your students? (See 4.2.2.)

Yes ☐ *No* ☐ ⌐*Comment* ――――――――――――――――――――――――――

4 Is 'new' language introduced in motivating and realistic contexts? (See 4.2.3. and Chapter 6, especially 6.1.1 and 6.1.2.)

Yes ☐ *No* ☐ ⌐*Comment* ――――――――――――――――――――――――――

5 Where the materials encourage practice, is the practice motivating for your students? (See 4.2.5, 5.4.2 and the many examples of practice activities in Chapter 7.)

Yes ☐ *No* ☐ ⌐*Comment* ――――――――――――――――――――――――――

D – Skills

1 Do the materials include and practise the skills your students need? (See 2.5 and the description of student needs on page 239.)

Yes ☐ No ☐ ┌Comment _____

2 Do the materials have an appropriate balance of skills for your students? (See especially questions 2 and 3 in the description of student needs on page 239.)

Yes ☐ No ☐ ┌Comment _____

3 Is the practice of individual skills integrated into the practice of other skills? (See especially 5.5 and the many examples of skill integration in Chapters 6–9.)

Yes ☐ No ☐ ┌Comment _____

E – Language type

1 Is the language used in the materials realistic – i.e. like real-life English? (See, for example, 7.1.4(2) and 9.2.2. The comments about signification and value in 4.2.4 also apply here.)

Yes ☐ No ☐ ┌Comment _____

2 Is the language used in the materials at the right level for your students? (Note that when a coursebook is advertised as, for example, intermediate, this level is not necessarily the same as what the term 'intermediate' means for you.)

Yes ☐ No ☐ ┌Comment _____

3 Is the language in the materials the right type of language for your students? (See especially question 4(b) in the description of student needs on page 239 and the comments on page 241.)

Yes ☐ No ☐ ┌Comment _____

4 Is the progression of 'new' language appropriate for your students? (See the comments on page 241.)

Yes ☐ No ☐ ┌Comment _____

F – Subject and content

1 Is the subject and content of the materials relevant to the students' needs? (See especially question 1 in the description of student needs on page 239.)

Yes ☐ No ☐ ┌Comment _____

_____

2 Is the subject and content of the materials realistic at least some of the time?

Yes ☐ No ☐ ┌Comment _____

_____

3 Is the subject and content of the materials interesting for the students? (See 11.4(d).)

Yes ☐ No ☐ ┌Comment _____

_____

4 Is there sufficient variety for your students in the subject and content of the materials?

Yes ☐ No ☐ ┌Comment _____

_____

G – Guidance

1 Do the materials contain clear guidance for the teacher about how they can be used to the best advantage (for example in a teacher's book)?

Yes ☐ No ☐ ┌Comment _____

_____

2 Are the materials clearly written for your students and are the objectives clearly stated for both students and teacher?

Yes ☐ No ☐ ┌Comment _____

_____

H – Conclusion

1 Would you recommend adopting (or continuing with) these materials for your students?

Yes ☐ No ☐ ┌Comment _____

_____

_____

The materials evaluation form, then, is designed to get the teacher to answer the central questions about what they need and expect from the materials which are under consideration. The teacher will complete the form on the basis of the previous student needs profile which tells him what kind of materials will be appropriate for his students. The issues raised in the materials evaluation form are precisely those which have formed the content of this book.

If the teacher is able to answer 'yes' to all the questions (which is unlikely) then it is probable that his conclusion will be to use the materials. Usually, however, there will be a number of 'no' answers as well. Particularly where two books or sets of materials are being compared, however, the answers to the questions on the materials evaluation form will be most revealing and will help to facilitate the choice between the two.

Exercise

Complete the student needs profile for a group of students you teach or are familiar with. On the basis of this profile use the materials evaluation form to assess the relative merits of two textbooks that might be appropriate for the students you have been considering.

References

1 A different type of evaluation form can be found in L Van Lier (1979). Some good general points about materials evaluation are made in L Mariani (1980) and T Buckingham (1978) makes some excellent remarks about what good materials should contain.

Bibliography

ABBS, B and FREEBAIRN, I *Starting Strategies* (Longman 1977)

ABBS B and FREEBAIRN, I *Building Strategies* (Longman 1979)

ABBS, B and FREEBAIRN, I *Developing Strategies* (Longman 1980)

ALEXANDER, L G *Mainline Beginners A* (Longman 1978)

ALLWRIGHT, R 'Motivation – The Teacher's Responsibility' (*English Language Teaching Journal* 31/4 1977a)

ALLWRIGHT, R 'Language Learning Through Communication Practice', (*ELT Documents* 76/3, The British Council 1977b), reprinted in Brumfit and Johnson (eds.) (1979)

ARNOLD, J W and HARMER, J *Advanced Writing Skills* (Longman 1978)

BADDOCK, B 'Creative Language Use in Communication Activities' (*English Language Teaching Journal* 35/3 1981)

BARR, P, CLEGG, J and WALLACE, C *Advanced Reading Skills* (Longman 1981)

BRAZIL, D, COULTHARD, M and JOHNS, C *Discourse Intonation and Language Teaching* (Longman 1980)

BRIÈRE, E 'Quantity and Quality in Second Language Compositions' (*Language Learning* 16/3 and 4 1966)

BRINTON, E, PLUMB, W and WHITE, C *Active Context English Book 2* (Macmillan 1971)

BROUGHTON, G *Success with English Coursebook 1* (Penguin 1968)

BRUMFIT, C J 'Correcting Written Work' (*Modern English Teacher* 5/3 1977)

BRUMFIT, C J 'Communicative Language Teaching: an Assessment' in Strevens (ed.) *In Honour of A. S. Hornby* (Oxford University Press 1978)

BRUMFIT, C J, *Problems and Principles in English Teaching* (Pergamon Press 1980)

BRUMFIT, C J 'Teaching the "General" Student' in Johnson and Morrow (eds.) (1981)

BRUMFIT, C J and JOHNSON, K (eds.) *The Communicative Approach to Language Teaching* (Oxford University Press 1979)

BUCKINGHAM, T 'Some Basic Considerations in the Assessment of ESL Materials' (*Mextesol Journal* 3/2 1978)

BULLARD, N 'Take your Partners' (*Modern English Teacher* 8/3 1981)

BYRNE, D *Progressive Picture Compositions* (Longman 1967)

BYRNE, D *Teaching Oral English* (Longman 1976)

BYRNE, D *Functional Comprehension* (Longman 1977)

BYRNE, D *Materials for Interaction* (Modern English Publications 1978)

BYRNE, D *Teaching Writing Skills* (Longman 1979)

BYRNE, D and HOLDEN, S *Follow It Through* (Longman 1978)

BYRNE, D and HOLDEN, S *Going Places* (Longman 1981)

CASTRO, O and KIMBROUGH, V *In Touch* (Longman/IMNRC 1979)

CHOMSKY, N 'Review of Verbal Behaviour' (*Language 35* 1959)

COE, N 'Comprehension Inside and Outside the Classroom' (*Modern English Teacher* 6/1 1978)

CORDER, S P *Introducing Applied Linguistics* (Penguin Educational 1973)

COULTHARD, M *An Introduction to Discourse Analysis* (Longman 1977)

DAVIES, E and WHITNEY, N *Reasons for Reading* (Heinemann 1979)

DAVIES, P, ROBERTS, J and ROSSNER, R *Situational Lesson Plans* (Macmillan 1975)

ELLIS, R 'Informal and Formal Approaches in Communicative Language Teaching' (*English Language Teaching Journal* 36/2 1982)

GARDNER, R and LAMBERT, W *Attitudes and Motivation in Second Language Learning* (Newbury House 1972)

GARTON-SPRENGER, J, JUPP, T, MILNE, J and PROWSE, P *Encounters* (Heinemann 1979)

GEDDES, M and MCALPIN, J 'Communication Games – 2' in Holden, S (ed.) *Visual Aids for Classroom Interaction* (Modern English Publications 1978)

GEDDES, M and STURTRIDGE, G 'Jigsaw Listening' (*Modern English Teacher* 6/1 1978)

GEDDES, M and STURTRIDGE, G *Listening Links* (Heinemann 1979)

GERWITZ, A 'Resource-based Learning and Class Organisation for Adult EFL Learners' (*English Language Teaching Journal* 33/3 1979)

GIRARD, D 'Motivation – The Responsibility of the Teacher' (*English Language Teaching Journal* 31/2 1977)

GORE, L *Listening to Maggie* (Longman 1979)

HARMER, J 'What is Communicative?' (*English Language Teaching Journal* 36/3 1982)

HARMER, J and ARNOLD, J W *Advanced Speaking Skills* (Longman 1978)

HARTLEY, B and VINEY, P *Streamline English: Connections* (Oxford University Press 1979)

HEATON, J *Composition Through Pictures* (Longman 1966)

HICKS, D, POTÉ M, ESNOL, A and WRIGHT, D *A Case for English* (Cambridge University Press 1979)

HILL, L *Picture Composition Book* (Longman 1960)

HOADLEY-MAIDMENT, E 'The Motivation of Students Studying EFL in London (*English Language Teaching Journal* 31/3 1977)

HOLDEN, S *Drama in Language Teaching* (Longman 1981)

JOHNSON, K 'The Deep End Strategy in Communicative Language Teaching' (*Mextesol Journal* 4/2 1980) and in Johnson (1982)

JOHNSON, K 'Some Background, Some Key Terms and Some Definitions' in Johnson and Morrow (eds.) (1981)

JOHNSON, K *Communicative Syllabus Design and Methodology* (Pergamon Press 1982)

JOHNSON, K and MORROW, K (eds.) *Functional Materials and the Classroom Teacher* (CALS University of Reading 1978)

JOHNSON, K and MORROW, K (eds.) *Communication in the Classroom* (Longman 1981)

JORDAN, R *Looking for Information* (Longman 1980)

KERR, J *Picture Cue Cards* (Evans 1979)

KINGSBURY, R and SCOTT, R *It Happened to Me* (Longman 1980)

KRASHEN, S 'The Monitor Model for Adult Second Language Performance' in Burt, M, Dulay, H and Finnochiario, M (eds.) *Viewpoints on English as a Second Language* (Regents 1977)

KRASHEN, S 'The Input Hypothesis' in Alatis, J (ed.) *The Georgetown Round Table on Language and Linguistics* (Georgetown University Press 1982)

KRASHEN, S 'Acquiring a Second Language' (*World Language English* 1/2 1982)

KRASHEN, S and TERELL, T *The Natural Approach* (Pergamon Press 1982)

LEE, W R *Language Teaching Games and Contests* (Oxford University Press, new edition 1980)

LITTLEWOOD, W *Communicative Language Teaching – An Introduction* (Cambridge University Press 1981)

LONG, M *Natural Dialogues* (*Modern English Teacher* 1/3 1973)

LONG, M 'Groupwork in the Teaching and Learning of English as a Foreign Language – Problems and Potential' (*English Language Teaching Journal* 31/4 1977)

LYONS, J *Chomsky* (Fontana 1970)

MACKAY, R 'Identifying the Nature of the Learners' Needs' in Mackay, R and Mountford, A (eds.) *English for Specific Purposes* (Longman 1978)

MACKAY, R and MOUNTFORD, A 'The Teaching of English for Specific Purposes: Theory and Practice' in Mackay, R and Mountford, A (eds.) *English for Specific Purposes* (Longman 1978)

MCLEAN, A 'Destroying the Teacher: The Need for Learner-centred Teaching' (*Forum* 18/3 1980)

MCLEAN, L 'Options for Classroom Organisation' (*Mextesol Journal* 3/2 1978)

MALEY, A 'Games and Problem Solving' in Johnson and Morrow (eds.) (1981)

MALEY, A and DUFF, A *Sounds Interesting* (Cambridge University Press 1977)

MALEY, A and GRELLET, F *Mind Matters* (Cambridge University Press 1981)

MARIANI, L 'Evaluating Coursebooks' (*Modern English Teacher* 8/1 1980)

MARKSTEIN, L and GRUNBAUM, D *What's the Story?* (Longman 1981)

MATTHEWS, A and READ, C *Tandem* (Evans 1981)

MORROW, K 'Teaching the Functions of English' (*English Language Teaching Journal* 32/1 1977)

MORROW, K 'Principles of Communicative Methodology' in Johnson and Morrow (eds.) (1981)

MOSKOWITZ, G *Caring and Sharing in the Foreign Language Class* (Newbury House 1978)

MUGGLESTONE, P 'Active Listening Exercises' (*Modern English Teacher* 3/2 1975)

MUGGLESTONE, P 'The Primary Curiosity Motive' (*English Language Teaching Journal* 31/2 1977)

MUGGLESTONE, P *Holiday English Book 5* (Mary Glasgow Publications 1979)

MUNBY, J *Communicative Syllabus Design* (Cambridge University Press 1978)

O'CONNOR, J *Better English Pronunciation* (Cambridge University Press 1967)

PLUMB, W 'An Analysis of Classroom Discourse' (*Mextesol Journal* 3/1 1978)

PLUMB, W 'Are Short Responses a Help or a Hindrance?' (Paper presented at the Vth Mextesol Convention 1979)

REVELL, J *Teaching Techniques for Communicative English* (Macmillan 1979)

RICHARDS, J 'Answers to Yes/No Questions' (*English Language Teaching Journal* 31/2 1977)

RIXON, S 'The "Information Gap" and the "Opinion Gap" – ensuring that Communication Games are Communicative' (*English Language Teaching Journal* 33/2 1979)

ROSSNER, R, SHAW, P, SHEPHERD, J, TAYLOR, J and DAVIES, P *Contemporary English Book 1* (Macmillan 1979a)

ROSSNER, R, SHAW, P, SHEPHERD, J and TAYLOR, J *Contemporary English Book 2* (Macmillan 1979b)

ROSSNER, R, SHAW, P, SHEPHERD, J and TAYLOR, J *Contemporary English Book 6: Pilot Edition* (Macmillan 1980)

SALIMBENE, S 'Non-Frontal Methodology and the Effects of Group Co-operation and Student Responsibility in the EFL Classroom' (*English Language Teaching Journal* 35/2 1981)

SCOTT, M *Read in English* (Longman 1981)

SCOTT, R 'Speaking' in Johnson and Morrow (eds.) (1981)

SCOTT, R and ARNOLD, J *Starting Points* (Longman 1978)

SKINNER, B *Verbal Behaviour* (Appleton-Century-Crofts 1957)

STATMAN, S 'Peer Teaching and Group Work' (*English Language Teaching Journal* 34/2 1980)

STEVICK, E *Memory, Meaning and Method* (Newbury House 1976)

STEVICK, E *Teaching and Learning Languages* (Cambridge University Press 1982)

STREVENS, P *New Orientations in the Teaching of English* (Oxford University Press 1977)

SUÁREZ, J 'Reading Comprehension' (*Modern English Teacher* 6/6 1979)

TENCH, P *Pronunciation Skills* (Macmillan 1981)

TRUDGILL, P *Sociolinguistics: an Introduction* (Pelican 1974)

TURNBULL, R M 'An Application of the Interview Role-play' (*English Language Teaching Journal* 35/4 1981)

VAN EK, J *The Threshold Level for Schools* (Longman 1978)

VAN LIER L 'Choosing a New EFL Course' (*Mextesol Journal* 3/3 1979)

WATCYN-JONES, P *Pair Work: Activities for Effective Communication* (Penguin 1981)

WATSON, J B and RAYNOR, R 'Conditioned Emotional Reactions' (*Journal of Experimental Psychology* 3/1 1920)

WEBSTER, M and CASTAÑON, L *Crosstalk Book 2* (Oxford University Press 1980)

WHITE, R V *Teaching Written English* (Heinemann 1980)

WIDDOWSON, H 'The Teaching of English as Communication' (*English Language Teaching Journal* 27/7 1972)

WIDDOWSON, H *Teaching Language as Communication* (Oxford University Press 1978)

WIDDOWSON, H 'The Communicative Approach and its Application' in Widdowson, H *Explorations in Applied Linguistics* (Oxford University Press 1979)

WILKINS, D A *Linguistics in Language Teaching* (Edward Arnold 1972)

WILKINS, D A *Notional Syllabuses* (Oxford University Press 1976)

WILLIAMS, E 'Elements of Communicative Competence' (*English Language Teaching Journal* 34/1 1979)

WILLIS, J *Teaching English Through English* (Longman 1981)

WRIGHT, A, BUCKBY, M and BETTERIDGE, D *Games for Language Learning* (Cambridge University Press 1979)

Index

Accent 25
Accuracy 37, 38, 44, 45, 56, 140,
    206
Accuracy work 64
Accurate reproduction 35, 36, 56, 57,
    59, 223
Accurate reproduction stage 43, 55,
    65, 66, 67, 68, 70, 72, 81, 201, 205,
    208, 221
Acquisition see Language acquisition
Activities 227–8, 230, 231, 235, 240,
    242 see also Balanced activities
    approach, the, Communicative
    activities
— change of activity 7, 214, 215
Activity and class organisation see
    planning
Adaptability see Teacher, the
Adolescents 7, 9, 53, 206, 209, 213,
    216
Adult advanced students 8
Adult beginners 7
Adult intermediate students 7
Adult learners 4, 9
Advanced students 82, 194
Aids 85, 86 see also Planning
— blackboard, the 5, 56, 58, 59, 65,
    67, 71, 72, 93, 111, 154, 222
        blackboard drawing 85
— flashcards 85, 88, 90, 222
— pictures 85, 115, 136, 191
— realia 85
— tape recorders 177, 197, 222, 230
— tapes 176, 222, 230
— using the tape recorder 197
— wall pictures 85, 89, 222
Allwright, R 31, 32, 33
Anti-social behaviour see Discipline
Appropriacy 13, 14, 15
— channel 14
— setting 14
— participants 14, 16, 44
— purpose 14
— topic 14
Appropriate language 34
— appropriate language use 98
Appropriateness 13
Assessor see Teacher, the
Atmosphere 5
Attitude to language learning 4, 225
    see also Motivation
Audio-lingual method 30, 31, 33
Aural stimuli 110, 112 see also Visual
    stimuli
Authentic material see Types of text
Authentic spoken English 190

Balance 235, 240, 242
Balanced activities approach, the 38,
    39, 200, 220 see also Planning
Behaviourism 29, 30, 33, 40
Behaviourist model of language
    acquisition 30
Behaviourist philosophy 34
Blackboard, the see Aids

Challenge 6, 8, 9
— high challenge 6
— low challenge 6
— realistic challenge 8
— unrealistic challenge 8
Changeable units 54, 55
Checking meaning 64–5, 72
— information checking 64
Children 4, 7, 9, 206, 209, 213, 216,
    221
Chomsky, N 12, 13, 14, 18, 30, 31
Choral repetition see Repetition
Class management 200–17, 223 see
    also Discipline, teacher, the (role of
    the teacher), Student groupings
Classroom, the 4, 5, 8, 21, 33, 177 see
    also Different contexts, Physical
    conditions
Cognitivism 30, 33, 39, 40
— cognitive abilities 32
Cohesive devices 107, 109, 145, 147,
    168 see also written practice
    (cohesion and coherence)
Communication continuum 42
Communication output 34, 37, 38, 39,
    40, 200, 220, 242 see also Output
Communicative activities 32, 33, 34,
    37, 38, 39, 45, 46, 47, 113–141, 200,
    201, 202, 213, 221, 222, 223, 228,
    240 see also Oral communicative
    activities, Written communicative
    activities
Communicative approach, the 38
Communicative competence 13, 23,
    24, 27, 42
Communicative efficiency 23–6, 27,
    37, 38, 42, 202, 206
Communicative events 41
Communicative purpose see Purpose
Communicative situations 32, 33
Competence 13, 14, 30, 31 see also
    Communicative competence
Comprehensible input 32, 40
Comprehension task 151, 152, 153,
    197 see also Language skills
    (receptive skills)
Conditioning 29, 30, 39 see also
    Behaviourism

— reinforcement 30
        negative reinforcement 30
        positive reinforcement 30
— response 30
— reward 30
— stimulus 30
Conditions see Physical conditions
Conscious learning 32, 33, 34, 35, 37,
    39
Content 44, 45, 124, 140
— content in texts 142–3
Content feedback see Feedback
Context 36, 51, 52–3, 239 see also
    Different contexts
— interaction with context 15
Controlled techniques 45 see also
    Drilling
— controlled oral drills 87
— controlled practice 56, 59, 220,
    222, 223, 228
— controlled writing 87, 112
Controller see Teacher, the
Correction 60, 62–4, 201, 202 see also
    Feedback
— correcting written work 140–41
— correction techniques 63–4
        student corrects student 60, 141
        teacher corrects student 63
— gentle correction 64, 98, 201, 204
— showing incorrectness 60, 62
        denial 63
        echoing 62
        expression 63
        repeating 62
        questioning 63
— symbols for correction 140
Cue-response drills 60, 61, 66, 72, 88,
    89, 90 see also Drilling
— cue 61, 201
— instruct 61, 201, 203
— nomination 44, 60, 61, 201
Culture 2, 4
— cultural stereotype 23
— culture of target language
    community 3, 4
Curriculum 2

Deep experience 31, 40
Describe and draw 115–16, 129, 203,
    234, 235 see also Games
Desire to communicate 44, 45, 46
— creating desire to read/listen 150
Dialogue 71–9, 83, 87, 221, 234, 235
— parallel dialogue 73
Different contexts 33, 52 see also
    Introducing new language
— classroom, the 52, 53, 66–8